Even

Good
Food
Shop
Guide

Jane Charteris

ESB

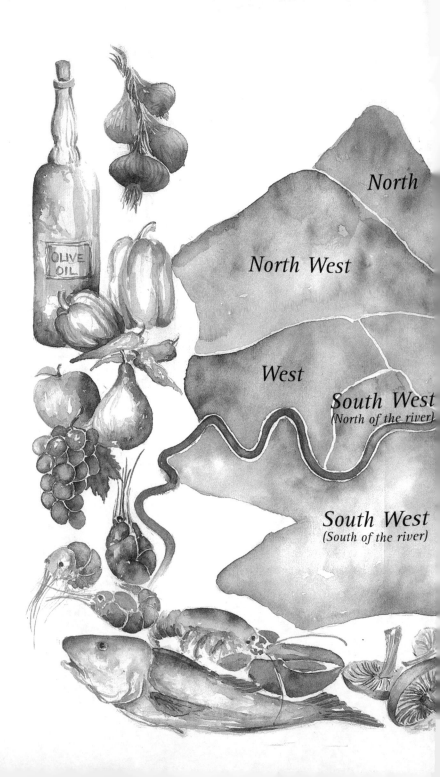

North

North West

West

South West
(North of the river)

South West
(South of the river)

Contents

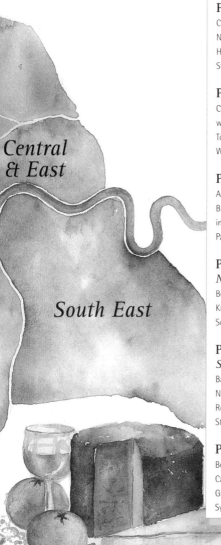

Central & East

South East

To Mum

First published in Great Britain in 1996 by
EVENING STANDARD BOOKS
Northcliffe House, 2 Derry Street, London W8 5EE

ISBN 1 900625 05 9

Publishing Manager Joanne Bowlby
Editorial Manager Charlotte Coleman-Smith
Production Manager Roger Hall

Designed by Nick Cave
With thanks to Peter Howes and Clare Emery

A CIP catalogue record for this book is available
from the British Library

Printed and bound in Great Britain by BPC Hazell Books Ltd, Aylesbury, Bucks.

This book may be ordered by post direct from the publisher,
but please try your bookshop first.

Corporate editions and personal subscriptions of any of the
Evening Standard Guides are available.
Call us for details. Tel 0171 938 6774

Also published in the series:

Children's London (ESB)
Best Of...London (ESB)
London Restaurant Guide (Pavilion Books)
London Wine Guide (Pavilion Books)
London Pub Guide (Pavilion Books)

Introduction

Few cities can rival the diversity of London's food shops. Thanks to the many ethnic communities that have sought refuge here over the years, Londoners have Italian delis galore, can buy lox-filled bagels in the small hours, find fresh Thai vegetables and treat themselves to a sushi lunchbox – in fact, eat their way round the world.

There are, of course, the flagship stores, such as Harrods and Fortnums, which have for decades provided quality produce. Cheesemonger Paxton & Whitfield has been around for nearly 200 years and the first Italian deli opened its doors over 100 years ago. The Jewish, Polish, Asian, Chinese and Greek-Cypriot communities have long ensured that their preferred foodstuffs were available. And there have always been good, traditional British butchers, bakers, greengrocers and fishmongers.

The *Good Food Shop Guide* is about all these, be they smart and expensive or ramshackle and cheap. Any shop listed is good for something, if not everything, it sells. There are no supermarket chains listed; independent retailers, who work against long odds set by competing superstores, deserve the support of all food lovers. I hope this book helps those who like good food to find it (if your favourite shop is not here, let us know!).

Enormous thanks go to journalist Christopher Hirst who introduced me to South East London's delights, to Katie and William Joll, whose intimate acquaintance with Soho was a life-saver, and to chef and food-writer Anissa Helou without whose explanations of some Middle-Eastern terms I would have muddled my kishk and my kashk. I am not the first to have tramped the streets of London in search of the best food shops, so thanks to Elaine Hallgarten and Linda Collister, Jenny Linford and Henrietta Green, all of whose works have been immensely helpful. Thanks are, of course, due to the hundreds of food retailers who spared precious minutes of their pressured time to talk to me. And to Jo Bowlby and Charlotte Coleman-Smith for their infinite patience.

I have divided London into broad points of the compass, corresponding with postal districts, then into main neighbourhoods, within which shops are listed alphabetically under category. Couldn't be simpler!

JANE CHARTERIS

Eros Awards

Central & East

The heart of London, stretching from The City to Mayfair and from Marylebone down to the river, is not what it once was when it comes to food shops. Happily, the area is still served by Fortnum's, Paxton & Whitfield, a re-vamped Selfridges, the old Italian delis and French pâtisseries of Soho. And, of course, Chinatown makes this one of the best and liveliest places to shop for oriental essentials. Among the newcomers, Villandry, Carluccio's and Neal's Yard Dairy stand out in the dwindling crowd. One species of shop which appears to do better here than anywhere else is the coffee specialist – there are no less than six within a stone's throw.

Bethnal Green

Delicatessen

Paris and Rios

93 Columbia Road E2. Tel: 0171 729 1147

Mon-Wed, Fri & Sat 9am-6pm, Thu & Sun 9am-2pm

This pretty stretch of Columbia Road is quiet during the week but comes alive at the weekends, particularly Sundays when London's last remaining flower market is open. Isabelle Rios started her charming deli 14 years ago; it is well stocked with Continental staples, the emphasis being Spanish; tinned seafoods, Serrano ham, spicy meatballs, plump tortilla and other tapas-type dishes, morcilla (Spanish black pudding) and other meats, Spanish cheeses, etc. There are also pastas, Bonne Maman preserves, loose coffee beans, paella and arborio rice, and the very special Tormesina beans, including judion, grown 1,000 metres above sea level in the Sierra de Grados and costing a staggering £11.99/1,000g. They are also now sold loose, which brings the price down a fraction.

The City

Butchers

R Ashby Ltd

8 & 9 Leadenhall Market EC3. Tel: 0171 626 3871

Mon-Thu 6am-4pm, Fri 6am-5pm

An old-style British butcher, established for over 50 years, with Scotch grass-fed beef, Kentish lamb and pork, homemade sausages, wild venison, own-cooked hams, ox tongue, turkey, pork. Free-range and organic meats and chickens can be ordered, but according to the friendly, knowledgeable staff, City folk don't ask for it much. Bacon is cut to order. Eggs are free-range. The entire range of the excellent Wiltshire Tracklement condiments seem to be in stock, and there's a small but select cheese counter.

Butcher & Edmonds

1, 2 & 3 Leadenhall Market EC3. Tel: 0171 626 5816/623 5946
Mon-Fri 6.30am-3.45pm

Alan Butcher is the third generation of this fittingly named family to preside over what is primarily a game dealership. He is supplied by local dealers in the great game areas — Norfolk, Yorkshire and Scotland, mainly — stocking grouse, pheasant, partridge, teal, widgeon, woodcock, mallard, wild rabbit and hare (which they will prepare with its blood should you want to jug it). Out of season, they revert to straightforward butchery — Scotch beef, English lamb, Dutch veal, barn-reared poultry — supplying more Directors' dining-rooms than anything else. Well worth a trip in winter if you're a game fanatic.

Fishmongers

Ashdown (Leadenhall) plc

23-25 Leadenhall Market EC3. Tel: 0171 626 0178 (24-hr answerphone)
0171 626 1949 Fax: 0171 626 5889
Mon-Fri 6am-3.30pm

The shop is at street level, spilling over with everything the sea can throw up; to one side is the 'kitchen' where such delectables as paella and curry (in the huge divided cast-iron frying pan), salmon and potato fishcakes, tuna and roasted peppers, salmon en croute are made daily; downstairs is the lobster and oyster pool; upstairs, Beauchamp's fish restaurant. Everything is fresh (except tiger prawns), and everything means just that, from coley and herrings to tuna and swordfish. Smoked salmon (London and Scottish cures), Iranian caviar, seasonal game and Ledoult sauces. City deliveries. Mad (in the nicest possible way) staff.

H S Linwood & Sons Ltd

6 & 7 Leadenhall Market EC3. Tel: 0171 929 0554
Mon-Fri 6am-3.30pm

Officially incorporated in 1883, when the covered market was built, Linwood the fishmonger had been trading for several decades before making it a truly venerable family outfit. Alan Linwood is the present chief. The smart black delivery van, with its Royal Warrant emblazoned on the side, can often be seen scooting around City streets. Cornish octopus, fat monkfish tails, Colchester oysters, sea bass, turbot, halibut, soles, tuna, Scottish salmon, are all beautifully displayed. Their smoked salmon is a London-cure and they sell three times as much of it as anything else.

Clerkenwell

Delicatessens

Gazzano & Son Ltd

167 Farringdon Road EC1. Tel: 0171 837 1586
Tue-Thu 8am-5.30pm, Fri 8am-6pm, Sat 8am-5pm, Sun 10.30pm-2pm

Beaten by Terroni & Sons (see below) to the title of oldest Italian deli in London, Gazzano's never the less takes the winner's rosette for remaining the longest in the same family: there has been a Gazzano in charge since 1901, and the fifth generation is learning the trade. The shop retains the old wooden, glass-fronted drawers in which loose pasta was stored for easy identification, and Signor Gazzano still uses them for storing packets of pasta and loose rice. The atmosphere here is authentic and unfussy - there's Rana fresh pasta, an extensive display of salami and other cured meats (no San Daniele - 'people round here seem to prefer Parma'); another of cheeses, including eight or so Pecorini; basic olive oils and antipasti. Breads come from Il Fornaio - huge Toscano loaves are wonderful. The only concession to modern tastes are a few gimmicky pastas.

L Terroni & Son

138-40 Clerkenwell Road EC1. Tel: 0171 837 1712
Mon-Fri 9am-5.30pm, Sat 9am-3pm, Sun 10.30am-2pm

Clerkenwell was the location of choice for the 19th-century Italian immigrants congregating around St Peter's Church, and Signor Terroni had the nouse to open London's (nay, Britain's) first Italian deli next door in 1878. Now owned by the Anessa family, it is a spacious shop with a vast range of dried pastas, biscotti, and other staples of the Italian larder. There is also Dell Ugo fresh pasta; breads from an Italian bakery in Bedford (where Signor Anessa used to live), including Pugliese loaves; rough-hewn crags of Parmigiano Reggiano; spicy Italian sausages; a small selection of salami and hams, and really delicious home-made pesto sauce.

Sausages

Simply Sausages
341 Central Markets Farringdon Street EC1.
Tel: 0171 329 3227 Fax: 0171 248 0312
Mon-Fri 8am-6pm, Sat 9am-2pm

Martin Heap opened his first sausage emporium on what used to be known as Hart's Corner, handy for Smithfield Market's meat traders, and initially manufacturing was all based here. The bulk has now moved to the Berwick Street shop (see p38), but some sausages are still made here at busy times. It's a small, cosy place with all the most popular sellers from Heap's innovative list. Small, plump and delicious handmade haggis from Mr & Mrs Kennedy in Scone, Perthshire, are good sellers. This is also the mail order HQ.

Covent Garden

Baker

Neal's Yard Bakery Co-operative
6 Neal's Yard WC2. Tel: 0171 836 5199 Fax: 0181 960 1840 (office)
Mon-Fri 10.30am-5.30pm, Sat 10.30am-4.35pm (or earlier if sold out)

Although established in 1980 long after hippies had given way to punks, something of the 1960s' ethos and atmosphere informs this pleasant bakery, not least because it is a collective owned by eight 'members' who pay themselves on a profit-related basis. And all power to them. Their breads are highly thought of, although they might be a bit on the dense side for some tastes. They only use 100 per cent organic flours from Shipton Mill in Gloucestershire and seasalt, getting through about a ton a week on their wholewheat, three-seed (linseed, sesame and poppy), 100 per cent rye, cheese & herb, olive & garlic, and breakfast fruit & malt loaves. These breads have never met sugar – where sweetening is needed, honey and fruit juice are used. Lunchtime trade in soups and quiches and suchlike (all vegetarian) is brisk. And yeast is sold here!

Cheesemonger

Neal's Yard Dairy

17 Shorts Garden WC2. Tel: 0171 379 7646 Fax: 0171 240 2442
Mon-Sat 9am-7pm, Sun 10am-5pm

'If British cheeses are now firmly on the culinary map, it is due in no small measure to the sterling work of the entire team at Neal's Yard', writes Henrietta Green in *The Food Lovers' Guide to Britain.* The team is led by Randolph Hodgson, cheese-maker, affineur and proselytising cheese crusader, who buys only from small-scale farmhouse producers in Britain and Ireland still making their cheeses in traditional ways. He is passionate that people should have the opportunity to taste the difference between a Cheddar like Montgomery or Keen's and a commercially produced one, that they should understand that 'unpasteurised' does not equal 'Listeria' and that real cheese is not only a delicious food but a pre-eminently safe one. Of his 50-70 varieties of cow's, sheep's and goats' milk cheeses, 95 per cent are made from unpasteurised milk – it just makes better cheese. Downstairs are the humidity- and temperature-controlled cellars where hundreds of hard and soft rounds are stored and matured, regularly turned by hand until *à point.* Then, and only then, are they uplifted to the small shop above, where they are packed floor to ceiling, ready to be tasted by the punters. 'The only way to buy is to taste,' says Ralph, particularly when the same cheese, say Duckett's Caerphilly or a Stilton, is stocked at various degrees of maturity. All the top names in British cheesemaking are here: Kirkham's Lancashire, Appleby's Cheshire, Smart's Double and Single Gloucesters, Botton & Loch Arthur from the Camphill Village Trust in

Scotland, Mrs Seator's Orkney, Wealdon and Perroche from their own Creamery in Kent... and on and on. There also Clarke, Bagatelle and Innes breads, yoghurts and créme fraîche. Mail order.

Coffee/Tea

Monmouth Coffee Company
27 Monmouth Street WC2. Tel: 0171 836 5272 Fax: 0171 240 8524
Mon-Sat 9am-6.30pm, Sun 11am-5pm

This handsome dark red shop has a literally breath-taking smell, so powerful are the aromas of freshly roasted beans. They have some eight carefully chosen Arabic beans from around the world, which are roasted dark or medium, daily on the premises, and sold whole or ground. The two roasts can be blended for subtly different flavour, but no two coffees are ever mixed. We are talking serious coffee, here. Once roasted, beans do not stay on the shelves for more than 48 hours, but will keep in the freezer for up to three months. The best thing is that each coffee roast can be tasted in tiny cups to help you make up your mind. Or you can sit at a table with a bigger paid-for cup and a Sally Clarke pastry. Of particular interest are the organic coffee from Papua New Guinea and the exclusive Guatemalan which rejoices in the name of Huehuetenango Cuchumatan. Raw beans are also sold for those with home-roasting expertise and equipment. Chocolate coffee beans, and handmade chocolates from a small family business near Lyons, gift-wrapped boxes (of coffee), mail order, Central London deliveries (for orders over £29 and at a cost of £4.50, on Tuesday and Thursdays), and discounts on volume sales are all available.

The Tea House
15 Neal Street WC2.
Tel: 0171 240 7539 (Mon-Fri 10am-5pm only) Fax: 0171 836 4769
Mon-Sat 10am-7pm, Sun 12-6pm

Reports that the shop 'smells like the Body Shop' were not encour-aging but, when I visited, it smelt mostly of tea and perhaps slightly fruity – they do, after all, carry a lot of whole-fruit and fruit-flavoured varieties. Altogether there are over 100 different teas, ranging from the familiar – Earl Grey and English Breakfast, Assam and Darjeeling - to South African Rooibos, Japanese green tea and South American maté (herbal), and including some 30 fruit-and-spice-flavoured black China teas and half-a-dozen whole-fruit caffeine-free types, whose names one would not normally associate with the great afternoon ritual: apple and lemon; strawberry and kiwi; Christmas Pudding – actually, as is explained, a blend of rose-hip, hibiscus, red and black currants and rose petals – which rather naughtily changes its name to Summer Pudding at the relevant time of year. Masses of 'teaphernalia' – infusers, novelty pots (if you like that sort of thing), mugs, caddies, pottery. Jams, honey and biscuits.

R Twining & Co Ltd

216 Strand WC2. Tel: 0171 353 3511
Mon-Fri 9.30am-4.30pm

Delightfully old-fashioned, with its marble floor, fine old wooden lockers and a golden lion over the door guarding the threshold, the Royal-Warranted Twinings was established in 1706 and its current director is the ninth generation to run it, making it possibly the oldest family firm in the capital. It started as a coffee-house, of which there were over 2,000 in the City alone, called Tom's (after the first Twining) the particular attraction of which, confusingly, was tea. And tea is still the main draw, coffee having been reduced to 12 or so. The range of teas includes all the main ones from China, India and Ceylon (in tea circles Sri Lanka does not figure), including the exclusive Lady Grey (no relation), a blend of China tea with orange peel and bergamot, and lots of caffeine-free fruit teas. Some teabags (6p each) are sold individually, so you can pick and mix different brews. Gift items include presentation tins and pressed tea-bricks, tea-pots, etc, and there are bottled 'iced teas' in various flavours (including raspberry!). At the back is a charming 'museum', opened on request, devoted to the Twinings and tea – old photos, documents, memorabilia and portraits of tea potentates including a copy of that painted by Hogarth of Thomas Twining in the 18th century (the original is in the head office in Andover).

Delicatessen

Carluccio's

28a Neal Street WC2. Tel: 0171 240 1487
Mon-Thu 11am-7pm, Fri & Sat 10am-6pm

'Why would people come to us instead of a supermarket?' muses Priscilla Carluccio, tireless helpmeet of chef/patron, TV star, author and fungiphile, Antonio. The question, one feels, is rhetorical. If you can afford it, and there's no avoiding the fact that it is an expensive shop, Carluccio's is a food-loving Italophile's heaven and a most pleasurable shopping experience. Antonio and Priscilla spend a great deal of time looking for the best ingredients for their own-label products (now available in a diversity of delis London-wide). Everything has to be 'made in the right place and in the right way' before it is considered for inclusion. Antipasti include various fungi, char-grilled vegetables, peperoncini farciti, peperoni agrodolce, caprice di canelli (peppers with tuna and capers), Sicilian salted anchovies, salted capers. Bottarga (air-dried tuna or mullet roe for sprinkling over seafood pasta, pasta sepia or mozzarella), is a Sardinian speciality and must come from that island. Pasta comes fresh and dried – the fresh is made with free-range eggs – own-brand and other makes: Gerardo di Nola pasta from Naples is exclusive to Carluccio's; truffle and saffron taglioni is 'expensive, quick – and exquisite'. Carluccio's Carnaroli risotto rice, grown in the Po Valley, is among the best I've ever used – big, succulent grains that behave themselves. Cheeses are imported every two weeks. The gastronomia counter, as you'd expect of a deli attached to a restaurant of The Neal Street's repute, is a wonder, with a constantly changing array of palate-pleasuring dishes. There are lots of fine oils and vinegars at fine prices, magnificent breads from Italy's regions, such as Pugliese loaves, brittle sheets of carta da musica and hard fresella bread; a small selection of fresh vegetables and when available edible wild herbs, such as dandelion, rocket and ransom; and, of course, in season the wild fungi for which Antonio is famous – St George's, morels (both spring arrivals), chanterelles, puffballs, parasols, honey fungus, ceps. These are all very definitely 'made in the right place in the right way'.

Health Food

Neal's Yard Wholefoods

23 Short's Garden WC2. Tel: 0171 836 5151

Mon-Fri 9am-7pm (Thu till 7.30pm), Sat 9am-6.30pm, Sun 11am-5.30pm

Now owned by Holland & Barrett, this long-established health food store is completely organic: rice, beans, muesli, cereals, cracked wheat, seeds, nuts and more nuts, dried fruits, cake, mushroom and garlic pasta sauce. Among the non-alcoholic drinks are the refreshing Ame, which hits the spot even with an old soak like me, raspberry cordial (a bit sweet) and Dorset ginger. Lots of herbal teas, their own very crunchy peanut butter, chutneys. Cheeses from neighbouring Neal's Yard Dairy (though why miss the exhilaration of a visit there?).

Finsbury

Health Food

Freshlands

196 Old Street, EC1. Tel: 0171 250 1708

Mon-Fri 10.30am-6.30pm, Sat 10.30am-4.30pm

Until two years ago this was Clearspring, the macrobiotic food specialists. When the whole caboodle was taken over by a Japanese company, which wanted the name and the distributing arm, the retail arm detached itself and has managed to grow a new body... as it were. Being surrounded by office workers, Freshlands' team concentrates on the lunchtime take-away market: a help-yourself salad bar is replenished daily, and there are spinach and tofu larties, soya cottage pie, spinach quiche, mushroom and nut or carrot and onion cutlets – all of which need only a microwave to render them edible. Much of the stock is organic, gluten-free, macrobiotic and vegan (they still carry a lot of Clearspring products). Orgran organic and wheat-free pastas, Mrs Gill's Indian Kitchen frozen meals, Duskin's single-variety apple juices, Rocombe Farm ice-cream, Breton cider are all stocked. There's a very small organic fruit and veg selection, including the interesting burdock root ('a little goes a long way'), and a comprehensive range or grains, pulses, rice and flours.

Hackney

Baker

Ridley Bagel Bakery
13-15 Ridley Road E8. Tel: 0171 241 1047
Mon-Sun 24hrs

Possibly the most famous bagel producer in town, this is an informal, fast turn-over joint, popular with members of Hackney's many communities. Everything is made on the premises, from the bagels to the French pâtisseries, taking in gingerbread men, doughnuts and American-style chocolate muffins. Breads include granary, rye and wholemeal; cholla from Thursday to Saturday. The deli counter holds bright yellow Jamaican patties, small packets of smoked salmon ends, kosher cooked meats and salt beef, and of course anything you might conceivably put in a bagel. Prices go up by 10 pence after 11pm. If you live nearby it is advisable to get to know what you like and phone your order through to avoid the inevitable queues in the evenings and at weekends. Branches at: 105 High Road, E2 (tel: 0181 442 0019); 515 Roman Road, E3 (tel: 0181 980 2385); 116 Upper Clapton Road, E5 (tel: 0181 806 1770); 3 Watford Way, NW4 (tel: 0181 203 8153), not all open 24 hours.

Emporium

Turk Gida
89 Ridley Road E8. Tel: 0171 254 6754/7355
Mon-Wed, Sat 8am-7.30pm, Thu & Fri 8am-8pm

A 20-year-old Turkish food market that seems to change name every few years while remaining in the same hands. The stock, thankfully, is a constant: masses of pulses, grains and rice, huge tubs of ghee, jars of pickles, spices, halva, many different feta, olives, labne (strained yoghurt, usually to be found shaped into balls and floating in oil, but sometimes available fresh), and lots of fresh fruit and veg. Through a linking archway, partially blocked by a revolving cabinet of wedding cakes, is the bakery - spacious and delicious smelling. There's a good range of baclava, some with nuts, kadayife, Turkish petits fours; of breads — the great flat pide (a kind of naan), Cyprus round breads and corek; and of savoury take-aways — borek, gozleme, kofte and the like which can be heated up in a handy microwave. From the outside, Turk Gida looks rather time-worn, but do not be deterred — it's good inside, particularly the bakery.

Market

Ridley Road Market E8
Mon-Sat 9am-5pm

As with all markets, this is better the later in the week you go and best at the weekend. It is unclassifiable, having a bit of every-thing — Afro-Caribbean, English, and Middle-Eastern fruit, veg, fish, meat. Underneath the railway arches, behind the stalls on the south side, are various shop-caves selling Afro-Caribbean fruit and veg, wet fish, dried fish, pigs' tails and snouts, Jamaican breads and buns.

Marylebone

Butcher

Wholefood Butchers
31 Paddington Street W1. Tel: 0171 486 1390
Mon-Thu 8am-6pm, Fri 8.30am-6.30pm, Sat 8am-1pm

Probably London's, if not the country's, oldest organic butcher, having been established 35 years ago. There's not a frozen piece of meat in sight, nor any prepared cuts, nor any meat containing preservatives or colourings, nor any from animals that have been intensively reared or improperly fed. John and Andy deal direct with farms, the grazing and rearing of whose herds have the imprimatur of the Soil Association, and certificates of authentication and proofs of origin are happily shown to doubters. Beef and pork are English, lamb English and Welsh. No veal. It is 30-40 per cent more expensive than non-organic meat, but probably worth it to know that it's clean. Homemade sausages are rusk-free. Game in season includes rabbit, pigeon, hare and mallard.

Delicatessen

Villandry

89 Marylebone High Street W1. Tel: 0171 487 3816 Fax: 0171 486 1370
Mon-Sat 8.30am-7pm, Sat 8.30am-5pm

An extremely knowledgeable food-loving friend declares 'this must be the best delicatessen I have ever been into', and it is true to say that in his seven and a half years, Jean Charles Carravini has established a reputation for tip-top produce from around the world, though the emphasis is European (Britain included). Jean Charles sources most of his produce from small producers, dismissing such distinguished names as Fauchon as 'a packaging job'. The list of goodies is endless and what's mentioned here only a sample. There are, in no particular order: Dean and Deluca beans; San Angel Mexican salsas; German chocolates; Ballymaloe chutneys and relishes; Wendy Brandon's preserves from Wales; South African jams; many honeys, some exclusive (one from Regent's Park, another from medlar-browsing Sicilian bees), Carved Angel Christmas puddings; Calabrian dried fruits; a £50 bottle of balsamic vinegar; red rice from the Camargue; dried cherries with or without a coating of white chocolate; Roger Woodall's bacon; mi-cuit foie gras, pâté and charcuterie; Neal's Yard and Philippe Olivier cheeses (a large selection, some of them exclusive); breads from Sally Clarke, Neal's Yard, plus Philippe Dadet's sourdough and (more exclusivity claimed here) Max Poilâne's woodfired-oven sourdough (as opposed to brother Lionel's — they've been having a blood-row for 12 years about whose is the authentic, even though both started under their esteemed father!), and the huge and beautiful Italian pagnotta, baked in chestnut-fired ovens, and baguettes courtesy of Delices de

France. Fresh fruit and veg, seasonal mushrooms and herbs comes direct from the great Rungis market in Paris. Sandwiches are made to order, and there's a small coffee-shop-cum-restaurant at the back. Booking for dinner essential.

Emporia

The Green Valley
36 Upper Berkeley Street W1. Tel/fax: 0171 402 7385
Mon-Sun 8am-10pm

This Lebanese supermarket stocks all imaginable ingredients for the various Middle Eastern cuisines and comes recommended by Lebanese chef and food-writer Anissa Helou, who says that 'it is just like Beirut' – although even she acknowledges that being a regular customer oils the wheels of service. There is an excellent selection of vegetables and fruit, including small oval aubergines, white courgettes and, in season, unusual produce like fresh m'lookhiyeh (which is otherwise known as Jew's Mallow, is more often found dried, and is difficult to cook), vine leaves, butter beans, jujube fruit and white figs. The deli section has samosas, kebabs, tabbouleh, stuffed vine leaves, falafel, manakish (small pizza lookalikes with strong thyme and normally eaten for breakfast), delicious shankeesh cheese balls (chop up with fresh tomato, a little oil or lemon juice, parsley). Dried goods include grains and rices, pine nuts, burghul, freekeh (roasted green wheat) and za'atar (a seasoning mixture of dried thyme, sumac and sesame seeds). Then there are the drinking syrups, such as jellab (made from date and grape molasses) and tamarind, lots of Arab breads, cooking utensils, conical Turkish coffee pots, hookah pipes and fresh loofahs.

Selfridges
400 Oxford Street W1. Tel: 0171 629 1234 Fax: 0171 493 0568
Mon-Sat 9.30am-7pm, (Thu till 8pm)

For years the poor relation of the capital's smart food halls (Harrods, Harvey Nicks and Fortnum's), Selfridges' have been revolutionised into a gleaming white-tiled, elegant collection of counters and 'islands', each dedicated to a particular product or national cuisine. The changes are largely due to Claire Reuben who joined in 1994, and her ideas have produced a grazer's paradise: s/he can stroll across the world on a Saturday morning, from Jamaica to Japan, leisurely buying examples of each cuisine. Ready-made food, not in geographical order, such as fresh pasta (14 different types), Mexican dishes, Jamaican patties, sushi, Chinese stir-fries, balti chicken, tandoori pomfret, meat or vegetable borek, felafel, kibbeh, stuffed vine leaves, kosher gefilte fish, baclava and halva, etc, are mostly made by small London producers exclusively for the store. There's even halal foie gras and kosher Coke and Pepsi (which says a lot about the local population). The olive 'island' is the most comprehensive in London, boasting 31 varieties, from very young and green Lucernes Royales and very young and black Coquilles Niçoises from France to wizened, raisin-like Throumbes from Greece (good for cooking). Twice-weekly deliveries ensure freshness and quality. Two hundred different cheeses from 15 countries, with the largest range of Spanish in town and a surprisingly high number of Scandinavian, make cheese-buying particularly taxing. All of Europe is represented in the charcuterie counter, plus South Africa with a bewildering array of biltong. There's a choice of some 80 different fish – bourgeois from the Seychelles, kingfish from The Gulf, carp rouge from Senegal, as well as sole, plaice, cod, halibut, mackerel, etc from nearer home; shellfish cooked (in store) and raw – Gulf blue crabs, Welsh mussels, cockles, winkles and whelks; brown shrimps, tiger prawns; many smoked varieties, including salmon (traditional and London smokes), Loch Fyne kippers, Finnan undyed haddock, halibut, tuna, and marlin. The butchery department has Cornish and Anglesey lamb, Inverurie beef, Norfolk free-range pork, English veal; Richard Woodall dry-cured bacon from Cumbria; Lorne sausage; chicken gizzards and necks, pigs' and lambs' hearts, calves' feet; 30 different locally-made sausages. Most meat is sourced directly, hung in store and cut to order. Game in season. Oil and vinegar shop, with produce from California to Crete. Entire Fauchon and Cordon Bleu ranges (through exclusive deals with each). There's an excellent bakery, very fresh (and some organic) fruit and veg (lots of wild mushrooms in season), Godiva and Leonidas chocolates, and an Oyster Bar. Phew!

Fishmonger

John Blagden

65 Paddington Street W1. Tel: 0171 935 8321 (24-hr answerphone)
Mobile: 0831 318000
Mon-Fri 7am-5pm, Sat 7am-1pm

A truly delightful shop: purpose-built in 1890 facing north to keep the fish cool, it retains its handsome glazed blue bricks, and boasts extremely helpful, informative and friendly staff – namely, the three partners David Blagden and brothers Peter and Albert Curd. Fresh sea bass, brill, red mullet, John Dory, and many soles all come from Devon; wild Scottish salmon is smoked in East London by East Europeans 'who are best at it'; lobsters are exclusively Scottish, never Canadian; shucked scallops are fresh and white; much-prized Rossmore oysters from Ireland and rock oysters from the River Exe are both reasonably priced; Baxters' potted shrimps now, sadly, have to be frozen by EU law, but are still good. There's a small range of frozen exotics – crevettes, tiger prawns, etc – and a wide choice of seasonal game – snipe, woodcock, wild duck, teal, grey-legged partridge, all in the feather and hung and plucked on the premises. Recipe/fact sheets are available at the cash desk or can be printed out while-u-wait (extremely useful for unfamiliar fish), as is a Product List, with trenchant remarks, such as 'Red Mullet – the woodcock of the sea, hence cook with liver in'; 'Woodcock – difficult to shoot, difficult to eat'; 'Boiled cod roe – brief season January to March'; 'Smoked duck breasts – interesting with raspberry vinegar', and so on. Free delivery over a wide area of London.

Health Food

Wholefood Ltd

24 Paddington Street W1. Tel: 0171 935 3924
Mon-Thu 8.45am-6pm, Fri 8.45am-6.30pm, Sat 8.45am-1pm

Established as long ago as 1960 under the aegis of the then-young Soil Association, this must be one of the oldest health shops around and is run by the same Trust as Wholefood Butchers over the road. It's a large calm shop, in which everything is organic if possible –

where it is known not to be, or cannot be vouched for, white price tickets alert the customer. White sugar and white flour are banned from the premises, and nothing stocked contains chemicals, colourings, artificial flavourings or preservatives (other than natural ones). There's a range of cereals, rices and pulses – whole, flaked or milled; organically grown dried fruits from trusted growers in California, France and Israel, sugar-free preserves, cold-pressed honeys, organic wines and ciders, free-range and organic eggs, breads from organic flours, soya products, etc. The organic vegetables are usually in excellent condition, and included when I visited shiny Swiss chard and fat, bouncy Savoy cabbages. Much of it comes from Wales. Sadly, they no longer sell fresh yeast.

Pâtisserie

Pâtisserie Valerie at Maison Sagne
105 Marylebone High Street W1. Tel: 0171 935 6240
Mon-Fri 8am-7pm, Sat 8am-6pm, Sun 9am-6pm

Wonderfully old-fashioned salon de thé, established in 1921 and now run by Pâtisserie Valerie. It is more spacious than the Old Compton Street branch, with seating for around 60, but refurbishment has not entirely destroyed its air of faded grandeur, despite the chandeliers being newly gold-leafed: the original murals and mirrors are still in situ, though the old photos of various visiting celebs have gone. The chocolates, gateaux, glazed fruit tarts, Danish pastries, palmiers, sablés, Viennoiserie (morning goods) are all of the high standard on which this Soho institution has built its reputation – a few more years and the new name will doubtless be as firmly established in Marylebone as in Soho.

Sausages

Biggles
66 Marylebone Lane W1. Tel: 0171 224 5937 Fax: 0171 935 8454
Mon & Sat 9.30am-4.30pm, Tues-Fri 9.30am-6pm

Pipped to the post from being London's first dedicated sausage-maker by O'Hagan's of Greenwich (who actually claims to be the world's first such), Biggles nevertheless manages a spoiler by advertising itself as the first 'in London's West End'! Started by Colin Bailey in 1989, its logo (a bewinged porker in flying goggles and scarf) seems to suggest that if pigs could fly, they would produce bangers like these. There are over 60 varieties, handmade daily in the basement of the small shop, in natural skins, containing a minimum of 85 per cent meat, and no rusk, MRM (mechanically recovered meat) or additives. The range is wide, from traditional county types (Cumberland, Oxfordshire, Lincolnshire) and Welsh leek and pork through well-known foreigners (Toulouse and Perigord; Bratwursts; chorizo; Italian spicy) and some less known (Swedish potato; Armenian lamb; Romanian beef) to the 'gourmet' selection (Madeira and pistachios; Champagne; Beaujolais Nouveau; chicken and lemon). I cannot pretend to have tried them all, but those I have, including some of the 'shires', chicken tikka, and pork/chilli/coriander, were excellent. BSE is not a worry to Colin because all beef is organically fed Aberdeen Angus. Delivery, depending on size of order. 48 hours notice for special orders.

Mayfair

Butcher

Allens Ltd
117 Mount Street W1. Tel: 0171 499 5831 Fax: 0171 409 7112
Mon-Fri 3am-4pm, Sat 6am-1pm

It is hard to believe that Mayfair residents rise early enough to benefit from Allens's extraordinary am-opening times – but chefs certainly do, and the orders marked 'Connaught' or 'Savoy' attest to the quality of the meat. Do not be intimidated, however, by these grand names (or by the antler-bedecked walls), any butchering job is cheerfully and knowledgeably undertaken – as manager Richard Garrett says, 'we get mostly butlers and chauffeurs in here' – though whether for themselves or their masters is not divulged. This is a serious old-style butcher, with no pre-cut or packaged meat in sight, just great carcasses and sawdust on the wooden floor, seasonal game hanging outside (weather permitting). Beef is from Elgin in Scotland, lamb and mutton from the West Country. A sculptor in Geneva is apparently trying to buy the famous wooden chopping block and you can see why: a wonderful mushroom-shaped affair, history ingrained in it. A friend who knows her brisket from her skirt says 'all chefs swear by Allens, and they are absolutely right to do so'. Central London deliveries and mail order are available.

Caviar

Caviar Kaspia
18 Bruton Place W1. Tel: 0171 493 2612/0879 Fax: 0171 408 1627
Mon-Sat 10am-11pm

The sister shop of the famous and eponymous Paris haunt of Diaghilev and other names of the times, started by Arcady Fixon in 1927, the London branch was opened in 1987, 10 years after M. Fixon's death (both places remain in the family's hands). This may not have quite the chachet of Place de la Madeleine, but is a fun way to indulge that craving for the mighty sturgeon's eggs. Beluga, Golden Osietra, Osietra, and Sevruga, ranging in price (for 125g, until summer '96) from £170 down to £63, all come in Kaspia's own-brand tins and keep for three months under sealed vacuum. Get proper buckwheat blinis here (canapé size available, and take your pick of 25 flavoured vodkas (including one with gold leaf!). Caviar and vodka should be well chilled, and if you divulge that you plan to eat it with extras like chopped onion and hard-boiled eggs, you will be firmly advised, in the words of Charles Ryder in *Brideshead Revisited*, 'to try it without first'. There's also take-away borscht, fresh foie gras to order, Fauchon teas, Belgian chocolates, gravadlax and smoked salmon fillet a la Russe.

Chocolates

Charbonnel et Walker
1, The Royal Arcade 28 Old Bond Street London W1.
Tel: 0171 491 0936/493 6768 Fax: 0171 495 6279
Mon-Fri 9am-6pm, Sat 10am-5pm

In 1875 the Prince of Wales (the future King Edward VII) persuaded Madame Charbonnel away from Maison Boissier in Paris to establish an English confectionery house in Bond Street with Mrs Walker. Three addresses and 121 years later it retains its Royal Warrant, high standards, charm and expense. But who counts the pennies with chocolate this good? Made in Tunbridge Wells, their chocs use a minimum of 70 per cent cocoa solids, and come in various assortments and wrappings. The Boite Blanche spells out a personal message in chocolate letters; the be-ribboned Theatre Box, a Victorian invention, is designed to avoid the rustling of paper during a performance and makes, we are told, 'the perfect gift for a lady'; the Plain Assortment comes in the 'classic' C & W blue-and-white box; at Christmas there are crackers full of bittermints. Bestselling products are rose and violet fondants; St Valentine's Day sees hearts and lips and what have you. C & W drinking chocolate is famous for its depth of flavour, as is their Chocolate Truffle Sauce (dark rum, white cognac, grand marnier and original, to accompany ice-cream, pears, crêpes, or to be used as a dip). Then there are the 'enrobed orange peel', nut fondants, crèmes Parisiennes, and yet others, available in various assortments, and, if you like, in handmade boxes covered in silk, moirée or Liberty prints. Your wish is their command. They do a same-day courier service within London, mail order, private accounts, and overseas postage all possible.

Lessiters

75 Davies Street W1. Tel: 0171 499 3691
Mon-Wed, Fri-Sat 10am-6.30pm, Thu 10am-7.30pm

The first Lessiters opened in 1911, fittingly in Swiss Cottage, the business being exclusively about Swiss chocolates, better than which there is no other, not even Belgian, according to Peter and Hans Luder, the brothers who own and run it. All the chocolates are made in their factory in Hatfield. The Lessiter philosophy, whch has been successful for over 30 years in Mayfair, is to concentrate on what they are good at, and that is good enough for Anton Mossiman, whose truffles come from here. Sadly, the City branch has closed due to the Mansion House redevelopment, so one can no longer say, wittily, 'my chocolates come from Poultry'. Also at 167a Finchley Road, NW3 (Tel: 0171 624 5925), which is the mail order branch as well.

Coffee

H R Higgins (Coffee Man) Ltd

79 Duke Street W1. Tel: 0171 491 8819 Fax: 0171 629 3913
Mon-Wed 8.45am-5.30pm Thu, Fri 8.45am-6pm Sat 10am-5pm

This is an airy, street-level shop adorned by black-and-white photographs and antique machinery with a four-table tasting area downstairs where Mr David Higgins (third generation) or his aunt, Miss Audrey Higgins, will, if not too busy, talk coffee with you. Established in 1942 in South Molton Street, where roasting took place on-site, Higgins has a large and loyal clientele, many of whom maintain standing orders to ensure regular supplies of their favourite coffee or tea. Around 50 different variants of bean/roast, blended or original, are available, including the popular Chagga from Tanzania and Harar Longberry from Ethiopia. Handsome red or green and gold gift boxes contain four 125g packs of different coffees. There's a wide range of pots and crockery, including a useful line of lidded mugs for take-away. Mail order and discounts on orders above 3kg.

Pâtisserie

La Madeleine

5 Vigo Street W1. Tel: 0171 734 8535 Fax: 0171 287 9554
Mon-Sat 8am-7pm

Affiliated with the excellent Filéric in South Kensington, this is a very French set-up – brasserie, café and pâtisserie rolled into one, and run by genial young Frenchman David Hocdé. Everything is baked to a very high standard on the premises by French staff. Particularly to be praised are Eden, a three-layer cake of black-and-white chocolates and caramel mousses; Religieuses, little pouffes of choux pastry with coffee cream and coffee fondant; pains chocolats; flan (which sounds much nicer as custard tart); handsome fruit tartelettes and lovely buttery croissants. Seasonal specialities include Galettes des Rois for Twelfth Night, Easter Notions and Christmas Bûches de Noël.

St James's

Cheesemonger

Paxton & Whitfield

93 Jermyn Street SW1. Tel: 0171 930 0259 Fax: 0171 321 0621
Mon-Fri 9am-6pm Sat 9am-4pm

This 200-year-old shop had a re-fit last summer (the charcuterie moved to the front, some fixtures and fittings were modernised and the back office turned over to wine and relevant books), but essentially not much has changed. Arthur Cunynghame, the owner for the past four years, and his staff certainly know their business and will happily help customers put a board of complementary tastes together from the 120-130 cheeses usually in stock (don't forget that some cheese, especially sheep's and goats', are seasonal). An erstwhile reputation for conservatism has been properly scotched: Cheddar and Stilton (Montgomery or Quickes and Cropwell Bishop respectively) may still be their bestsellers, but they also have Cornish Yarg, Bonchester, Vulscombe (soft goats'), Ticklemore (hard goats'), Beenleigh Blue (blue sheep's), Dorset Blue Vinney (the farmhouse variety as opposed to the commercial kind) and Lanark Blue (salty Scottish sheep's blue, so nearly lost to EU regulations) among an impressive show of British cheeses. Foreigners include all the favourites, plus some special treats such as Livarot from Brittany (a favourite of mine) and appellation contrôlée Camembert Fermier. Arthur is full of tips: 'cheese before pudding, and preferably on its own with a good wine'; 'a cheeseboard should be harmonious – don't put an 18-month-old Cheddar with a fresh soft cheese, it shocks the palate'; 'crudités clean the palate between tastes, but celery is probably too strong'; and 'as soon as you make a rule about cheese, it gets broken'! P & W run a Cheese Society for aficionados, membership of which entitles you to a quarterly newsletter, invitations to special tastings, such as the W G Grace event (all Gloucestershire cheeses) or British Cheeses and Ports, special offers, and for an extra monthly payment of about £20, a monthly Cheeseboard Selection delivered to your door. Ordinary mail order for 'postable' cheeses also available.

Emporia

Fortnum & Mason
181 Piccadilly W1. Tel: 0171 734 8040 Fax: 0171 437 3278
Mon-Sat 9.30am-6pm

The history of F & M is long and illustrious, and includes unbroken Royal connections going back to the reign of Queen Anne in 1707 (the year Mr Fortnum and Mr Mason joined forces); food-parcel support for 'our boys' in various wars, from the Napoleonic to the Falklands; being the first to offer ready-to-eat meals (in about the 1850s) and to sell Heinz products, Horlicks and Baxters soups; supplying 'delicacies' for the suffragettes; and a list of customers whose names filled the social columns of each decade. There have been changes, of course, but F & N is still essentially a high-class 'grocer and provisioner', still sends parcels to Brits all over the world. The majority of its customers may now be tourists, and, although some staff still wear morning coats, there is a more demotic feel to the place, notwithstanding the air of pomp and ritual provided by carpets and chandeliers. Sixty per cent of packaged goods is own-label stuff, supplied by small producers who adapt recipes to F & M's specifications. In this area there is a wide range of choice chutneys, mustards, jellies, sauces, pickles, jams, honeys and marmalades (including Sir Nigel's Marmalade, named after a past peer of the realm who complained about the sweetness of the brands on offer – his is a bitter, more robust concoction). Cakes and biscuits tend towards the traditionally English (and Scottish), though Continental visitors, such as Sacher Tortes, are gone by lunchtime on the day of making. Fresh foods include caviar and smoked fish; cooked meats and cheeses; and fruits, exotic and domestic with apples and pears from Brogdale Horticultural Trust taking pride of place. Teas and coffees have for ever formed, and still form, a substantial part of F & M's trade – there are some 30 teas, from Assam to Yunnan, including 'the Beaujolais Nouveau' of teas, First Flush Darjeeling, and another from Japan, Gyokuro, only drunk by the Emperor and costing £50/125g – and some 16 coffees. English chocolates are handmade mostly by 'Audrey's in Hove', a very small and traditional firm. Finally, the famous hampers and 'instant picnics', fruit and fruit-and-flower baskets remain bestsellers.

Natural Food

Japan Centre
212 Piccadilly W1. Tel: 0171 434 4218
Mon-Sat 10am-7.30pm, Sun 10am-6pm

Buried in the basement of the Travel Centre is this tidily arranged supermarket dedicated to all things Japanese. Unusually, there's no fresh fish counter, but there are appealing sushi lunchboxes, chilled fish balls and canapes. Lots of teriyaki sauces, beansprouts, dried noodles, pot noodles, etc. Not everything is given in translation, so non-Japanese speakers might feel handicapped − but staff are happy to explain to those interested.

Soho & Chinatown

Soho

Butcher

Slater and Cooke, Bisney and Jones Ltd
67 Brewer Street W1. Tel/fax: 0171 437 2026
Mon-Fri 7.30am-5pm, Sat 7.30am-1pm

The lamented demise of Randall & Aubin has left Slater and co. to hog Soho's butchery business, though it has always enjoyed a brisk trade. The owner Mr Van Flyman and manager Mr Dunning are efficient and straightforward in their approach, rather like the display of meat, which is extensive but perhaps a little clinical in atmosphere. Beef is Scottish and grass-fed (via Mathers of Inverurie) and is hung for up to ten days in the shop; lamb comes from the West Country, pork is free-range. They make about five different sausages on the premises (two pork, Toulouse, Merguez, Cumberland) but will take special orders. Bacon is an excellent Suffolk sweet dry-cure, and there's a good range of East Anglian game and poultry.

Coffee/Tea

Algerian Coffee Stores Ltd
52 Old Compton Street W1. Tel: 0171 437 2480 Fax: 0171 437 5470
Mon-Sat 9am-7pm

Established in 1887, the ACS have long been supplying their beans to the bars and restaurants of Soho and to the cognoscenti among the public. The shop is tiny and crammed with some 60 coffees, 140 teas, coffee machines and other related bits of equipment, chocolates and sweetmeats, and squeezed into a corner an espresso machine from which you can have a cup of delicious steaming dark liquid while you make your selection. Their coffees divide into Blends, of which the Velluto Nero and the too-technologically named Megamix are both excellent; House Specials, of which Lebanese with Cardamoms and Arabic with Spices are recommended; Originals – single beans from Colombia, Jamaica, Indonesia, Kenya, Nicaragua, etc; and Specialities – Guatemala Antigua, Colombian Supremo Popayan, Marargogype (the largest bean in the world), Monsoon Malabar, etc. Everything is roasted twice weekly on the premises. Then there are the flavoured coffees, American-style, which purists rail against, but vanilla, hazelnut and cinnamon are my three favourites. In addition to the usual Indian and China teas, there's a long list of herbal and those Black China fruit-flavoured types, whose names inspire suspicion rather than desire for a cuppa – Blue Lady, indeed! sounds more like a cocktail. Sugared almonds, caramelised nuts, chocolate-covered coffee beans and figs, and Valrhona chocolates to bring dinner to a splendid finish. Worldwide mail order and free delivery in W1 area.

A Angelucci Coffee Specialists
23b Frith Street W1. Tel: 0171 437 5889
Mon-Sat 9am-5pm (Thu till 1pm)

Ormond Angelucci and his sister are the last of the family – 'there will be no one left to run it when we're gone,' they confide sadly. And sad it will be indeed if this characterful Soho shop (est.1929) becomes just another cigarette or fast-photo booth – being barely more than a gap between two walls, it's too small to be much else. So, if you've never tried their 'own secret blend' Mokital coffee, hurry, hurry before it's too late! Mokital comes with the slogan 'A Morning's Necessity An Evening's Pleasure', and indeed it does make both delicious cappuccino and espresso. There are 35 other types of coffee, roasted somewhere in the City, green beans for home-roasters, a few Italian staples (arborio rice, pasta, oils), no 'coffeephernalia' and no teas. A reference to 'Angelucci's' in Dire Straits' song 'The Wild West End' has brought numerous fans to the door (thanks to Jenny Linford for this piece of information).

Ferns

27 Rathbone Place W1. Tel: 0171 636 2237 Fax: 0171 580 2869
Mon-Fri 8.30am-5.30pm, Sat 10am-4pm

Established as a Covent Garden coffee-house in 1893, modern rents and rates forced Ferns to move to the northern fringes of Soho. However, Ferns retains a sense of the past, with lovely mahogany cabinets, arithmetic done on the back of paper bags, and proper old-fashioned, knowledgeable, civil service (lots of 'hello, dear', 'morning, Albert'; parcels wrapped). A stream of regular customers is firmly managed ('No, sir, too mild a blend for you I think'). Several grades of grind are offered of the 14 coffees, including water-processed decaffeinated. The beans are roasted at the HQ in Basingstoke and then rested for 12 hours in order to 'de-gas' before being bagged. They do a special line in loose fruit teas. Own-brand packaged teas are sell-by dated (many don't bother), and they also stock Twinings and Jacksons in the confidence that their own brand is superior.

Java Java

26 Rupert Street W1. Tel: 0171 734 5821
Mon-Thu 10am-10pm, Fri 10am-11pm, Sat 11am-11pm, Sun 1-8pm

A friendly little shop-cum-café with perhaps too self-conscious a 'groovy' atmosphere: the opening times are billed as 'Hours of Joy', and there's a Mirror of Fame, on which you can write immortal prose in lipstick or whatever. About 12 freshly ground coffees and some

60 loose teas are available, the world's largest, Maragogype or elephant bean, being listed among the former but, unfortunately, not in stock when I called. Jumping on the Seattle bandwagon (that West Coast city whose fame as being the birthplace of Jimi Hendrix has been supplanted by Meg Ryan, coffee bars and grunge), Java Java also sells Da Vinci syrups in 20 flavours for adding to your coffee – including marshmallow, vanilla, hazelnut, etc. Personally I prefer the taste of the flavoured coffee beans which are less sweet. There are six high-stooled tables where Soho types pass the 'Hours of Joy', homebaked cakes and quiches, etc, coffee-making machines and an exclusive range of Berkshire-made teapots and mugs.

Delicatessens

I Camisa and Son

61 Old Compton Street W1. Tel: 0171 437 7610 Fax: 0171 494 2214
Mon-Fri 8.30am-6pm, Sat 8am-6pm

Alphabetically, the first (just) of Soho's three long-established and first-rate Italian delis, each of which has its loyal supporters who claim that X is the best. Confusingly, there is no longer any connection (except a bit of cousinship) between the two Camisas (see next page for history). This one has been part of the Old Compton Street bustle for nearly 40 years and hasn't changed much in that time: its narrow and slightly cramped shop space, with dry goods to the right of the counter and everything perishable to the left, seems old-fashioned but works well enough if you kow what you're after. Among the notable offerings are fresh pasta, own-brand olive oils from Liguria and Tuscany, an excellent range of cured meats, an impressive array of olives, freshly baked breads, homemade pasta sauces, and fresh white truffles in season from Piedmont.

Fratelli Camisa

1a Berwick Street W1. Tel: 0171 437 7120 Fax: 0171 287 1953
Mon-Sat 9am-6pm

The history: there were two Camisa brothers who started a Soho deli in 1929; they worked together until the early 1960s, when one left to start his own business (I Camisa and Son); in time, the sons

(Alberto and Francesco) of the other took over the original shop, ensuring that the name still means something. The shop: old-fashioned in the best sense, hams hanging from the ceiling, huge kite-like pieces of baccala, coffee ground to order, 12 different home-made pastas, fresh buffalo Mozzarella every day, La Fornaia breads, black and white truffles in brine (separately, naturally), a large range of oils and antipasti, 20-year-old balsamic vinegar at £29/250ml, top-quality salamis, punchy Italian sausages, panettone, Italian flours, biscotti, etc. Camisa Direct is the thriving mail order arm, which can be reached on 0181 207 5919 for a catalogue. A newer branch at 53 Charlotte Street, W1 (tel: 0171 255 1240) is larger and carries a wider range of the same stock.

Lina Stores

18 Brewer Street W1. Tel: 0171 437 6482
Mon-Fri 8am-5.45pm, Sat 8am-5pm

Being higher and wider than many Soho premises, there is more room to manoeuvre round other customers when it is busy - and this is the norm - but you are still expected to be decisive in your ordering. Once accepted as a serious punter, however, discussion of the finer points of Italian cuisine is definitely allowed, either with one of the current proprietors (Antonio and Gabriella Saccomani, whose parents bought it in 1978 from the original family), or with the friendly and markedly Italian staff. Of the many excellent breads, the focaccia is especially good; the choice of fresh, made-on-the-premises pastas is exceptional (they are famed for their pumpkin ravioli; new to the range are quattro fromaggio tortelloni and squid-ink tagliatelle); there are fresh porcini in season, whole wheels of Parmesan, sacks of beans, rice and lentils, freshly cut herbs and homemade Italian sausages.

Products from Spain

89 Charlotte Street W1. Tel: 0171 580 2905
Mon-Fri 10am-5.30pm, Sat 10am-1pm

Like the coffee merchant Ferns, this delicatessen is not, strictly speaking, in Soho, but the indefinable area that used to be called 'Fitzrovia'. The Lopez brothers' father set up an import-export business for Spanish food over 30 years ago, and this straightforwardly-named shop is where much of it ends up. There is fine Serrano ham, lots of chorizos of varying spiciness, many tins of the seafood so beloved by Spaniards, Manchego and other cheeses, olives and olive oils, vinegars, and much more.

Emporium

Arigato
48-50 Brewer Street W1. Tel: 0171 287 1722
Mon-Sat 9am-9pm, Sun 11am-8pm

This is a fairly stark outlet, with a good range of Japanese ingredients stocked, from rice crackers to udon noodles and wasabi horseradish, by way of pickled vegetables and miso paste, and Yakult, a surprisingly good fermented milk drink containing a bacterium which is, apparently, particularly good for the gut. Japanese breadcrumbs are very good for coating fish or potato cakes. The sushi lunch boxes are particularly popular – you can take-away or eat-in (this area is about to be expanded).

Fishmonger

Richards (Soho) Ltd
21 Brewer Street W1. Tel: 0171 437 1358
Tue-Thu 8am-5pm, Fri 8am- 5.30pm, Sat 8am-3pm

The only remaining wet-fish shop south of Selfridges, east of Mayfair, west of Covent Garden and north of Belgravia, is a high quality operation in spite of its determinedly low-key appearance. Breath was generally held a few years back when Richards shut its old doors for ever, promising to open at new premises; the collective Soho sigh of relief was almost audible when it did re-open further down the street, even though it seems a smaller, drabber place, the fishy presence of which is no longer announced by an impressive frontal display open to the pavement (hygiene regulations apparently). The chaps who run this shop are knowledgeable and laconic, and, like most Soho people, do not gladly suffer pretension or pomposity; however, 'helpful advice' is proffered where necessary (e.g. 'Do you really want this sea bass filleted?'). Fish is mostly from British waters; where it isn't, as in tuna and swordfish, it is imported direct. Smoked salmon is always wild, Scottish and sliced to order. Shellfish and other smoked fish are invariably excellent.

Market

Berwick Street Market W1
Mon-Sat 9am-5pm

Being in Soho, the market doesn't really get going until midmorning, but once it does it is surely London's best traditional food market. The vendors shout out their bargains, stalls are beautifully arranged, and there are usually seasonal delights to be found. At the southern end, the 'Raymond's Revue Bar passage' leads to Rupert Street where there are further stalls worth a visit. Shop around.

Pâtisserie

Maison Bertaux
28 Greek Street W1. Tel: 0171 437 6007
Mon-Sat 9am-7.30pm, Sun 9am-1.30pm; 3.30pm-7.30pm

Stealing 55 years on its Old Compton Street rival (see below), Maison Bertaux can justifiably claim to be the oldest café-pâtisserie in Soho, with a long tradition of supplying coffee and pastries to Sohobes and theatre people alike (the theatre conection extends to Shakespeare productions which take place in an upstairs room that can be no more than 20-foot square). Mouthwatering profiteroles, strawberry tarts, croissants, petit fours, gateaux, etc, are all made on the premises, where you can squash on to one of the three tables. The atmosphere here is cosy and friendly — staff get two hours off for lunch on Sunday, which is perhaps why one delightful lady has worked here going on 40 years. Birthday and wedding cakes (including croquembouches) can be made to order if you give them 24 hours notice. Cakes delivered locally.

Pâtisserie Valerie

44 Old Compton Street W1. Tel: 0171 437 3466
Mon-Fri 8am-8pm, Sat 8am-7pm, Sun 10am-6pm

O pened in Frith Street in 1926 by the Belgian Madame Valerie, this bustling café-pâtisserie was an instant success with 'starving artists and Bohemians' (according to the literature) and remained that way until it was bombed during the War, when Madame and her staff upped sticks to the present site. This is cramped and jolly, intimacy unavoidable at the closely-packed tables, but nowadays you are more likely to bump into celebs and thespians than garrett-living painters. Chef Ugo Amato makes everything on the premises, daily – fruit tarts, gateaux, petits fours, Viennoiserie (croissants, etc), light snacks and sandwiches. Easter eggs are a specialité de la maison, as are custom-made cakes for birthdays, weddings, retirement parties, christenings.

Sausages

Simply Sausages

93 Berwick Street W1. Tel/fax: 0171 287 3482
Mon-Sat 8am-6pm

N ot the original but now the main branch of the business started by Martin Heap four and a half years ago, and where the bulk of the sausages are made, using best quality meat, natural skins and no additives. There are some 35 different flavours on a list that changes quarterly and features British Regional, such as Kentish Hop (pork, hops and real ale), or John Nott's, reproduced from his 1720 'cook's diary' and made of pork, spinach, marjoram and savoury (bright green), International (Toulouse, Thai, Meguez, Spanish, etc) and Gourmet (duck with apricot and orange, wild boar with apple and calvados). This last menu is the one that changes most frequently – pigeon and foie gras had become guinea fowl and foie gras, and had lost nothing in the substitution. Other base ingredients include, smoked salmon, beef, lamb, turkey, venison, ham. There's a vegetarian selection, and a high proportion of the meat ones are gluten-free. Stock is made daily in quantities that will sell out by the end of the day – so go early or order in advance.

Chinatown

Like other Chinatowns in large non-Sinaean cities round the world, London's has been given a facelift for tourists — pedestrianised streets, red and gilded dragon arches guarding the boundaries — but it remains, as they all do, resolutely Chinese. It is still stuffed with restaurants and, of course, food shops, which vary little from one to another save in the range of stock and quality of fresh fruit and vegetables on offer. It is really a matter of exploration and, in some cases, courage. Those listed here are thought to be the best for food, though not necessarily for service. For most fun, go on a Sunday when Chinese families are out in force.

Baker/Pâtisserie

Far East
13 Gerrard Street W1. Tel: 0171 437 6148
Mon-Sun 10am-7pm

An unusual bakery and tea-shop where you can sit and watch the commerce of Gerrard Street. Along with a pot of cha you can sample unusual Chinese cakes and pastries, such as char-siu buns, curry puffs and custard tarts.

Fishmonger

Good Harvest Fish and Meat Market
14 Newport Place WC2. Tel: 0171 437 0712
Mon-Sun 11am-7pm

An unusually friendly joint and Chinatown's one and only fishmonger. There are tanks of carp, eel and lobsters, and on the slabs pomfret, Emperor bream, oysters, scallops, catfish and, naturally, prawns.

Emporia

Loon Fung Supermarket

42 Gerrard Street W1. Tel: 0171 437 7179
Mon-Sun 10am-8pm

This is Soho's largest and oldest Chinese supermarket, being around 30 years old, in which any serious cook in any Oriental style should find everything required (most of it is in translation). There's always an extensive range of fresh fruit and vegetables – lychees, pak choi and its many relatives, Chinese chives and cabbage and broccoli, bitter melon, lotus root, fresh bamboo shoots, sugar cane, and several kinds of chillies; seas of frozen fish – scallops, indecently large prawns, whole pomfret, crab claws, dace fillets – and dim sum (won ton, dumplings, buns, spring rolls, etc); a whole wall of different teas, including chrysanthemum; myriad noodles and rice; great pillows of dried Japanese mushrooms; preserved duck eggs; birds' nests (expensive) for that prized soup; fresh tofu. A useful butchery section has basic cuts, plus pig bits – tails, tongues, ears, and so on. Wines include 'Greatwall' (unfortunately I didn't get the opportunity to taste this unusual-sounding wine on my visit here) and sake. Crockery and wokery are also sold, along with chopsticks, satay sticks and, rather surprisingly, mothballs.

Newport Supermarket

28-29 Newport Court WC2. Tel: 0171 437 2386
Mon-Sun 10.30am-8pm

A super-abundance of Chinese and domestic fruit and vegetables takes up most of the pavement around this corner-supermarket. Inside, it's spacious and neatly arranged so that browsing is easy, as in Loon Fung (see above). Newport Supermarket also stocks the usual range of Oriental ingredients from noodles and rices to spices and frozen fish and dim sum.

Spitalfields

Asian Sweets

Ambala
55 Brick Lane E1. Tel: 0171 247 8569
Mon-Sat 10am-8pm, Sun 9.30am-7.30pm

When the Sunday market is in top gear, the queue snakes out the door and down the street. Here are all the concoctions for which Ambala (main branch in Drummond Street, NW1) is famed. There are helpful colour photographs for those not well-versed in the difference between barfi and gulab jaman, or cham cham and ladoo.

Baker

Beigel Bake
159 Brick Lane E1. Tel: 0171 729 0616
Mon-Sun 24hrs

Even on non-market days (i.e. Monday-Saturday) this slightly run-down looking shop has an almost permanent queue – on Sunday you might have to wait tens of minutes for a bagel to be stuffed with lox and cream cheese, chopped herring, chopped liver, or whatever. Some say that these are the best bagels in town, though naturally every other bagel baker would demur. Also on sale are cholla, rye and black breads, and some French pâtisserie.

Emporium

Eastern Grocers
23 Hanbury Street E1. Tel: 0171 377 1824
Mon-Sun 9am-8.30pm

A large supermarket-cum-greengrocer with all the Asian staples and a very good range of fresh imported root and leaf veg, some of which I had never seen before, not even in Southall and Wembley – perhaps because the community in these parts is largely Bangladeshi, rather than Indian or Pakistani. Sadly, none of the staff on duty was able to supply English names, or even transliterated ones. Worth visiting for those adventurous enough to try anything once.

Market

Brushfield Street, E1
Sun 10am-5pm

A ll that remains of the once-thriving markets of the City – now removed to E10 (veg) and E14 (fish) – is this small confluence of organic growers' produce – everything from veg and fruit to meat, and all to Soil Association standards.

Wapping

Butcher

Hussey's
64 Wapping Lane E1. Tel: 0171 488 3686
Mon-Sat 7am-6.15pm

I an Hussey, a butcher here for 28 years, has responded to the yuppi-fication of Wapping with free-range eggs, smoked salmon (which happens to be kosher 'because it's the best'), fresh pasta, duck eggs, fresh foie gras and a very superior make of the foie gras pâté (definitely *not* the long-life tinned variety). But first and foremost he is an excellent butcher, stocking in his tiny shop grass-fed Scotch beef, West Country and Welsh lamb, free-range pork from Plantation Pigs in Sussex. His mum and oth-ers make authentic-looking steak-and-kidney, mince-and-onion pies and puddings (individual portions). 'Local' game, pheasants and wild rabbit, come from Essex and at £5 for an oven-ready brace and £2 a bunny, are stupendous value. There's good beef dripping, and even pigs' ears for dogs ('Scott saw them in a pet shop for £1.50, so he thought why not bung them in the oven and sell them for 50p, so we did').

Whitechapel

Delicatessen

Rogg's

137 Cannon Street Road E1. Tel: 0171 488 3368
Mon-Fri 9am-5.30pm, Sun 7am-2.30pm

Old photographs of Barry Rogg's shop, an East End landmark since his grandfather started it in 1916, show it lined floor-to-ceiling with heavily laden shelves of groceries, the counters groaning with plastic tubs and trays containing the many different herrings, fried fish, and his home-pickled cucumbers that have made him famous. It has, sadly, changed, as the once-strong Jewish presence has been diluted by other nationalities: Barry no longer stocks the huge range of dry goods and so has reduced shelving ('I lower them as I get shorter,' he cracks), and he has introduced fresh fruit and veg ('people seem to want it,' he says in a tone that implies he cannot imagine why they would). But the tins of his young green cucumbers floating in their garlic, bay leaves and chilli pickle still stand around the floor, changing colour from green to almost white as they mature. There are ten different herring preparations, chopped liver, egg and onion, and all the fried fish, of which I tried fresh from the pan in the back kitchen and delicious croquettes. Breads include cholla, pumpernickle, bagels, rye.

North

The vastness that is North London varies enormously. The affluent neighbourhoods of Islington and Highbury have many superior shops, from butchers and fishmongers to sleek modern delis and pungent cheese specialists. Finsbury Park and Haringey boast excellent Turkish and Greek Cypriot bakers, grocers and greengrocers, as well as a healthy showing of Afro-Caribbean stores. Holloway, of course, is the home of Gibber, one of London's best known greengrocers. Crouch End and Muswell Hill are both out-of-the-way localities stuffed with small, independent specialists, some old as the hills, such as Dunn's the baker and Martyn's the coffee-roaster. Others are bright and new, like baker/pâtisserie/tea-room Le Papillon. Finchley offers everything from chocolates and coffee to a Japanese fishmonger and a kosher bakery.

Canonbury

Delicatessen

Amalfi

240 St Paul's Road N1. Tel: 0171 359 4398
Mon-Sat 9am-7pm

A traditional, cram-packed Italian deli which has occupied this site in the no-man's-land between Highbury and Islington for 16 years. Mrs Fattorusso and her sister-in-law offer a wide selection of basic groceries – pastas, pasta sauces, antipasti, biscotti, oils, pulses, risotto rice – as well as more up-market items, such as Rana and Dell Ugo fresh pastas, Casa Manzi ice-cream (from Marine Ices, see page 83), cold-pressed oils from Sardinia and mature balsamic vinegar. Numerous different salamis, coppa di Parma, bresaola, Parma ham, ventricini, and cheeses, including the less-often seen ewes' milk Caciotta from Sicily, fill the deli counter. A huge wheel of Parmesan hides in a cupboard under the window, from which customers' needs are cut to order. They also make their own ravioli, salads (olives, tomatoes and Mozzarella; aubergine, peppers and artichoke hearts), pesto and marinated olives (using nothing more than a good oil, lots of garlic and fresh herbs).

Gallo Nero

45 Newington Green Road N1. Tel: 0171 226 2002
Mon-Sat 8.30am-6.30pm

R oberto Mori has been supplying the neighbourhood with the best of Italy for some ten years and makes a charming and trust-worthy guide to what's what (his parents started with a restaurant in Stoke Newington, now deli number two run by brother Michele, Signor and Signora Mori having sensibly retired to Italy's warmer climes). Home-made items include familiar and unusual pesto sauces – one using mint is particularly good on baked potatoes or grilled vegetables – and small and large tiramisu, all made by

Michele. Monti's huge fresh tortelloni stuffed with salmon or mush-rooms are among a wide choice of up-market pastas on display. Roberto de-bones his Parma hams, and his San Daniela is 'riserva', which guarantees a 14-month cure. There are lots of different salamis and Italian cheeses, including Torta Basilica, that sumptuous creation of Mascarpone, basil and pine kernels, and a spicy Pecorino a Peper-oncino. The larder stock covers everything you would expect from a good Italian delicatessen – good-quality oils, top-range commercial pastas, cantuccini and other biscotti, dried porcini, pasta sauces, antipasti... Daily breads come from Il Fornaio, but Roberto recom-mends his country Italian loaves, which come from a bakery based in Bedford on Wednesdays, Fridays and Saturdays. Also at 75 Stoke Newington High Street, N16 (tel: 0171 254 9770).

Emporium

Camlik
13 Green Lanes N16. Tel: 0171 226 5925
Mon-Sat 9am-8.30pm

This shop was established more than 20 years ago and is a wonderful jumble of Cypriot produce. It is long and narrow with a central wooden counter piled high with aubergines, fennel, chillies, spinach and spinach-like leaves from Cyprus, Iranian melons, apricots, figs, cherries, quinces and other fruit and vegetables. Yoghurt comes in huge tubs or small earthenware pots which can be re-used once you have devoured the delicious contents. There's cow and sheep feta, and tulum (a hard, strong sheeps' cheese which is matured in a dried hide), halva, superior Turkish Delight, and jezerique, a most peculiar (to the English palate) chewy Turkish sweet made of grapes, pistachios, coconut and carrot. Pide (Turkish bread) comes plain or with walnuts and coconut.

Crouch End

Bakers

Dunns
6 The Broadway N8. Tel: 0181 340 1614
Mon-Sat 7.15am-6pm

A long-established, trusted bread and cake shop, whose current owner is the fifth generation of masterbaker in his family. The wonderfully comforting smell of fresh baking hits you before you cross the threshold; once inside, the goods live up to that early promise. There are old-fashioned cottage loaves and bloomers, trendy black olive ciabatta with extra virgin olive oil; 100 per cent stone-ground wholemeal; granaries and oaties (this last a flavoursome stunner); Lionheart (oats and wheat bran); crusty rolls, floury baps, buttery croissants (Dunn's was one of the first English bakeries to make them, over 30 years ago). All breads are animal-fat free and made with untreated, unbleached flour. On the cake side, there are American muffins, Bakewell tarts, rock cakes and scones. At lunchtimes the place is packed with hungry workers queuing for soup, pies, quiches, baked potatoes and Cornish pasties. Easter sees hot cross buns a-plenty, and in December Christmas cakes and puddings (with china bowl thrown in).

Stella's Bakery
43 The Broadway N8. Tel: 0181 341 7789
Mon-Sat 7.30am-7pm, Sun 8am-5pm

Cypriot Steve Pashallis has named his shop after his young daughter and filled it with all manner of delicious breads and pies, which he makes himself in the small rear kitchen. Rye and soda breads, Greek loaves, granary and wholemeal; carrot cake and pecan pie; haloumi and olive breads; cholla and bagels and hot cross buns – there seems to be nothing Steve cannot bake. Of particular note are the sensational and enormous, buttery croissants. Also on sale are useful bags of breadcrumbs.

Butcher

Freemans
9 Topsfield Parade N8. Tel: 0181 340 3100
Mon-Sat 9am-6pm

Steve Freeman is a second-generation butcher who took the decision some eight years ago to go 'real', turning to organic and
free-range producers. Organic lamb, pork and chickens are delivered
every Wednesday. Beef is Scotch, grass-fed, and hung for a minimum of
14 days. He stocks Simply Sausages, wild boar and venison bangers;
kangaroo and ostrich steaks; McSween's haggis; Martin Pitt eggs and
Wiltshire Tracklement condiments.

Delicatessen

Bunces
10 Broadway Parade N8. Tel: 0181 340 1720
Mon-Sat 10am-7pm, Sun 10am-5pm

A good Continental deli run by Gloria and Joseph Foradaris, who
took over here four years ago and try to supply top names from
various countries. There are coffees from Martyn's of Muswell Hill, Dell
Ugo fresh pasta, jams from Wilkin & Sons and Bonne Maman, Fern's
and Patak's pickles and chutneys, Taylor's of Harrogate teas. The meat
counter holds chorizos and cabanos, as well as Hungarian, German,
Italian and Danish salamis, pastrami and Parma ham. Home-made foods
include stuffed vine leaves, moussaka, Greek feta salad, pasta sauces,
sun-dried pepper pesto, dips, samosas and bhajis. Herrings are soused in
dill, or mustard, or sherry. Parmesan is 18 months old, and chocolates
are Belgian.

Health Food

The Haelan Centre
41 The Broadway N8. Tel: 0181 340 4258 Fax: 0181 292 2232
Mon-Sat 9am-6pm, Sun 11am-3pm

Haelan is an Anglo-Saxon word meaning 'to make whole', and Nino Booth, who set up shop as long ago as 1971, stocks his shop accordingly — i.e., he tries to make sure that no product on his shelves contains added sugar (in fact, he won't even sell organic sugar), hydrogenated fats, preservatives or additives, or anything else that might make holes in the body rather than heal it. In his 25 years in the business, Nino has noticed ordinary people have become much more interested in what they eat, with the result that organic produce and unadulterated foodstuffs are far more available. His stock is 50 per cent organic; vegetables are 100 per cent organic. There are a few things that the non-vegetarian might sniff at, such as 'scheese', a soya-based solid which comes as 'Cheshire-style', 'Cheddar-style', or 'Mozzarella-style'. But there are also goodies such as Duskin's apple juices, Tropical Wholefoods, sun-dried fruits, organic buttermilk, Green and Black organic chocolate, La Terra e Il Cielo organic pastas, De Rit honeys and other products, Mr Bean's soups, lots of pulses, nuts and grains (including kasha and bulgar), Celtic Bakery breads, Miel des Pyrenees single-blossom honeys (rhododendron, raspberry) and Meridian 100 per cent fruit jams.

Central Finchley

Baker

Marlene's Bakery & Deli
6 Hendon Lane N3. Tel: 0181 349 1674
Mon-Thu 6am-5pm, Fri & Sun 6am-1pm

Marlene Harris is renowned for her egg cholla as far afield as Brighton and Bournemouth, made every Thursday and Friday, but like all good Jewish bakeries she also does a brisk trade in bulka, the 'everyday' loaf, and bagels, the 'all-night' roll. Her team of bakers work round the clock, with the day-shift producing the cakes and biscuits, and the night-shift the breads — wholemeal and granary, white and baguettes in addition to the Jewish loaves. For lunchtime snackers there are salads, soup, gefilte fish, hot potato latkes, filled bagels and pizzas.

Emporium

Marimo

350-356 Regent's Park Road N3. Tel: 0181 346 1042
Tue-Sun 10am-8pm

One section of this large store is entirely given over to shelf after shelf of videos, all in plain white covers with titles in Japanese, which lends a decidedly 'inscrutable' air to the place. Thankfully, the edible side is more recognisable – here are the freezerfuls of frozen fish and fish heads, the jars of pickled radish, ginger, cucumber and assorted veg, the bottles of sukiyaki and teriyaki sauces, the packets of quick noodle soups, the sheets of seaweed, the rice crackers, dried fungi, sai-fun noodles and green teas that you'd expect from a good Japanese supermarket. At the back is a wet-fish counter where they prepare take-away sushi and sashimi.

Fishmonger

Pedro

95 Ballards Lane N3. Tel: 0181 346 8525
Tue-Sat 9am-6pm

Supermarkets can survive without selling fish – we can't,' declares the notice in Pedro's window, a challenge to his customers that was probably unnecessary ten years ago when he first set up shop. Inside, the mild-mannered Pedro serves loyal customers (Spanish and Portuguese in particular) with fresh fish of the day: cuttlefish and con-ger eel, tilapia and snappers, sea bream and red bream, codling and whiting. Being Spanish, he is unfazed by requests to 'save the ink' from cuttlefish and squid – indeed, it is second nature to him, so that he usu-ally has a little plastic bag of it tucked away (either creature cooked in its own ink is a far superior dish to any other method). His freezers hold raw, frozen tiger prawns, prawns in filo pastry (to be fried in oil and garlic) and what little fish has not sold on its 'fresh' day – these are labelled in red when they are brought to the slab again, for instant identification.

Greengrocer

C & D Fruiterers

54 Hendon Lane N3. Tel: 0181 346 5076
Tue 6am-6pm, Wed 6am-7pm, Thu & Fri 6am- 6pm, Sat 7am-5pm

You'd think that the ex-personnel officer of a major oil company would have a special way with customers – well, Carol Warren does, but not in quite the way you'd expect. Hers is less soothing tact, more abrasive up-front jollity, but since she took over this 35-year-old veg shop some four years ago her manner seems to have endeared her to the well-heeled housewives of Hendon. Apparently, they don't mind at all being told: 'If you want to play with the tomatoes, buzz off down the supermarket' (although her language is somewhat stronger), and being greeted with raucous familiarity. The quality of her produce might have something to do with their tolerance, all good stuff from Spital-fields market, where Carol feels she has more control over what she buys – tender, young pak-choi, baby red onions, several different vari-eties of potatoes, lovely dark green Savoy cabbages, papayas, mangoes and much more, all piled precariously high on either side of her tiny narrow shop.

T J Ellingham

179 Ballards Lane N3. Tel: 0181 346 1721
Mon-Sat 6am-5.30pm

The Ellinghams certainly know their onions, as it were. A real costermongering family, they started out with a barrow in a long-vanished market some 50 years ago, taking cover in Ballards Lane around 1965. Now they are affectionately known simply as 'Ellie's' by their many long-standing customers, one of whom volunteered that they beat the supermarkets on quality *and* price. Gary Ellingham is helped out by two brothers-in-law, one sister, one nephew and Dave 'the Leek', so-called because of his handy way of arranging said veg-etable. Everything is checked for quality before being put on display, and inferior produce sold off cheap; root vegetables are cleaned up, sugar snaps topped 'n' tailed, sprouts stripped of their outer leaves.

South African peaches and nectarines are available from about January onwards, Chilean cherries shine redly in November. In summer months the shop almost disappears behind salad leaves (Gary has a good selection year-round, but reckons that people like a break). And there are always huge, luscious pineapples, strawberries, raspberries and blueberries. What you might call a peach of a shop.

Ice-Cream/Coffee Shop

Friends
146 Ballards Lane N3. Tel: 0181 346 0904
Mon-Thu 9.30am-8.30pm, Fri-Sun 9.30am-10.30pm

Mr Ellinas ran a popular Greek deli at this address for years, but the end of 1995 saw him yield to the pressures exerted by local supermarkets and turn his deli into Friends. The ice-cream is Cypriot (no animal fats, no colourings or preservatives, only fresh fruits), and damn fine it is too. His coffee beans are still supplied by Martyn's of Muswell Hill. In addition, he has Greek cakes, taramasalata, hommmos, and makes kleftiko and moussaka for lunchers. The walls are decorated with posters of Elvis and Marilyn Monroe. Mr Ellinas seems a little saddened by the change, as doubtless will be many of his customers. But come the summer, it's to be hoped that they will flock back for the excellent ice-cream.

East Finchley

Baker/Pâtisserie

Chorak
122 High Road N2. Tel: 0181 442 0370 Fax: 0181 442 0372
Mon-Sat 8.30am-6pm

Parvin and husband Javed started this business three and a bit years ago, and have clearly filled a niche in the area – apart from a branch of Ridley Bagel Bakery across the street, there isn't another decent bakery/pâtisserie in Finchley. Displayed on a wall is a certificate from the Grands Moulins de Paris, authenticating their baguettes and other French loaves; there are also granaries, farmhouse, wholemeal, speciality loaves, such as cheese and onion, and on Fridays ciabatta, cholla and Arab barberi. On the sweet side, there are Danish pastries, palmiers, apple tarts, chocolate slices, cream puffs, American muffins (incredibly popular), cookies and other biscuits. At lunchtimes queues form for the soups, take-away sandwiches, quiches and pies. Everything is made on the premises.

Butcher

Grahams
134 East End Road N2. Tel: 0181 883 6187
Tue-Sat 8.30am-5.30pm, Sun 8.30am-1pm

Sunday opening, which started about 18 months ago, is just one aspect of this traditional butcher which attests to the Mien family's adaptability. Graham bought these tiny premises over 25 years ago, since when he, his sister Ann, and now his son David have been responding to the demands of the area with imagination and cheeriness. The South Africans of Finchley called for biltong and boerewors, so they found a supplier for the former and learnt to make the latter from their customers' recipes, experimenting with the variations until a consensus was reached. Finchley families seem keen on barbecues, so in summer Graham produces tons of ready-spiked kebabs, home-made hamburgers ('to Delia's recipe') and, of course, sausages, of which he makes 10-15 different kinds (available year round). Nowadays, the cry is for 'real' meat, so they sell nothing but free-range, humanely treated, naturally reared meat and poultry. Beef is either Welsh Black from Black Mountain Foods (which now accounts for 70 per cent of Graham's beef sales) or free-range Aberdeen Angus; pork is from Plantation Pigs which rootle around Sussex fields; lamb and poultry, including duck and geese, come through Pure Suffolk Foods and with their guarantee of quality. Bacon is traditionally dry cured from free-range Gloucestershire pigs. They carry a few salamis and good old-fashioned pressed tongue.

Organic meat can be ordered, but Graham is keen that customers should understand that 'organic' simply refers to the condition of the soil the animals are reared on – not to the quality of the breed ('lots of organic farmers didn't start with good stock'), of animal husbandry or whether the beasts are medicinally treated (even so, I was sorely tempted by a joint of organic smoked lamb). Ever enterprising, the Miens make Christmas pudding at the relevant time of year. They describe themselves as 'traditional butchers with a modern slant', possibly one of the few promotional slogans not to be ripe for review under the Trades Description Act.

Delicatessen

Amici

78 High Road N2 Tel: 0181 444 2932
Mon-Sat 8am-7pm, Sun 9.30am-1pm

When I called upon what I thought was going to be long-established Philip Baretta's delicatessen I found Amici, whose doors had only been open for a matter of hours. Mr Baretta had retired due to ill-health, and his premises had been taken over by his young friends, Renato and Maurizio. They have made a few changes: there is now seating around a couple of the tables at the front of the shop and along a counter running down one side, where you can hang out with a steaming cup of espresso or cappuccino; the deli proper is hidden at the back, so that from the street you might not recognize it as a source of good Italian produce. This would be a pity as the new owners are attempting to continue the tradition of quality supplies, even to the point of eventually re-introducing hand-carved and hand-tied Parma ham on the bone (a rarity in this country), for which Mr Baretta was famous. It would be unfair to judge a shop on its first few hours of business; suffice it to say that although stock was not extensive, what there was on display seemed excellent: Renato has been running L'Europa in Seven Sisters Road for seven years and his experience will doubtless tell here, even if he and Maurizio are going for a more 'nineties' look and feel.

Fishmonger

A Scott & Son
94 High Road N2. Tel: 0181 444 7606
Tue-Thu 8.30am-5.30pm, Fri 8.30am-6pm, Sat 8.30am-5pm

The business may only have been in the Scott family for 15 years, but Trevor (second generation) and his partner Clive Matthews are justly proud that they are maintaining a long tradition – this is the only shop on the street which has not changed its purpose in 100 years. And in keeping with the shop's pre-technology past, Trevor and Clive let nothing frozen through its doors. They smoke their own haddock, cod, salmon, and occasional kippers, boil their own lobsters and crabs, carry other smoked fish, such as sprats, tuna and halibut, from reliable suppliers, and do not shy away from jellied eels; but the emphasis is on wet and fresh, and the cod steaks I bought were excellent. They have the biggest plaice I think I've ever seen ('families round here like their fish whole'), plus the whole range from turbot to jacks (aka scad or horse mackerel). On Saturdays, shellfish almost take over – winkles, whelks, cockles, mussels. They will get anything to order, prepare your squid for you (preserving the ink), and even fillet a red mullet (although Trevor would advise against anything so wasteful).

North Finchley

Chocolates

Exclusive Chocolate Shop
797 High Road N12. Tel: 0181 446 2560
Mon-Sat 9.30am-6pm

Mrs Shah describes her shop as 'a bit of the West End in North Finchley' and you could not fault her. It's a very classy joint, with Valrhona, Belgian truffles (of which the Champagne variety sell fastest), creams, nuts, pralines and marzipans, English mints etc, all prettily arranged. There's also a good choice of sugar-free diabetic chocolates (Belgian), plain, milk or white. Apart from the mints, top-brand English chocolates are not in evidence, but as Mrs Shah says, 'people do not expect to pay top prices' for the home-grown sort. Mail order can be arranged by special request, and they'll fill and custom-wrap almost any kind of container for gifts. Unrelated sidelines include masses of teddy bears, aromatherapy oils and floating candles.

Delicatessen

Lina's

601 High Road N12. Tel: 0181 446 6011
Tue-Thu, Sat 8.30am-6pm, Fri 8.30am-7pm, Sun 10am-1pm

Lina Centanni's husband is a wholesale coffee merchant, so she carries a wide range of recently roasted beans in her well-stocked but spacious shop. She also has fresh pasta, her own tiramisu, which she makes in party quantities, and daily breads from Il Fornaio. Otherwise, this is a good basic deli with lots of pastas and sauces, risotto rice, biscotti, salamis and hams, and a small selection of wines, including sake for the Japanese community (Lina gets advice from the helpful staff of Atari-Ya).

Fishmonger

Atari-Ya

595 High Road N12. Tel: 0181 446 6669 Fax: 0181 446 6728
Tue-Fri 10am-6.30pm, Sat & Sun 10am-7pm

There's long been a strong Japanese presence in Finchley, and this branch of Atari-Ya (there's another in Acton, see entry) has been providing it with good fresh fish for some years. One counter contains the prepared species – kingfish, salmon, sea-urchin roe, sea bass, turbot, bluefin tuna, squid and octopus, all beautifully filleted in readiness for sushi or sashimi. The other displays the same varieties before the knife-artist got to them, plus those that would not be eaten raw (gurnard, scad, sardines), cured and salted kinds and shellfish. There's a minuscule section of Japanese dry goods and thinly sliced beef.

Finsbury Park

Emporia

Mehboob

35 Stroud Green Road N4. Tel: 0171 263 7654
Mon-Thu 8.30am-8.30pm, Fri-Sat 7.30am-8.30pm, Sun 8.30am-7.30pm

An Afro-Caribbean store offering lots of different flours (from yams, cassava, potatoes), West African dried fish, beans and rice, hot sauces, tinned ackee, ogbono (the kernel of the African bush mango), egusi (pumpkin seeds), as well as fresh fruit and veg - plantains, chow-chow, yams and sweet potatoes, sorrel flowers, okra, pigeon peas, papaya, mangoes, breadfruit and jackfruit, coconuts, soursop, etc.

Pak Cash & Carry

25-27 Stroud Green Road N4. Tel: 0171 272 3370
Mon-Sun 8am-9pm

The largest of the Afro-Caribbean stores along Stroud Green Road, this has a vast selection of flours, rices, pulses, gari (pounded cassava), in industrial quantities; Patak pickles; tins of soursop soup, callaloo (green leaves of the potato-like dasheen plant used to make the soup of the same name), ackee (a red-skinned fruit often cooked with saltfish), coconut milk, palmnut concentrate; the flavoured syrups so popular with Jamaicans; and hard dough breads, spicy breads and 'buns' — actually dense loaves with sugar, caramel, vanilla and currants. Outside are yams, plantains, cassava, mangoes, papayas, guavas, etc.

Stroud Green Food Store

65 Stroud Green Road N4. Tel: 0171 272 0348
Mon-Sun 8am-9pm

This jolly shop specialises in Jamaican groceries, so there's an abundance of hot sauces, tinned veg, herbal bitters, Constitution bitters (good for 'general debility'!), syrups, sorrel drink, salt-cod, etc.

Outside are bonnet peppers, Ghanaian garden eggs (small, yellow and aubergine-like), karela, chow-chow, yams, red sorrel flowers (from which the drink is made), fresh peanuts and lots more.

Fishmonger

France Fresh Fish
99 Stroud Green Road N4. Tel: 0171 263 9767
Mon-Sat 9am-7pm

The charming France Ng was a BT engineer before swapping his telephones for fish over 12 years ago. Ninety-five per cent of his stock is fresh British fish coming from Billingsgate Market, but most being imported direct from his homeland of Mauritius, the Seychelles, Florida, the Gulf and the West Indies. This inevitably means that some have to be frozen for the journey, and these are clearly marked as such. There are fresh redfish, snappers and tilapia, barracuda, parrot fish, jackfish, conch, frozen lobsters, as well as the more prosaic red mullet, salmon, etc.

Haringey

Baker/Pâtisserie

Barnaby Pâtisserie
8 Grand Parade Green Lanes N4. Tel: 0181 802 0275
Mon-Sat 8.30am-10pm, Sun 10am-8pm

'We have 400 different lines,' says Nicos Georgiou proudly, not wanting to be characterised as a strictly Greek Cypriot baker. And indeed, alongside the kadayife and baclava, you'll find granary and wholemeal loaves, Victoria sponges, French fruit tarts and petits fours, apple pies and American muffins. A speciality of this popular, smart shop is vassilopitta, a Greek New Year's sponge cake ('but not the English kind of sponge') flavoured with orange juice and peel. Everything is made daily on the premises, staff are friendly and well-turned-out.

Yasar Halim

495-7 Green Lanes N4. Tel: 0181 340 8090
Mon-Sat 8.30am-10pm, Sun 8.30am-9pm

This large popular Turkish-Cypriot bakery has been going since 1981. Baking goes on all day in the rear kitchens, so you will almost certainly bump into something oven-fresh and still-warm – corek, the traditional Turkish bread, round Cypriot loaves, olive and cheese breads, huge flat ones like plates. There are gozleme, like pancakes, with spinach, cheese or mincemeat fillings; kofte, cracked-wheat balls with spices and mince; pilavna; halouli, sultanas and dried mint in a pastry case; borek, vegetable pies; tahini and cinnamon pastries. And, of course, sweet pastries galore – ladies' fingers, baclava, kadayife, deep-fried honey-balls, aniseed biscuits, etc.

Emporia

Ozgur Supermarket

397 Green Lanes N4. Tel: 0181 348 1074
Mon-Sun 7am-11pm

The first thing you notice on entering this small, friendly Turkish store are the necklaces of dried aubergine, courgette, red pepper and okra skins. Further exploration reveals bottles of 100 per cent natural turnip juice ('very good for the stomach'), Turkish sausages and salamis, several different kinds of feta, the hard strong sheep's cheese called tulum, to be eaten with, I was advised, 'hand-made' Turkish butter, hot pepper and tomato sauces, pide and somun (breads).

The Turkish Food Centre

385 Green Lanes N4. Tel: 0181 340 4547
Mon-Sun 8am-9pm

A spacious store, with heaps of good fresh veg, fruit and herbs – peppers, aubergines, white courgettes, baby cucumbers, flat white cabbage leaves, long green chillies, plump tomatoes, spinach, quinces, prickly pears, mint, coriander, dill. There's black olive paste and tarhana (a mixture of fermented yoghurt and wheat, used as a soup base), dried

white mulberries, rose petal jam and sour cherry juice, Turkish ice-cream,
lots of nuts, rice and pulses, tins of prepared vegetable dishes (aubergines
in tomato sauce, stuffed peppers, stuffed vine leaves), Turkish and Arabic
breads, a big choice of olives and cheeses, and a halal butchery.

Andreas Michli & Sons

405 St Ann's Road N4. Tel: 0181 802 0188 Fax: 0181 802 3681
Mon-Sat 9.30am-7.30pm, Sun 11am-3.30pm

'I am only a village shop,' says Andreas, twiddling his black mous-
tache and grinning widely. Would that all 'village shops' were
like his – eccentric and delightful. From the ceiling hang dry gourds,
wickerwork, ceramic birds, crucifixes; a saucepan of freshly cooked
beetroot sits on the floor; plastic tubs of marinated olives line the window – it's all very informal and friendly. Andreas has been in the area
for 32 years and is well known to lovers of Cypriot produce. He has
endive, rocket, spinach, parsley, coriander, hollyhock leaves (for soup),
mustard, fennel, lemons with stem and leaf, all what he calls 'wild',
grown on the hills of his homeland. (He's so keen on veg and herbs that
he is trying to buy his own farm here in order to grow them.) There are
masses of dried herbs and spices, Greek cured meats (basta – smoked
boneless rib of pork; chiromeri – smoked leg of pork; pastourma – fillet
of beef, wrapped in a paste of garlic and spices), Greek and Turkish
breads (including vassilopitta at Christmas and lambropsomo at Easter),
young dried broad beans (which Andreas swears are an aphrodisiac),
and sougoukkos, dried grape juice on a long string. Andreas will happily explain unfamiliar items and offer recipes.

Fishmonger

Andreas Fish Bar

445 Green Lanes N4. Tel: 0181 347 5310
Mon-Sun 8.30am-8.30pm (Fri & Sat till 9.30pm, Sun till 7.30pm)

It seems entirely natural for a take-away fish 'n' chips joint to sell
wet-fish as well, and surprising that more don't. Andreas and his
mum have been successfully combining the two for eight years now.

The window display is beautifully arranged with black bream, grouper, herrings, fresh snappers, voper (a Greek fish), tilapia, sardines, cuttle-fish, oysters and mussels, all fresh from the market that morning. Of course, there's also plaice, haddock and cod, ready to be freshly fried.

Highbury

Butcher

Frank Godfrey

7 Highbury Park N5. Tel: 0171 226 2425
Mon-Sat 8am-6pm

One of the few remaining traditional breeds of sheep native to this country is the North Ronaldsay which feeds on seaweed on the shores of that island in Orkney. So rare is it that the Rare Breeds Survival Trust removed some for safekeeping to the uninhabited island of Linga-holm, where the flock is culled annually. Said to produce similar meat to the pre-sale lamb of the Brittany salt-marshes, it is damnably difficult to get hold of – the two islands together produce only about 200 carcasses a year. However, brothers Chris, Jerry and Phillip Godfrey, who get their grass-fed Aberdeen Angus-cross beef from Orkney Meat in any case, have recently started to take North Ronaldsay lamb when they can, and it is well worth trying. Although known as 'lamb' (because the breed is natu-rally small and grows slowly – what wouldn't on a diet of seaweed? – and therefore produces small joints), the age of the animals at slaughter (between one and three years) means that strictly speaking this is mutton, and it should not be dressed otherwise. Traditionally, in the Orkney Islands, it is slow-roasted, or pot-roasted with vegetables, making a fine, rich dish with a distinctly different flavour from cultivated lamb – which, of course, the Godfreys also have. Pork is Sussex free-range from Broom-lye Estate Plantation Pigs, poultry from Organic Farmers and Growers Association approved breeders. The brothers Godfrey also dry-cure their own bacon with cloves, juniper berries and a bit of sugar, salt their own brisket, make their own sausages using fresh herbs, leeks, etc, and stock a few fancy French items such as rillettes d'oie. If this all sounds too much of an elaborate thing, be assured that this is still a real butcher's, with all the usual joints and cuts and some things not so often seen, particularly at the cheaper end, such as skirt, caul fat and ham bones for broth.

Cheesemonger

La Fromagerie
30 Highbury Park N5. Tel: 0171 359 7440
Mon 11am-7.30pm, Tue-Sat 9.30am-7.30pm, Sun 10am-4.30pm

Patricia Michelson's maturing room, presided over by Eric, the French affineur, must be one of the most pungent places in London. Over 200 cheeses, aged from a few days to two years and including some 30 goat varieties, sit on straw matting gaining taste and texture. The majority are French and Italian, searched out under Patricia's instructions by contacts in each country. She's a self-taught cheese buff, having become interested in the stuff on skiing holidays, then setting up a kind of maturing-room/shop in her garden shed some five years ago. Among the many, many interesting cheeses she has are Fourme au Sauternes, crumbly and sweetish, to be served, according to Eric, 'as an aperitif'; Foglie di Noce, a Pecorino matured in a pit with walnut leaves and shells for about nine months; Astuzias, a cows'/goats'/sheep's milk mix, strong and blue; and a two-year-old Beaufort, which is sheer heaven – face-tinglingly strong, but still creamy. There are also home-made tarts and quiches, tortelloni, Poilâne pain de campagne delivered weekly from Paris ('the perfect cheese accompaniment'), chocolates from Burgundy, lingue crispe biscuits ('mother-in-law's tongue'), Sally Clarke's breads at weekends, and made specially for Patricia a dark rye with pecan nuts.

Delicatessen

Da Rocco
67 Highbury Park N5. Tel: 0171 359 2670
Mon-Sat 8am-7pm

Before landing on this unprepossessing stretch of road six months ago, Rocco Donvito traded for seven years from premises round the corner in Gillespie Road, and it is tempting to imagine homeward-bound Arsenal football fans stopping off for a little higher sustenance than hotdogs and burgers. For, although Rocco carries the basic Italian groceries, hams, salamis and cheeses, the nub of his business is home-made pasta which he makes in the small backroom, where great sheets of it can be seen hanging up to dry. From these, he makes ravioli with lobster and crab, or veal; tortelloni with saffron and orange, spinach and basil, sun-dried tomatoes, or mushrooms; paglio fino; and tagliatelle. He also makes pesto and bolognese sauces, and is happy to do lasagne to order.

Highgate

Butcher

The Highgate Butcher
76 Highgate High Street N6. Tel: 0181 340 9817
Mon-Fri 7.30am-5.45pm, Sat 7am-5pm

Mother-and-son partners Phyllis and Lee Harper run a small, old-fashioned, no-frills butchery. Beef is grass-fed best Aberdeen Angus, lambs are Welsh, pork from free-range Cherry Tree Farm pigs which have rootled about a bit in fields. Chicken, ducks and turkeys are all free-range, they have a game licence and will pluck and draw. Lee is particularly proud of the 20 different sausages he makes – chicken, lamb, pork and garlic, beef and Guinness, a rusk-free Toulouse, all in natural skins. There's a selection of cheeses and free-range eggs.

Holloway

Delicatessen

L'Europa
78 Seven Sisters Road N7. Tel: 0171 700 3132
Mon-Sat 9am-6.30pm

A good Italian deli run by brothers Renato and Gianni Paganuzzi for the past six and a half years (Renato also has a share in Amici in East Finchley). There are lots of pastas and accompanying sauces, bacala, wines and liqueurs, a wide range of salamis and hams, including the delicious speck from the Tyrol, coppa di Parma, Spanish chorizo piccante and dolce; Pecorino, Provolone and Manchego cheeses; pasteis de nata, those yummy little Portuguese custard tarts. Fresh sandwiches are available daily at lunchtimes, and they will cater for buffets as far afield as Barnet.

Fishmonger

Fresco Fish

60 Seven Sisters Road N7. Tel: 0171 700 1939
Tue-Thu 7am-6pm, Fri & Sat 7am-7pm

Tony and Sophie Sophocli, London-born Greek Cypriots, stock fish for all tastes, from jellied eels to flying fish and Cornish shark steaks. Eighty-five per cent is fresh, much flown in direct (on Tuesdays and Thursdays) from the Caribbean – kingfish, jackfish, tilapia, snappers, etc – and assistant Paolo goes to France twice a week for Continental supplies. They also use Billingsgate. Squid and cuttlefish are lovely and inky (they will keep the ink if requested, and also sell the little sachets of it). There are also 'cod pieces', and salmon heads and skins for stock, soups or cats.

Greengrocers

Gibber of Holloway

116 Seven Sisters Road N7. Tel: 0171 607 5449
Mon-Thu, Sat 8am-6pm, Fri 8am-7pm

Although this famous, 30-year-old shop went self-service about five years ago, there is still an army of men and women shifting boxes, re-arranging displays, and willing to offer advice, suggestions and help. The Gibbers are a costermongering family – Albert started out as a barrow-boy in the long-vanished Seaton Street Market, his son Michael is now doing most of the day-to-day ordering, and they have always been very much part of the local community (during the last long postal strike in the 1970s, they made up bags of fruit and vegetables for pensioners, who were unable to collect their pensions, to ensure they didn't starve). They have what Michael calls a 'Mediterranean profile of customers' – Greek, Italian, Spanish, French, Egyptian and Moroccan – which perhaps explains why his three key lines are cucumbers, lemons and garlic. The Russian trade delegates, who visit en masse once a week, presumably come for Michael's excellent cabbages, beetroot and potatoes. Gibber also sell their produce wholesale to surrounding restaurants, so there are Thai and Chinese vegetables as well. In addition there are baby strawberries, Italian new potatoes, kologassi, fresh coriander, wild rocket and nuts galore. Special offers include such things as mixed bags of peppers and garlic for the knock-down price of 70 pence. Fruit is often on offer by the box (popular, apparently, with the Stamford Hill Orthodox Jewish community). Apart from those items on special offer, it is not necessarily the cheapest greengrocer around, but then Michael says they go for quality and value rather than the rock-bottom prices.

Seven Sisters Greengrocers
70 Seven Sisters Road N7. Tel: 0171 607 9070
Mon-Sun 7am-8pm

There are Afro-Caribbean fruit and vegetables a-plenty at Seven Sisters Greengrocers – plantains, yams, cassava, chow-chow, bonnet peppers, fierce little red, green and yellow chillies, sorrel flowers, mangoes, guava, papaya, a few fresh herbs, and the rest. It is also a supermarket with varied stocks ranging from flavoured syrups, malt drinks, pulses, rices and hot sauces to Jamaican spiced bread, ghee, jasmine oil and palmnut soup.

Hornsey

Baker

Queen of Tarts

173 Priory Road N8. Tel: 0181 340 1854
Mon-Sat 8am-5.30pm, Sun 8am-2.30pm

Sumptuous French fruit tarts, traditional English breads – granary, wholemeal, bloomers – spicy kebab rolls, vegetable spring rolls, chicken and sweetcorn pasties, samosas, meat and vegetable pies, doughnuts, croissants, pains au chocolat, doughnuts, almond slices, cream sponges, fruit cakes, eclairs – Mr Mounti, 15 years a master baker, makes everything imaginable and all of it excellent.

Butcher

L R Daniel

304 Park Road N8. Tel: 0181 340 1720
Tue-Fri 8am-5.30pm, Sat 8am-4pm

Half-way between the 'villages' of Crouch End and Muswell Hill, this good old-fashioned butcher of 38 years' standing keeps the independence flag flying against the odds (he still has Queen of Tarts round the corner for company, but the greengrocer has gone and with it some custom). However, moving with the times Les, the manager, went 'real' about a year ago, getting pork, and lamb and beef from Pure Suffolk Foods. He tries to have some of each in stock all the time, but supplies are limited so it's probably best to order in advance if you're set on organic or a particular joint (in organic beef, for instance, Les usually only has about 7-9kg (15-20lb) of stewing steak and a couple of ribs at any one time). Chickens are free-range from PSF. In addition to the organic, there's 'ordinary' English lamb and Scotch beef (grass-fed, naturally reared, Les assures me: 'we try to avoid anything intensively farmed'). Finally, there's Irish smoked salmon and free-range eggs, and Home Farm jams, pickles, mustards.

Islington

Baker/Pâtisserie

Bliss

248 St John Street EC1. Tel: 0171 837 3720
Mon-Fri 8am-7pm, Sat & Sun 9am-6pm

In the early 1970s there were plenty of places like this. A wall covered in hand-written ads for rooms-to-let/wanted, services offered, theatre projects, lost cats, etc, attests to its community spirit, it's painted brightly in blue and red, and staff are young and friendly - indeed, the only things that distinguish it from its predecessors are the lack of dope-smoke and the vastly superior quality of the food. Baker Tim Jones trained as an architect and the building industry's loss is the croissant-lover's gain – his almond one is sublimely light and is justly famed in the area. There are also pecan, hazelnut and walnut tarts, summer fruits on crème pâtissière or cheesecake, wild berries on frangipane, cheese and tomato croissants, mushroom/cheese filo parcels, walnut/onion/courgette/ham quiche, pizzas, cream cheese/apple/coriander/pesto sandwiches, and fruity cakes. Breads include walnut and onion, olive and herb, basil and sun-dried tomato, sesame, poppy, black rye, and organic. The coffee is good and strong and there's enough seating for about a dozen dawdlers. In keeping with the democratic spirit of the place, Bena, Kamal, Jenny and David must also be mentioned, who bake or serve in this extremely pleasant, relaxed place.

Butchers

James Elliott

96 Essex Road N1. Tel: 0171 226 3658
Mon-Sat 6am-6pm

A long-established family business with a huge local following which is in no way deterred by the sides of beef, dark of flesh and yellow of fat, in the window (many butchers have yielded to 20th-century squeamishness by banishing the carcasses to a backroom cold store). The naturally-reared free-range beef is from the highly respected Mathers of Inverurie and is hung for three weeks, lamb and free-range pork comes from Devon (the last going into the home-made sausages). Bacon is dry-cured from Bourne's of Raynham. Game is well represented in season – pheasants, mallard, teal, wild boar, etc. At Christmas (notwithstanding their reputation for radicalism, Islingtonians are apparently a traditional bunch when it comes to festivities), almost the entire shop is given over to Norfolk free-range turkeys which hang in plump-breasted rows, naked bar the white neck ruff, like so many dowager duchesses who have forgotten to finish dressing for the ball. Apart from the meat, there is an excellent selection of farmhouse cheeses – Harbourne Blue, James Aldridge's Celtic Promise and Tornegus, fresh unpasteurised goats', Cashel Blue and Keen's cheddar among them – and delicious Wiltshire Tracklements.

J R Wall

399 St John Street EC1. Tel: 0171 837 1781 (answerphone)
Mon 9am-1pm, Tue-Sat 9am-5pm

Mr Wall's shop is a beaut from the outside, attractively clad in shiny tiles. Inside, it is minimalist and old-fashioned, but comes recommended by several meat-loving friends of mine. All the beef, huge sides of which sit on the stone window ledges, is from naturally-reared, grass-fed Scottish animals, and Mr Wall proudly says he has never sold anything else in his 40 years here. He hangs the sides of beef for 14 days minimum, and is prepared to hang it longer if asked (but, he explains, 'it mortifies itself' – i.e., loses weight and therefore increases in price). Lamb comes from the West Country, pork is antibiotic-free. Chickens, ducks, geese and turkeys are all free-range, pork/garlic, pork/herb and venison sausages are all home-made, and there's always plenty of game in season, hare and partridge included.

Cheesemonger

Barstow & Barr
24 Liverpool Road N1. Tel/fax: 0171 359 4222
Mon-Fri 10am-8pm, Sat 10am-6pm, Sun 10am-2pm

A small, pleasant two-year-old shop, run by Jennifer Barr and husband David and piled high with mature and maturing cheeses, 90 per cent of which are unpasteurised and British. Among the less familiar names from around the country are Tyning, a hard ewes' milk cheese matured for 6-12 months which, according to Henrietta Green, 'rivals any Pecorino', Bonnet and gold-medal-winning Swinzie (goats' and sheep's respectively) from Scotland, Isle of Mull, buttery Richard III Wensleydale from Yorkshire (apparently the nearest thing to the pre-mass production original). Then there are the old favourites – Kirkham's Lancashire, Ford Farm Cheddar, Cotherstone, Wigmore – and from Ireland Gubbeen, Durrus and Killorglin among others. Continental cheeses are not entirely absent, with French goats' particularly well represented. There are also Wendy Brandon pickles, Sally Clarke's breads, olives and biscuits.

Chocolates

Dugan's Chocolates
149a Upper Street N1. Tel: 0171 354 4666 Fax: 0171 837 4300
Mon-Sat 10am-6.30pm, Sun 11am-5.30pm

A nnie Dugan Webster's minuscule shop is more of a grotto, 'choc-a-bloc' with the stuff. Those walls not supporting 'choc-full' shelves are decorated with Victorian stick-on angels, flower baskets, birds and animals and there's barely room for Annie and assistants Jane and Evie, never mind the customers. While Annie is serious about chocolate, still eating it for breakfast after nine years, this is a delightfully frivolous place, where the connoisseur will find superior hand-made Belgian truffles, liqueurs and crèmes, and the child any number of amusing novelties – tool kits, ladybirds, cars, bears, rabbits, many of them by Ackerman. Most of the chocolates are bought in, but Annie does make her own sumptuously rich chocolate fudge. At Easter, they hand-foil Belgian eggs, filling them with their own selections; for Valentine's Day they fill chocolate hearts with truffles (and no doubt human ones with joy), decorating them by hand and piping suitable messages of 'lurve'.

Delicatessens

Limoncello
402 St John Street EC1. Tel: 0171 713 1678
Mon-Fri 8.30am-7pm, Sat 9.30am-5pm

Suzanne Heyd and Elizabeth Mitchell opened their delightful deli/gastronomia in September '94, painting it a mood-enhancing yellow and calling it after the Italian liqueur of which Elizabeth drank a good deal on a holiday on the Amalfi coast. They are both into quality food, to which end they stock a carefully chosen range of British goods - Martin Pitt's free-range eggs, farmhouse cheeses (Ticklemore, Keen's Cheddar, Innes, Beenleigh Blue), Wiltshire Tracklement mustards and other condiments, Fudge's biscuits, Duskin's single-variety apple juices, Richard Woodhall's Cumbrian dry-cured bacon, breads from Kolos in Bradford (Ukrainian rye), Innes and the Old Post Office Bakery in Clapham. But they're not chauvinist, also carrying French and Italian cheeses (including the Pecorini rosso and nero from the slopes of Mount Amiata in Tuscany), Seggiano oil and sweet chestnut honey, fresh pasta, salami and Parma ham. The gastronomia side is produced by two ex-Arts Café cooks, Gwen Sampe and Catherine O'Sullivan, in the downstairs kitchen. Their ever-changing menu includes dishes such as chicken and pork meatballs, couscous, roasted aubergine fritters, pot-roast boned leg of lamb, pepper-and-herb tortilla. In the summer, the garden out back fills with dawdlers, although there may be less room for them this year as Suzanne and Elizabeth plan to grow more herbs, such as sorrel and borage.

Monte's
23 Cannonbury Lane N1. Tel/fax: 0171 354 4335
Mon-Fri 9.30am-7pm, Sat 9.30am-6pm, Sun 10.30am-2pm

Julia Monte worked in various traditional delis until three years ago, when she decided there was a need for something a little different. She describes her shop as 'sort of New Age', which should not lead one to imagine a place full of quartz crystals and ambient muzak (though there is background music), but one selling 'modern Italian food in pleasant modern surroundings'. And indeed, the atmosphere is sleekly modern, metal shelving stacked with up-market produce such as elegant bottles of layered and multi-coloured flavoured salts (which Julia swears people use rather than just admire), estate-bottled oils, polentas and chestnut flour, persechelle (unripe baby peaches) in truffle oil, expensive and extraordinary 'fruit' pastas (cranberry, bilberry, sweet orange), baba sorrento with lemon liqueur, Vin Santo cake with aniseeds. Some might dismiss such things as mere faddishness, but Julia is clearly hitting a spot among the younger professionals with which the area is hotching. More traditionally, for no Italian deli can safely ignore the basics, there are lots of salami, hams and cheeses; home-made Italian sausages, ravioli and tiramisu; marinated olives; breads baked from imported frozen Italian doughs. Parties as well as dinner parties are also catered for.

Olga Stores

30 Penton Street N1. Tel: 0171 837 5467
Mon-Fri 9am-8pm, Sat 9am-7pm, Sun 10am-2pm

Z enaida Almonte, the charming and diminutive Filipina who runs, with Bettina and Donata (from Sicily and Vicenze respectively), this famous deli, could hardly have better credentials for the job. She worked first at Luigi's in Fulham and then Camisa in Soho, learning her now-faultless Italian off staff and customers because 'I loved the work'. There's a full range of general Mediterranean groceries which probably has not changed much in the shop's 43-year life, a dozen different home-marinated olives, several home-made pasta sauces (a spicy Napolitano pesto is excellent), olive paste, artichoke paste, grilled veg, mushroom/ricotta gnocchi, huge ravioli, tortelloni with sun-dried tomatoes, ricotta and Parmesan, and tiramisu. Hams and salamis include Tyrolean speck, toscana with fennel, piccante and a new product, salame fiocco, which is mixed with prosciutto to give an interesting hybrid of the two. There are about half a dozen different Pecorini, Asiago, Taleggio, Fontina (the vital ingredient of Piedmontese fonduta), Cacciota and Innes cheeses. About two years ago, Zenaida introduced a small selection of fresh veg and herbs for late-evening shoppers, including asparagus and vine tomatoes, tarragon and basil (year-round, for her pesto and to go with the buffalo Mozzarella). Another recent innovation is pre-grated Parmesan (cut from the block of Parmegiano Reggiano) for lazy cooks.

Saponara
23 Prebend Street N1 Tel: 0171 226 2771

Mon-Fri 9am-8.30pm, Sat 9am-8pm, Sun 11am-2pm

Described by one resident as 'Islington's best-kept secret', this unassuming shop has in fact won an award for its off-licence, but there is more to it than grappa, Vino Santo and, of course, an extensive range of wines. Brothers Vincenzo and Marco fill the shelves with such delicacies as little jars of black truffles, dried chanterelles, truffle oil, Green & Black's organic chocolate, smart estate-bottled oils and balsamic vinegars, dried fruits, risotto rices, antipasti in oil, Casa Manzi ice creams, Bonne Maman jams, Twining's and Jackson's teas. The meat counter holds a good selection of hams and salami, including ventricina and finocchione. They make a mean pizza topped with sun-dried tomatoes. A small chill cabinet contains fresh salad leaves and veg — fennel, corn salad and cress year-round, red and baby white onions, new potatoes. An additional attraction is Radio 4 burbling away in the background, though Vincenzo admits to playing Italian music occasionally for extra atmosphere.

Fishmongers

Cecil & Company
393 Liverpool Road N1. Tel: 0171 700 6707 Fax: 0171 700 5738
Mon 6am-12pm, Tue-Fri 6am-2pm, Sat 6am-11am

A small, spartan shop without an alluring window display, and at the 'wrong' end of Liverpool Road, to boot. Its peculiar morning-only opening times reflects its wholesale origins, but cannot exactly capitalise on passing trade home-bound from the nearby tube station (Highbury and Islington). Cecil & Company sell excellent lobsters, in addition to which they also have fresh bonito and redfish from Australia, Finnan haddock, snappers, squid, sole and salmon, etc, and cheap and cheerful oddities such as pout whiting, which owner Fergus Doyle says makes very good eating even if it is more usually used as bait!

Steve Hatt
88-90 Essex Road N1. Tel/fax: 0171 226 3963
Tues-Sat 7am-5pm

The 'legendary' Steve Hatt is a keen fisherman as well as monger: a modest notice on display in his shop advises customers that salmon that he's caught (and frozen) in September, taken from the mightiest river of them all, the Tay, is on sale in December so that a taste of the wild might be enjoyed in bleak mid-winter (availability obviously depends on Steve's luck with the rod). From a distance his display, with its coloured labels on sticks, looks like a flotilla of small boats; up close, these sails reveal delights such as 'wild sea bass direct off the boats only hours old' and 'award-winning Rossmore oysters'. Delicately smooth Brixham soles lie beside large and hairy John Dory, like Beauty and the Beast. Haddock, mackerel, trout, and occasional salmon are smoked on the premises. There's also game in season, including very reasonably priced hares. The Hatt family has been mongering fish here since the turn of the century, and the busy-ness of its business should ensure a livelihood for at least another four generations to come, by which time the family will surely have moved from 'legendary' to 'mythical' status.

Market

Chapel Market N1
Wed-Sat 8am-6.30pm, Tue & Sun 8am-12.30pm

Among the clothes, pots and pans, and household cleaning stuffs, there are still some pretty good costermongers plying their trade in Chapel Market. As in any market it pays to walk about a bit before plumping for one stall. Remember that the one with the longest queue isn't necessarily the best (but it might well be the cheapest). Some stalls specialise in seasonal produce, so depending on the time of year you might find one given over to nothing but nuts, or wild mushrooms, or fresh herbs. There's a decent fishmonger near the Liverpool Road end.

Muswell Hill

Baker/Pâtisserie

Le Papillon
241 Muswell Hill Broadway N10. Tel: 0181 372 7156
Tue-Sun 7am-5.30pm

Chris and Harpal Pollard took over this 75-year-old pâtisserie three and a half years ago, added an elegant, light tearoom above the shop, and haven't looked back since. Baking is in Chris's genes (a grandfather and an uncle were both master bakers in Sheffield), and Harpal is Cordon Bleu-trained in sugar-work and chocolate-work (she has even won a British Baking Industry award for the latter). She makes her own Champagne truffles, as well as all the pastry items (chicken and asparagus puffs, feuilleté des champignons), the mousses and French fruit tarts, leaving Chris to knead and fold his many different varieties of bread. Apparently, Maureen Lipman buys half a dozen of his 100 per cent rye at a time. His multi-seed loaf (sesame, sunflower, oats, poppy, cracked wheat and pearl barley) is gorgeous and extremely popular; he makes campaillou and Lionheart, which is so-called because it is supposed to lower cholesterol levels, onion and sage, sunflower and honey, and cheese and thyme loaves, pain du Midi at weekends; and he hand-rolls his baguettes. His stollen is drenched in rum, and there's foccacia, ciabatta, and rum-flavoured pistachio sweet bread. This is altogether a totally charming place that deserves to succeed.

Cheesemonger

Cheeses

13 Fortis Green Road N10. Tel: 0181 444 9141
Mon-Thurs 10am-5.30pm, Fri 10am-6pm, Sat 9.30am-6pm

A tiny, weeny shop stuffed with all sorts of cheeses, with British farmhouse ones well represented in the form of Montgomery Cheddar, Robin Congdon's Harbourne Blue and Ticklemore (both goats'), Duckett's Caerphilly, James Aldridge's Tornegus, Devon Oke (a Curworthy matured for about five months), Duddleswell (a ewes' milk from Sussex), among others. French cheeses are brought over once a week, ready for eating, as there is simply no room to store them. Proprietor Vanessa Wiley spent two years working for the previous owner before doing what her 'assistant', Trevor, calls 'a Victor Kiam' and buying the business off him. She's learnt the cheese business on the job, as it were, and makes a cheery, unpretentious guide to the various types. Trevor, who originally trained as a landscape gardener, has learnt it from her and by now has 'done a Jane Eyre and married the boss!

Coffee/Tea

W Martyn

135 Muswell Hill Broadway N10. Tel: 0181 883 5642
Mon-Fri 9.30am-5.30pm (Thu till 1pm), Sat 9am-5.30pm

P robably Muswell Hill's most famous shop, having been here, and in the same family, since 1897. The present Mr Martyn (also a William, like his great-grandfather) is the fourth generation to seduce passers-by with the smell of his roasting coffee-beans, which he still does in the ancient machine in the front window of the shop. He roasts about 16 blends and nine pure single-bean, at any time of day depending on demand, and discourages customers from buying too much at a time (although he will offer a discount on large orders). Some 20 different teas, from Assam to jasmine and herbal, nuts and dried fruits (apricots, figs, dates, peaches, pears and sultanas), together with the coffees, make up the backbone of the business (and his thriving wholesale dealings with about 100 restaurants and Kenwood House). Branch lines are various top-quality dry goods, for this is nothing if not a good old-fashioned grocer of which there were once so many — condiments, marmalades, preserves, biscuits, sauces, Dunn's cakes, cheese crackers, etc. 'Retailers of Fine Foods' is a just description.

Delicatessens

Mauro's

229 Muswell Hill Broadway N10. Tel: 0181 883 2848
Tue-Sat 10am-4pm, Sun 11am-4pm

Although you may never hear him admit it 'on air', this is Brian Aldridge's (of BBC Radio 4's The Archers) favourite shop and he always makes a point of visiting it on his trips to London — someone who, shall we say, shares a Barbour with him, vouchsafed this information when I called. Mauro's is really about home-made pasta, which comes dried, as twists and shells in about 60 different flavours, or fresh, as ravioli with walnut, fig and gorgonzola filling, for example, or salmon coloured pink with beetroot juice, and half a dozen other flavours; as tortelloni, with Parma ham; as tagliatelle, etc. Then there are home-made spicy pork sausages, sardines in fennel and balsamic vinegar, black pesto made with olives, grilled aubergines, marinated char-grilled onions and all sorts of other wonderful gastronomic pleasures, Casa Manzi's ice-cream, and a gleaming gold espresso machine just inside the door.

St James Deli

56 Fortis Green Road N10 . Tel: 0181 883 0117
Mon, Tue, Sat 9am-6pm, Wed-Fri 9am-7pm, Sun 8am-5pm

Attached to the next-door restaurant, which has been a favourite haunt of Muswell Hillbillies since 1949, this 11-year-old delicatessen is run by Nick and Jean Ward. It has a bit of everything that you would expect from a Continental deli, and then some samosas and bhajis made locally, Jamaican patties, bagels and French breads, salamis, hams and cheeses, pasta and sauces (including Paul Newman's charity-supporting brand – very good), Bonne Maman preserves and, a recent addition, Antonio Carluccio's own-brand products. A reassuringly unfussy, old-fashioned sort of delicatessen.

Stoke Newington

Delicatessen

The Cooler

67 Stoke Newington Church Street N16. Tel: 0171 275 7266
Mon Sat 9am-9pm, Sun 10am-3pm

An oasis of taste and refinement in what otherwise is a desert of mediocre shops (or worse), The Cooler has survived for some five years now, despite its wines being repeatedly looted. The wines have now been moved to the front shop for greater security, leaving the vulnerable middle room free for further treats or for expanding the rear café – Marcus Zauner hasn't quite decided on his best strategy. Whatever the space is filled with, it is sure to be good, since Marcus is intent on bringing 'best-quality food at decent prices to the community'. To this end he has farmhouse cheeses, such as Ribblesdale, Curworthy, Colston Bassett Stilton, Brie de Meaux, home-made sausages from Devon, Dorset bacon from free-range pigs, home-made haddock and Stilton mousses, smoked mackerel and salmon pâtés from Cumbria, Wiltshsire Tracklement condiments, game pies from Burbush's of Penrith, delicious soups from the Real Soup Company (Northumberland), Bakoven rye breads, soda bread from a local baker, Seggiano oil, roasted artichoke hearts and honey, D J Jardine hot sauces – and lots more besides.

Tufnell Park

Delicatessen

Salvino

47 Brecknock Road N7. Tel: 0171 267 5305
Mon-Sat 9am-6.30pm, Sun 10am-1pm

Brothers Tony and Steven Salvino have been running their smart
shop in Tufnell Park for 15 years, and though they are both
London-born, they are decidedly influenced by their Sicilian-Neapolitan
ancestry. They import a lot of Italian products themselves, such as
Bertucci Contadina oil, Russo pasta and Narello (a family brand-name)
vegetable and olive oil mix for cooking. A family friend supplies them
with large, hand-made tortelloni, plump with porcini and ricotta or
spinach and ricotta fillings. One of their aunts runs the Rosa Maria
Farm near Hemel Hempstead, where she makes delicious little goats'
cheeses, loose or in oil, plain or with chilli or black pepper. Home-made
pestos include a traditional Calabrian speciality made with sun-dried
peppers, basil and pine nuts. There's excellent mature Parmegiano Reggiano, the heavenly Basilico (Mascarpone, Parmesan, pine nuts and
basil), various Pecorini, including Amiata Rosso whose rind is coloured
with tomato pulp (I have yet to be convinced that this affects the
flavour much – but it certainly looks pretty), and 100 per cent buffalo
Mozzarella; on the meat front, there is prosciutto alle branche with
rosemary and garlic, San Daniele and Parma hams, roasted pork fillets,
coppa di Parma, bresaola, pancetta and countless different salamis.
Among the expensive treats on the shelves are whole black truffles,
truffle oil (add to mashed potatoes for a dish of divine miscegenation)
and saffron (add that to the mash, too). At Christmas and Easter the
place fills up with panettone and Columba cakes, in September and
October fresh porcini arrive.

Health Food and Organic Greengrocer

Bumblebee

30, 32 & 33 Brecknock Road N7. Tel/fax: 0171 607 1936
Mon-Sat 9.30am-6.30pm (Thursday till 8pm)

Started in 1980, these three shops have a well-established reputation for organic and healthy foodstuffs. No. 30 is known as 'the nut shop' or 'the original Bumblebee', and sells nuts, seeds, beans, tinned products, dried fruits, pastas, oils, honeys, jams, condiments, teas, coffees and soya drinks. Most of the top healthfood brand-names are represented – de Rit and Healthrite honeys, single-blossom Miel des Pyrenees (limeflower, herb, sunflower, raspberry), La Terra e Il Cielo organic pasta, Wiltshire Tracklement pickles and mustards, Meridian crunchy organic peanut butter and jams, Whole Earth products, St Dalfour jams There's a macrobiotic section with a lot of Clearspring products. At No. 32, 'the bread shop', are soft drinks, including Duckin's single-variety apple-juices, organic ales and wines, biscuits (Duchy Originals next to gluten-free brown rice sesame wafers), baby foods, fresh pastas, olives, grains, cereal products, hot and cold take-away food, all home-made and including quiches, vegetable pies, pizzas, organic wholemeal rolls, soups, casseroles and lasagne, and, of course, breads which come from Celtic Bakery, Innes, Neal's Yard and Crank's. 'The veg shop' at No. 33 is also the dairy, with a good selection of farmhouse cheeses, such as Montgomery Cheddar, Appleby Red Cheshire, Long Clawson Blue Shropshire, Colston Bassett Stilton, Pen-Y-Bont organic Welsh goats' cheese; Martin Pitt eggs; Botton Village ice-cream; organic milk and goats' milk. Fruit and vegetables are always organic (except ginger and bananas) and come from as far away as Egypt. There's usually a good range from potatoes and turnips to lettuces and artichokes. Loose herbs and spices are also here.

North West

North-west London straggles from the raffishness of Camden and Kentish Towns through the leafy boroughs of Hampstead, St John's Wood and Golders Green to Wembley, where some of the best Asian grocers and greengrocers are to be found. Golders Green is excellent for kosher food, while Camden has one of the best organic bakeries (Lou's Bakery) and Hampstead has one of the best and most expensive greengrocers. Panzer in St John's Wood goes from strength to strength, Ackerman's in Swiss Cottage continues to produce top-notch British chocolates, and Colindale prides itself on its stupendously smart Japanese mall.

Camden

Coffee

The Camden Coffee Shop

11 Delancey Street NW1. Tel: 0171 387 4080
Mon-Sat 9.30am-6pm (Thu till 1pm)

This has to be one of the most delightful and eccentric shops in London – and one of the best known, so much publicity does it get. It sells nothing but coffee – no teas, no gadgetry, no morning biscuits. There's nowhere to sit, and barely room for more than three people to stand. And it has been this way since 1955. George, who bought it in 1978 (from another Greek-Cypriot from the same village), is actually a qualified engineer, which is probably just as well since the machinery, from the roaster and dryer to the scales and grinders, is antiquated to say the least. He doesn't keep a huge range of beans, but roasts each kind in a variety of ways, from light blends to darkly strong single-bean. He custom-roasts to your specifications in quantities of 1.8kg (4lb) plus.

Emporium

The Spice Shop

115-117 Drummond Street NW1. Tel: 0171 916 1831
Mon-Sun 10am-10pm

One half of this comprehensively stocked Asian grocery is entirely dedicated to spices, chutneys, pickles and cooking sauces. All the top subcontinental brand names can be found here – Patak, Fern, Ashoka, Rajah – between them providing every spice imaginable, whole or ground, and all the sauce names familiar from your local take-away menu – jalfrezi, dopiaza, makhani, vindaloo, madras, tikka, masala, etc. This is a cheat's paradise, for those who can't be bothered with, or don't have time for, Madhur Jaffrey's half-teaspoon of this, three-quarter-tablespoon of that approach.

Indian Sweets

Ambala
112 Drummond Street NW1. Tel: 0171 387 3521
Mon–Sun 10am-8.30pm

Now an established enterprise with outlets all over the country, this tiny unadorned shop near Euston station is where it all started back in 1965. Indian/Pakistani sweets are an acquired taste, sometimes so cloyingly sweet that even devotees of mass-produced Western confectionery cannot swallow them. This is no doubt because their base is 'jaggery', a rich, brown sugar made from sugar-cane juice (great lumps of it wrapped in sacking can sometimes be seen in the bigger Asian Cash and Carries in Southall and Wembley). If you've never tried them, start here, where the green and brown barfi are pleasantly fudge-like. Flavours tend to be nut-based – almond, pistachio, cashew. Come here anyway for the best samosas I've ever had – really flavoursome, spicy vegetables in a wonderful crisp, non-greasy batter.

Chalk Farm/ Primrose Hill

Baker

Lou's Bakery
8 Ferdinand Street NW1. Tel: 0171 284 4644
Mon–Fri 9.30am–5pm, Sat 9.30am–4pm

Lou Landin started off baking her breads in Camden Market at weekends, until demand got so great she opened a shop. And thank God she did, for many would go out of their way to avoid Camden on a Saturday or Sunday and would therefore be strangers to the pure joy of Lou's loaves. I speak as someone who often finds so-called 'healthfood' or organic bread too heavy by half, each mouthful taking so long to chew that boredom sets in, thoughts drifting uncontrollably on a cottony cloud of white sliced and, when finally swallowed, sitting in your stomach like the raw dough from which it was unwisely made. Not so with Lou's: her 'Breakfast' loaf with fruit, nuts and spices is a wondrous start to the day, the spices gently waking the palate to the taste of fruits, the nuts giving the jaw a bit of work, but nothing too taxing. Toasting only intensifies all the flavours. And it has an unexpectedly long life, lasting a few days without undue deterioration. Other breads are sesame and sunflower, four-seed (sesame, sunflower, pumpkin and poppy), granary, wholemeal. Then there are pecan nut brownies, organic carrot cake, date flapjacks, daily soups, salads and sandwiches. If you like a sharp marmalade, try her organic orange and lemon mix. But don't forget that 'Breakfast' loaf.

Delicatessen

Austrian Sausage Centre
10a Belmont Street NW1. Tel: 0171 267 5412
Mon–Fri 7am–1pm, Sat 7am–1pm

Like Roman in Acton, this is a sort of 'industrial estate' purveyor of East European cooked and cured meats, housed in a works unit rather than a conventional shop. It is hard to find, as 10a is actually a five-storey warehouse building, which overshadows the single-storey concrete block where the sausages are. But seek and ye shall find – through the hanging strips of plastic, there are delicious wiejska (lean smoked 100 per cent pork, lightly spiced), boczek (cured, smoked and cooked), kassler (cured loin of pork), baleron (neck, pickled, smoked and cooked), German hams, Hungarian salamis, and much else.

Health Foods

Sesame Wholefoods
128 Regents Park Road NW1. Tel: 0171 586 3779
Mon–Sat 10am–6pm, Sun 12pm–5pm

Breads from Neal's Yard and The Celtic Bakery, sun-dried fruits from the fair-trading Tropical Wholefoods, Clearspring and Whole Earth organic products, single-bloom honeys from the Pyrenees, and plump and healthy-looking organic vegetables all make this an enticing local health store. Daily ready-to-eat dishes are made in the downstairs kitchen – a soup, a hot vegetable or pasta dish, quiches, pizzas and various salads – and are eagerly consumed by the street's other retailers and local residents. In the summer, pavement seating makes it even more inviting. A good place to go to before or after a visit to the zoo.

Ice-Cream

Marine Ices

8 Haverstock Hill NW3. Tel: 0171 485 3132
Mon–Sat 10.30am–10.45pm, Sun 11am–10pm

Summer gigs at the Roundhouse, sadly long since a thing of the past, were always preceded by a 'quickie' at Marine Ices across the road, and thus its renown became London-wide, at least among rock-concertees. Marine has been part of the Chalk Farm landscape since 1931 (when the shop front was designed as a boat, hence the name). Three generations of Manzis have been involved in devising and selling the 26 flavours of ice-creams (latest additions are amaretto, tiramisu and Italian toffee crunch); the additive-free sorbets; the wonderful creations like Knickerbocker Glory (a childhood post-dentist treat for me, it brings back many memories of gas and drills); and Vesuvius (vanilla, chocolate, marsala ice-cream scoops with crushed meringue, cherries and marsala-soaked sponge – mmm). Let's hope a fourth generation will continue to enjoy these marvellous ice-creams and see off the American invasion.

Ready-Meals/Caterer

Traiteur Pagnol

170 Regent's Park Road NW1. Tel: 0171 586 6988 Fax: 0171 916 1983
Mon–Fri 9.30am–8pm, Sat 9.30am–6pm

Melanie Pini trained as a cook in Provence and opened this classy joint about three years ago. Attractively presented in the window are fashionable dishes such as Brussels sprouts with roasted garlic, roast whole aubergines (the long thin kind), roast parsnip, swede and carrot (a hearty winter variation on the usual char-grilled variety), pasta — quattro formaggio, roast poussin with rosemary, tuna fishcakes and soya sauce. There are Neal's Yard British cheeses, a small but decidedly up-market selection of French ones (including a farmhouse Brie de Meaux), homemade jams and pickles, tarte tatin, lemon tart and walnut tart (both favourites with customers, apparently), breads from Sally Clarke and Baker & Spice, Valrhona chocolate, fancy pastas, and little muslin sachets of spices for delicious mulled wine. All very tasteful, if a bit chi-chi.

Colindale

Emporium

Yoahan Supermarket & Food Court
Yoahan Plaza 399 Edgware Road NW9. Tel: 0181 200 0009
Mon–Sun 10am–7pm (Fri–Sat till 8pm)

In an area thick with light industrial estates and shopping malls of Lego-like design, Yoahan Plaza shines out in silvered splendour. Inside, it is Little Japan, down to a bookshop and library, American Dry Cleaning, and a Segadome arcade in which to dump the kids while the shopping gets done. On entering the food mall, the first thing to hit the eye is the Minamoto Kitcho — a display of Japanese sweets — as much for the prices as the exquisite packaging: £36 for 12 pieces! Are they made of gold dust, or what? No, explains Alex Pritchard, they are largely made of red or white bean paste, mikasa-yaki cakes (rice beaten into a dough), chestnuts, plums and rice jelly, none of which staples of the Japanese larder would seem to justify the expense. However, 'they have the same status as Belgian chocolates', are given as presents on certain days of the year to important people (by less important people) and bring luck, honour, prosperity, happiness to the receiver. Besides that, they are imported from Japan, and the only other source in all Europe is Minamoto's Paris shop. Beyond Minamoto is the Food Court, a quadrangle of quick-food stalls, each dedicated to a different element of Japanese cuisine — yakitori, sushi, noodles and soup, etc — and the

Yamakazi Bakery, which offers red bean paste buns, curry doughnuts, corn rolls, sugar toast, cream marchen, and other oddities. The super-market check-outs line the fourth side of the quadrangle, and beyond them is everything the Japanese cook could possibly want. Fish, as you'd expect, is particularly enticing, skilfully prepared for a variety of dishes, from the krill-sized baby sardines called shirasu (fresh) or chiri-men (dried), which are eaten just as they come, to tuna and turbot and octopus tentacles. Meat is also beautifully presented, pork loin sliced transparently thin for sukiyaki. A 'deli' counter has ready-meals of udon noodles and other dishes, which come with cooking instructions. There's also a small Korean section.

Cricklewood

Butcher

Bifulco
182 Cricklewood Lane NW2. Tel: 0181 452 2674
Mon–Fri 7am–5.30pm, Sat 7am–1pm, (Deliveries)

The Bifulco family has suffered its share of problems from the vicissitudes of the food retail industry: after their popular shop in St John's Wood closed down in the early 1990s, a group of employees opened Quattro Bella in Portobello Road to carry on the traditions of good butchery. But their repute had always been north-westerly, and, Notting Hill business rates being what they are, 1992 saw them moving back to NW-land, when Anthony Bifulco rejoined them. Their butchery is based on the French seamed-out method (getting rid of as much of the fat as possible), so everything is beautifully trimmed and presented. Their beef is Scotch free-range (hung for a minimum of two weeks, but longer if requested), lamb is English, Welsh and Scottish, pork free-range, as are eggs and chickens, Norfolk Bronze turkeys and French Barbary ducks, and they'll get mutton to order in winter. They do have a game licence but do not keep much as there isn't much demand among their clientele: it is best to order. Home-made items are sausages, ham-burgers, breaded veal (Dutch) escalopes, kebabs and 'Kievs'. They deliver around the north-west and down to the West End and west London (call before 10am for same-day delivery). Let's hope that the burghers of Cricklewood and environs give Bifulco the support it deserves.

Emporium

Wing Yip
395 Edgware Road NW2. Tel: 0181 452 1478
Mon–Sat 9.30am–7pm, Sun 11.30am–5.30pm

If you are a serious and frequent cook of Chinese food, this is undoubtedly the place to stock up on ingredients. It's vast, and carries everything, clearly labelled and arranged. The freezers are crammed with industrial quantities of frozen fish (which looks a better bet than the rather tired wet variety), from barracuda heads and sultanfish to something merely called 'fish'. There is also frozen dim sum – dumplings and buns, won tons and Vietnamese spring rolls – oodles of noodles, including fresh types such as hofun and Chinese 'cannelloni' ('cheung fun' in restaurants), and a chill cabinet of fresh Asian vegetables flown in once a week. A small Japanese section is largely filled with ceramic bowls and utensils, but has a few packets and bottles of Japanese goods.

Golders Green

Bakeries

Cousins Bakery
109 Golders Green Road NW11. Tel: 0181 201 9694
Mon–Fri 7am–7pm (in winter 3pm on Fri), Sun 7am–7pm

Despite the presence across the road of famous rivals Carmelli, Zion Hasan and Nathan Chaso have kept their small, cosy bakery going for three years and seem unfazed by the competition. Among the baker's dozen breads are shining plaits of cholla. Bagels come plain, or with sesame or poppy seeds, and there's kipfel, kichel and strudel in a variety of flavours.

Daniel's Bagel Bakery

13 Halleswelle Parade Finchley Road NW11. Tel: 0181 455 5826
Mon–Wed 7am–9pm, Thu 7am–10pm, Fri 7am–(summer) 6pm, (winter)
3pm or 1hr before sunset

Nader, a partner in the enterprise, says that they are very famous for their cholla, in which are used only the best ingredients (eggs, sugar and oil), and the rolls I tried were still excellent at breakfast the next day – dense and slightly sweet: there are large, medium and small plaits and rolls of cholla, bagels, platzel, rye loaves, granary, wholemeal, all strictly supervised by the Beth Din. Bagels can be plain, poppy seed, sesame or rye, filled or not. The deli counter features salmon cutlets, tuna cutlets, gefilte fish balls, latkes, etc.

Kosher Baker

Carmelli Bakeries

126–128 Golders Green Road NW11. Tel: 0181 455 3063
Mon–Wed 7am–1am, Thu 7am–Fri 3pm, Sat 6.30pm–Mon 1am

The incredibly long opening hours attest to the immense popularity of this smart, gleaming, well-established bagelry, which expanded into the next-door premises two years ago. They sell 2000 bagels, most bulging with smoked salmon and cream cheese, every Saturday night alone. Everything, but everything (even the cream cheese), is made in the huge and visible rear kitchens. Apart from the bagels, other instant eats include pizzas, quiches, potato or cheese burekas. There are almond croissants and chocolate croissants, cheesecakes and chocolate yeast cakes, cholla, bulka, granary and wholemeal loaves, and a large 'Parev' section (neutral breads and cakes, containing eggs, but no dairy products, which can therefore be eaten with dairy and meat dishes). A speciality are the traditional wedding cakes, tiered and royally iced.

Coffee/Tea

Importers

76 Golders Green Road NW11. Tel: 0181 455 8186
Mon–Thu 9am–5.30pm, Fri 9am–5pm, Sat 9am–6pm Sun 10am–6pm

This branch of the chain has a larger restaurant than either Ealing or Beckenham (see entries) to accommodate the 70 per cent of customers who drop in for a snack and a cuppa, rather than a pound of Jamaican Blue Mountain or Continental Blend. Roasting none the less takes place every morning between 9.30 and 11.30 in the tiny, ancient-looking, gas-fired roaster which sits in the window, and there's the usual range of coffee/tea-related hardware. Also at 180 High Street, Beckenham (see entry) and 3 The Green, W5 (tel 0181 567 2981).

Delicatessen/Caterer

Platters

10 Halleswelle Parade Finchley Road NW11. Tel: 0181 455 7345
Mon–Sat 8.30am–5pm, Sun 8.30am–2pm

A Jewish but non-kosher deli-cum-caterer. Fish is Harvey Platter's speciality – he has umpteen ways of preparing herring, gefilte fish, and salmon into balls and cakes. There's chopped liver, egg and onion, an extensive choice of salads, potato latkes, freshly made sandwiches at lunchtime, hand-cut smoked salmon, salt beef, cheesecake, apple strudel and other puddings. Everything is made on the premises. He caters for weddings, dinner-parties, bar mitzvahs and funerals. Also at 83–85 Allitsen Road, NW8 (tel: 0171 722 5352).

Emporium

Maysun Supermarket

869 Finchley Road NW11. Tel: 0181 455 4773
Mon–Sat 9am–7.30pm

' Japanese, Korean, Thai, Indonesian, Filipino, Malaysian, Singaporean' announces the window-writing of this small but packed supermarket run for the past 16 years by Kin-Hoo Ho from Hong Kong. And the announcement does not disappoint. Thai veg – long beans, birds' eye chillies, bitter melon, green papaya, fresh young coconuts, etc – arrives fresh on Thursdays, the freezers are stuffed with dim sum and spring rolls, the shelves stacked with sauces and spices from all these countries. Mr Ho gave me a '1,000-year-old' egg ('really preserved for only a few months'), but I am afraid that its ammoniac smell was more than my feeble European sensibility was prepared for.

Fishmongers

J A Corney
9 Halleswelle Parade Finchley Road NW11. Tel: 0181 455 9588
Tue–Thu 8am–5pm, Fri 8am–4pm, Sat–Sun 8am–1pm

Although not a kosher establishment (hence the Saturday opening), Mr Corney knows his fish and from which community the bulk of his trade has come for the past 28 years. So this is a crustacea-free zone, his bestsellers are salmon (with whole fish at £1.95/500g (1lb), it is hardly surprising they shift) and smoked salmon; he minces selected white fish and fries gefilte balls every morning; 'Lasht' or freshwater bream and St Peter's fish from Israel are much in evidence. His stock, which also includes huge whole cod and plaice, comes from Cornwall, Devon, Grimsby and Billingsgate. He also has a branch at 81 High Street, Edgware (tel: 0181 952 0302/5447).

Sam Stoller & Son Ltd
28 Temple Fortune Parade NW11. Tel: 0181 458 1429
Mon 8am–2pm, Tue–Thu 7am–5pm, Fri 7am–4pm, Sun 8am–1pm

Long-established, large and very busy, shopping at Stoller teaches you to be choosy – not because of quality, which is beyond reproach, but simply because all the other customers are, rejecting one piece of cod tail for another seemingly identical. The staff are friendly and infinitely patient (as you would expect from an outfit recognised by the Guild of Mastercraftsmen under the Service and Retail Category). As at Corney, salmon (wild in season, farmed out of it, and smoked) is plentiful and cheap. 'Lasht' (fresh-water bream), whole haddock and cod, Greenland halibut, Brixham soles (small and delicious), John Dory (huge and wondrously ugly) feature in the large selection of other fish from Billingsgate and the coast. No shellfish.

Greengrocer

Blyth
24 Temple Fortune Parade Finchley Road. NW11. Tel: 0181 455 2383
Mon–Fri 7.30am–5pm, Sat 8am–1pm

A much-respected 26-year-old shop run by brothers Alan and Kenny Blyth. They turn over, for some reason, more fruit than vegetables, but everything is in tip-top condition, from the half-dozen varieties of potatoes to the strawberries and lychees. What with two of the better supermarkets just up the road, trade has slackened in recent years, but their attention to the quality of their produce keeps loyal customers coming. It would be a sad day indeed for north-westerners if the Blyths were forced to close their doors.

Hampstead

Baker

Rumbold
45 South End Road NW3. Tel: 0171 794 2344
Mon-Sat 8am-5pm

This century-old bakery has for the past six years been owned by Mr Brum the baker, helped out by Mrs and Master Brum, and a happy family it seems to be. It's a small, cosy corner-shop, shelves displaying a surprising range of breads, from farmhouse and bloomer to wholemeal and Bavarian rye (50 per cent rye) and light rye (30 per cent). The rye breads and bloomers are baked, tinless, on the oven floor, giving them a particularly intense flavour. Flour comes from Germany and Canada – 51 years' experience as a baker leads Mr Brum to rank

Canadian flour above European varieties, on the whole. He is, in his own words, 'a fanatic' about bread. There are bagels, croissants, fruit scones, banana and walnut muffins, apple strudels, cherry lambada, all of which look wonderful; however, for my money, Mr Brum's glory is his Combicorn, made with oats, rye, barley, wheat, linseed, sunflower and sesame seeds, which is a true staff of life.

Butcher

J A Steele
8 Flask Walk NW3. Tel: 0171 435 3587
Mon–Sat 7.30am–5.30pm

Forty years on and this traditional family-run butcher is now a Real Meat Company stockist, so you can be sure there's no trace of nasties in the free-range pork, lamb and beef, the last of which is hung for a minimum of two weeks. French Barbary ducks, guinea fowl, quail and corn-fed chickens are all popular with Mr Steele's customers, as is the Real Meat dry-cured bacon, cut to order. Game is dressed in season, and he'll jug a hare for you. Also a source of graisse d'oie.

Delicatessens

Belsize Village Delicatessen
39 Belsize Lane NW3. Tel: 0171 794 4258
Mon–Fri 8.30am–7pm, Sat 8.30am–6pm, Sun 9am–2pm

It is hard to believe that the current owners here are ex-Rosslyn Deli (see entry), the difference between the two establishments is so great (and that is not to pass judgement on either). For years a Polish deli, until the owners retired, Belsize has kept its Polish/French bias, but has perhaps branched out a bit, now carrying Duskin's single-variety apple juices, for instance. The ready-made dishes are still above-averagely good — a half-dozen different ways with herring, home-made pastas, chicken in mustard sauce, steak/kidney pie, salads — and the cured sausages still come from all over Europe. Go on a Thursday to be sure of the best choice of cheeses — that's the day they arrive fresh from wholesaler Philippe Olivier. There's the famed Ukrainian rye from the

Kolos Bakery in Bradford, ciabatta, multi-grain soda bread, and some items from Daniel's Bagel Bake in Golders Green.

The Delicatessen Shop

23 South End Road NW3. Tel: 0171 435 7315
Mon–Fri 9.30am–7pm, Sat 9am–6pm

Sandra Cavaciuti, whose husband was Britain's first Maître des Fromagers and one of the first to put a pasta machine in his shop-window, continues the tradition of fine home-made pastas and good farmhouse or artisan cheeses (there are no pasteurised ones). Pasta is made all day every day (they supply restaurants as well), so there's always plenty of choice, and a number of home-made sauces to go with them – the pesto is particularly fine. Other than that, Mrs Cavaciuti buys in the best of a wide range of goods, and although the emphasis is Italian, there's also French mountain honey, Wiltshire Tracklements, Belvoir cordials, free-range eggs from Norfolk, excellent locally-made breads (the wholemeal, treacle and oats is exclusive) and a counter full of extremely health-giving dishes, such as vegetable and lentil burgers, spinach and ricotta pancakes, spinach and brown rice flan.

Giacobazzi

150 Fleet Road NW3. Tel: 0171 267 7222
Mon–Fri 9.30am–7pm, Sat 9am–6pm

London-born Renata and Raffaele Giacobazzi take their culinary inspiration from Emilia Romagna, the region of Northern Italy from which both sets of parents hailed. Their home-made pastas are particularly influenced by that area's traditions – pumpkin raviolini, red pesto tortelloni, porcini tortelloni. Other ready-to-go dishes include hot bean salad, char-grilled vegetables, aubergine parmigiana, crespelle, bacala fritters, chicken escalopes, omelette alla Lucia (Raffaele's mum's recipe of Mozzarella, mortadello, bechamel sauce and Parmesan) and a seafood salad, bottled for them in Italy, the authenticity of which can be judged by the notice beside the brimming bowl: 'Please note: pieces of what appear to be plastic may be found in the seafood salad. These are NOT plastic, they are part of the squid which is in the salad'. Lasagne and cannelloni are made to order. Breads are home-made and include focaccia, olive loaves and rolls, ciabatta. They also sell raw pizza dough. The small deli side features packet pastas from De Cecco upwards, estate-bottled oils, lentils, and bottled sauces and antipasti.

The Pasta Place

42 Heath Street NW3. Tel: 0171 431 0018
Mon–Fri 10am–8pm, Sat 10am–6.30pm, Sun 11.30am–6.30pm

Marco's 14-year-old joint is a good source of made-on-the-premises dishes typical of an Italian gastronomia counter, from fresh pasta through baked ciabatta-and-veg slices, roast herby poussin, cauliflower/broccoli/zucchini salad to home-made tiramisu and the wondrous sorbet marmite: nothing at all to do with our dearly beloved jar of dark gooey stuff, this is a nougatine 'saucepan and lid' filled with balls of variously flavoured sorbets – mango, cassis, coconut, lemon, orange, raspberry, kiwi, among them. It looks a treat, serves up to 6–10 people and requires three days' advance notice. Deli goods include single-estate olive oils, nut oils, Vino Santo and accompanying biscotti (there's a wonderful chocolate-covered variety). Marco will do you a fine cocktail party or dinner.

The Rosslyn Delicatessen

56 Rosslyn Hill NW3. Tel: 0171 794 9210 Fax: 0171 794 6828
Mon–Sat 8.30am–8.30pm, Sun 8.30am–7pm

A glitzy, modern deli for the affluent professional, full of the kind of labels you'd never see in your workaday corner-deli. There's a fancy American section, Ledoult soups and sauces, Tradition du Pays de Gasconne tins of haricots à la graisse d'oie, choucroute garnished with Toulouse sausage and smoked chicken breast, pâté de chevreuil, and other delights for the game and hearty meat-eater, Rosslyn-label extravagances such as baby marinated figs, cranberry and raspberry relish, 'Aga-dried' tomatoes with capers (actually rather good) and flavoured oils and vinegars. And if that 'Aga-dried' sounds too much for you, stay awhile – there are also 120 different farmhouse cheeses, including a lot of unusual ones, lovely breads (six ryes, walnut, sesame and raisin, sunflower and apricot), much-praised Viennoiserie and pâtisserie, and a counter of scrumptious ready-made dishes to make your mouth water.

Fishmonger

Hampstead Seafoods

78 Hampstead High Street NW3. Tel: 0171 435 3966
Tue-Fri 7.30am-5pm, Sat 7.30am-4.30pm

Tucked away at the back of Hampstead Community Market, Andy and Emi Theodorou's establishment of nine years' standing is the only place to buy fish in NW3 — surprising, really, given the socio-economic class of most of the residents. The brothers come from a fish-mongering family, and go daily to Billingsgate to get Essex oysters, Cornish red mullet, fresh prawns from the Gulf, swordfish from the Sey-chelles, tuna, Dover soles, halibut, turbot, etc. They boil and dress their own lobsters and crabs, the latter apparently going down particularly well with the locals.

Greengrocers

Crescent Fruiterers

62 Belsize Lane NW3. Tel: 0171 435 9444
Mon-Fri 7am-7pm, Sat 7am-6pm, Sun 7am-1pm

Little Queen pineapples, sweet Medjoul dates, and bobby beans were among the unseasonal produce on offer when I visited one dark and drizzly November night. And I felt rather cheered as a result, since the order of banter between owner David, assistant Matthew and assorted customers was quite as high as the quality of produce, which comes daily from Spitalfields. Everything is prettily displayed. They say they're the best, and no-one in the shop gainsaid them. Certainly cheaper than Brian Lay-Jones (see next page).

Brian Lay-Jones

36 Heath Street NW3. Tel: 0171 435 5084
Mon–Sat 8am–6pm

The presence in November of wild rocket, small but perfectly formed Jerusalem artichokes, tiny thin asparagus, deep-sea-green watercress, wickedly red cherries, enormous strawberries gives the game away – Mr Lay-Jones is not constrained by the seasons. Much of his non-seasonal produce comes from Chile, which is apparently the foreign market at which to shop, and Australia. He does not, however, neglect home-growers – turnips, potatoes, swede, Brussels were all present (though some would argue that before the first frosts a Brussel is not worth a sprout). He has a rabbit's feast of different salad leaves and fresh herbs all year round. I especially enjoyed my £1.20's worth of custard apple, possibly because I'd been told I probably wouldn't, what with having to spit out so many substantial black seeds; they didn't interfere with the pleasantly rough texture and surprisingly peary taste. Be warned – there's a premium to be paid for so much exotica.

Pâtisserie/Tea Room

Louis Pâtisserie

32 Heath Street NW3. Tel: 0181 435 9908
Mon–Sun 9am–6pm

Hurry, hurry, hurry! The indefatigable Louis, now 66, shows signs of tiring: 'Fed up – the year two thousand, I finish'. Surely a family member will take over then? 'More likely little Chinese,' he says mysteriously. Whatever this means, it is bad news for more than just the population of Hampstead. For some 34 years, Heath-walkers have joined local residents in Hungarian Louis's tea-room, particularly on Sundays when it is packed, for a cuppa and a cake or a pastry. Louis came over to this country to 'go down mines', then worked with fellow ex-patriate Egon Ronay for a year or so, before opening his tea-room in 1962. Every day since, he has been there to create his sweet delights: petits fours; flans; gateaux; cream cakes; poppy-seed slices; almond horseshoes; chestnut slices; a chocolate sponge with fresh and chestnut cream; the sublime 'Louis cake', a deep dark chocolate sponge with chocolate cream, chopped cherries and brandy and, of course, his famous Hungarian confections, such as dobos, a vanilla sponge with chocolate cream butter and caramel.

Hendon

Bakery

Hendon Bagel Bakery

Church Road NW4. Tel: 0181 203 6919
Mon–Thu 7am–11pm, Fri 7am-6pm (summer) 3pm (winter)
Sat-Sun 6-11pm

Avi Avital calls his bakery 'French-style kosher', and indeed there are croissants and tartes aux pommes alongside the bagels, cholla, platzels and rye breads. Their bagels are 'the best' (is there a Jewish bakery that doesn't make 'the best bagels'?), and come variously filled with salmon, tuna, herring, or simply buttered. I tried one generously stuffed with tuna, which was delicious and kept me going for the rest of the day. There is a Parev (non-dairy) section, pitta breads stuffed with omelettes, cream slices, fresh pizzas, cakes and pastries. Everything is made out back on the premises by the French baker.

Kentish Town

Fishmonger/Butcher

B & M Seafoods

258 Kentish Town Road NW5. Tel: 0171 485 0346
Tue–Sat 9am–6pm

Ex-trawlerman Bob Birchenall has been invited to become an honorary member of the Association of Masterchefs of Great Britain – not because he can cook to save his life (though perhaps he can do that as well), but because of his 'contribution to improving the food chain'. Every bit of meat, poultry and game sold by him is organic and/or free-range: beef and lamb come from registered (by the Soil Association or Demeter) farms in Devon; pork is 50 per cent Devon organic/50 per cent Eldon Blue from Hampshire; veal from Devon is of the 'suckled' variety. Slaughtered locally (to avoid traumatising journeys), carcasses are then transported to Bob's 'farm unit' in Bedfordshire for hanging and butchery and other processing, such as curing and smoking (beef is hung for a minimum 10–14 days, but longer if requested). Sausages, both beef and pork, are home-made, bacon is cut from the piece and is a good not-too-strong dry cure. Pies and pâtés are made by the wife of one of their registered farmers. The Bedfordshire farm also produces hickory-smoked (sweeter than oak) turkey breast, chicken, pork ribs, pheasant breasts, briskets, whole pigeons – Bob is not bound by convention. On the fish side, everything comes from the coast, mostly the fleets at Brixham where Bob still has family and friends in fishing. There's an excellent choice, from the big 'uns down to little flat fish, such as dabs and megrim. Who could ask for more?

Fishmonger

Fish & Fowl Ltd

145 Highgate Road NW5. Tel: 0171 284 4184 Fax: 0171 482 1500
Fri-Sat 9.30am–5.30pm

Note those opening times: this is really a restaurant supplier, only open to the public at the above times when it displays its wares in the window. The rest of the week you have to take pot luck: if the metal shutter is half-drawn, someone is probably there and will sell you whatever isn't already bagged by London's chefs. Himself an ex-chef, Adrian Rudolf started up five and a half years ago. Apart from the daily deliveries from the coast (Cornwall mostly) – tuna, monkfish, swordfish, halibut, soles, etc – he carries seasonal game, Italian squab pigeons, French poultry, smoked poultry, French chips soups, kosher smoked salmon, Glenarm smoked salmon from Ireland (which he says is the closest there is to the wild taste), and a few deli items (oils and vinegars). Caviar to order.

Park Royal

Emporia

Hoo Hing

North Circular Road Park Royal NW10. Tel: 0181 838 3388
Mon–Fri 9am–7pm, Sat, and Bank Holidays 10am–7pm, Sun 11am–5pm

The new, western outpost of the Hackney store. The vagueness of its address is compensated for by its distinctive frontage – bright blue Chinese pagoda-type roofs. But you could still whizz past it going north on the North Circular from the Hanger Lane Gyratory System (otherwise known as a roundabout) as you have to take a nameless slip- road before you pass it. Once you've mastered the geography, you'll find a cool, airy hangar of Oriental produce. The emphasis is on Chinese cuisine, including a chill-counter of rarely-seen fresh dim sum treats (char-siu dumplings, cheug fung pancakes) and Chinese sausages made in France, but there's also a Japanese/Korean section, lots of fresh chilled Thai veg (four kinds of choi), lobster tanks, a wet-fish counter, and the usual vast choice of noodles, pickles, soy sauces, etc. Also at Eastway Commercial Centre, Eastway, E9 (tel: 0181 533 2811).

T K Trading

Unit 7 The Chase Centre Chase Road NW10 . Tel: 0181 453 1001
Fax: 0181 453 0606
Mon–Sun 10am–5pm

The retail arm of importers Yoshikawa UK Ltd, this small, tidy shop is up three flights of metal stairs, giving the impression that you're off to catch a plane rather than get the groceries. It is exclusively dry and frozen goods, and if there's a Japanese sauce, pickle, noodle or rice needed you'll find it here.

St John's Wood

Emporium

Panzer

15 Circus Road NW8. Tel: 0171 722 8596/8162 Fax: 0171 586 0209
Mon-Fri 8am-7pm, Sat 8.30am-6pm, Sun 8.30am-2pm

Peter Vogl believes that success for a local general grocery store lies in reacting to changes in its customer make-up. So, given its locality, Panzer has American (including a 'Tex Mex' subdivision), Japanese, French, Italian, Greek, Oriental and German sections, each of which stocks good-quality larder-staples of that cuisine. And his retail philosophy has clearly got something, since the place is as popular as ever after 40 years. Of course, Panzer is thought of first and foremost as a Jewish (but non-kosher) store, and the deli has gefilte fish, chopped liver, egg and onion, herring dishes, smoked salmon (a bestseller) along-side the salamis and cheeses from all over Europe. There is also a kosher section. Breads include bagels (turnover, 5000 a week), Sally Clarke's, ryes, Arab varieties, French and Italian sticks and slippers. Outside is a very impressive display of fruit and veg – black cabbage from Italy, yellow courgette, vine tomatoes, fresh wild mushrooms, Chilean cherries, Mexican raspberries, pitihayas and papayas. Tuesday is delivery day. All in all, Panzer is a wonderful 'general' store, in which bottled water and loo paper run a close second to the smoked salmon as money-spinners!

Fishmonger

Brown's

37-39 Chalbert Street NW8. Tel: 0171 722 6284
Mon-Sat 7.45am-5.30pm. Deliveries.

A repeated winner of the Seafood Authority's Award for Best Fish monger, most recently in 1995, Brown's is famous for its light London-cured smoked salmon and haddock. They also cook (and dress for table) lobsters and crabs, have samphire from Norfolk in season,

Cornish sea bass, monkfish and halibut, Venus clams, large and small, almond clams, squid, hake, oysters direct from Brittany and Normandy, and much else besides. They deliver as far as the West End.

Pâtisserie

Le Connaisseur
49 Charlbert Street NW8. Tel: 0171 722 7070
Mon–Fri 8am–6pm, Sat 8am–5pm, Sun 9am–1pm

A bakery since 1958, owned since 1975 by former employee Josef Keppeln, who is never away from his ovens, out of which come doughnuts and croissants, pecan tarts and apple tarts, Danish rings and rye breads, cream slices and fruit tarts, florentines and palmiers, and sumptuous-looking cakes. Much thought-of in the locality.

Swiss Cottage

Chocolates

Ackerman's
9 Goldhurst Terrace NW6. Tel: 0171 624 2742
Mon–Fri 9.30am–6pm, Sat 9.30am–5pm

The thin dark wafers produced here (actually in the small unassuming 'factory' in Pratt Street, Camden) are heavenly – smooth and rich, deeply satisifying. They come as plain, mint, orange or mocha, the first two being my favourites. But then, the truffles are irresistible, and the plain bars... and the nutty ones. How do the Queen and Her Mum, who have bestowed their Warrant on these exquisite sweets since 1961, ever make up their minds? Ackerman's has been going strong for over 50 years and must stand at the top of English chocolate makers (there is still a Swiss chocolatier at the helm). Their products can be found in the smarter retailers around town, and as far afield as America and the Middle East, where people will doubtless pay a premium for them. Mail order list available.

Wembley

There's a huge choice of Asian shops in Alperton, a sub-division of Wembley, most of them bunched along Ealing Road. I have listed only a few here, and, as ever, the best policy is to explore. Shop-keepers are friendly and only too happy to explain and advise. Don't make the mistake of thinking that you know all there is to know about Asian produce because you happen to have a good local store.

Emporia

V B & Sons
218 Ealing Road Alperton W10. Tel: 0181 795 0387
Mon–Fri 9.30am–5.45pm, Sat 9am–5.45pm, Sun 11am–5pm

Fudco
184 Ealing Road Alperton W10. Tel: 0181 902 4820
Mon–Sun 9.30am–6.30pm

VB & Sons is now run by the sons and is big. They have own-brand lines, in the manner of top British supermarkets, which tells you something about their status. All the usual array of rices, flours, pickles (some of which are sold from colourful plastic bins under a sort of covered-wagon stall within the shop) is in evidence. A less-often-seen item is jaggory – elephant-foot-sized lumps of cane sugar wrapped in sackcloth. Fudco is smaller and has a huge range of different flours, many of them milled at the back, and freshly ground spices.

Greengrocers

Big Market Retail Ltd
192 Ealing Road Alperton W10. Tel: 0181 903 5927
Mon–Sun 8am–8pm

Fruity Fresh
111–113 Ealing Road Alperton W10. Tel: 0181 902 9797
Mon–Fri 9am–8pm, Sat–Sun, and Bank Holidays 9am–9pm

Wembley Exotics

133–135 Ealing Road Alperton W10. Tel: 0181 900 2607
Mon–Sun 24hrs

Tuver, kantola, tindori, guvar, valor, karela, ravaya, papdi, gunda, tinda, dhudi, ginger, garlic, long beans – piles of them all, every-where. How to choose? Follow the crowds, or go for the best price, or the friendly faces of the staff, or the loudest music. Thakarshi at Big Market is a welcoming and jolly fellow. Wembley Exotics probably has the biggest range and is open 24 hours. I found sungora there – a sticky, black, bumpy root, which is boiled until it reaches the consis-tency of a cooked potato and then peeled – which I hadn't come across before, even in Southall. Everything to be found here makes for an exciting experience, if you're interested in trying new things.

Willesden

Butcher

Enzo Tartarelli

1 Sidmouth Road NW2. Tel: 0181 459 1952
Mon–Fri 7.30am–6.30pm, Sat 7.30am–6pm

Enzo Tartarelli proudly displays no fewer than three symbols of excellence which put the quality of his meat beyond doubt – Demeter, Soil Association and Organic Farmers and Growers Associa-tion. Although he's been here since 1984, he's only been selling organic meat for the past three years and finds it's going very well. He makes two Italian-style sausages – pork and chilli, pork and spices – which make hearty eating. Eggs and chickens are free-range, there's ham-on-the-bone and salamis. There's also fruit and veg, passata, Italian flour, pastas, daily breads (ciabatta, baguette) from Il Fornaio, dried mush-rooms, panettone and pandoro, and many other Italian delights.

West

The vast area that is west London, roughly W2 (Bayswater) to W13 (West Ealing), offers a varied and pleasurable shopping experience. There are the 'haut produit' enclaves of Holland Park and Chiswick, the Polish delis of Acton and Ealing, Middle-Eastern emporia of Bayswater and Kensington High Street, Spanish and Portuguese stores in North Kensington, an excellent market in Portobello Road, traditional English butchers scattered throughout – all this before you reach the subcontinental thrills of Southall, where tindori, tinda and dhudi rule. Hammersmith boasts the only Swedish deli in the capital, and Shepherd's Bush the only Yugoslavian (although a Serbian deli-café opened in the same road, too late, sadly, for inclusion in this book).

Acton

Delicatessen/Baker

Roman Ltd

Unit 20 Acton Park Industrial Estate W3. Tel: 0181 749 2123
Mon–Fri 10am–4pm

If you've been put off liver-sausage for life by the bland, smooth paste which passes for it in British brand-name tins, or you've had the real thing in New York or Germany and are pining for it, Roman Gawlak is your man. His Ponnath (a German firm for which he and partner Len Hiscock are sole importers) coarse-cut liver-sausage is sublime and a favourite of Sir Clement Freud. You could get many of their products – 'frankfurters' (they don't actually come from Frankfurt) that are to the hot dog as caviar is to cod's roe, German Blacky ham, lachiss-chinken, rusk-free biaka from Poland, Bavarian meatloaf – from places they supply, such as Harrods, Harvey Nichols or Partridges, but going to the source is more fun, cheaper and gives the chance to get some superb bread from Gert Guscher's bakery (sour dough rye, Greek olive, Iranian, stollen, and excellent pastries).

Fishmonger

Atari-Ya

7 Saxon Drive W3. Tel: 0181 896 1552
Tues 10.45am–6.30pm, Wed–Fri 10am–4.30pm, Sat–Sun 10am–7pm

An outpost of the North Finchley store, set up two years ago to cater to the local Japanese – there's a Japanese school round the corner and the London-Tokyo Property Agency across the road. Although none of the fish is imported from Japan (EU laws make this well-nigh impossible nowadays), some of it is unfamiliar – chirimen and shirasu, (minuscule sardines, dried and raw, respectively), nakaochi (off-cut tuna), razorshells, surf clams. It is all sparklingly fresh and Mr Sakai will make sashimi to order. The grocery side is small but carries everything you'd need for a Japanese meal.

Bayswater

Bakers/Pâtisseries

Maison Bouquillon

41 Moscow Road W2. Tel: 0171 229 2107
Mon–Sat 8.30am–9.30pm, Sun 8.30am–8.30pm

The delectable fruit tarts are made on the premises, everything else is made in their Hendon plant, from the mango and chestnut mousse (different item!) to the pepitos (fried croissants filled with custard), trifle and rice pudding. Empanadas (pastry filled with tomato, eggs and tuna) are a very popular lunchtime snack. Amazing-looking cakes go round and round in the revolving display cabinet, making it, if anything, even more difficult to choose one, since another comes into view just as you're on the point of decision. The deli counter has saucisson and chorizo, Manchego, Spanish jams and Spanish tins of their favourite dishes, such as fabada asturiana. Chocolates are French and Belgian.

Pierre Pechon

127 Queensway W2 Tel: 0171 229 0746
Mon–Wed 7.30am–6pm, Thu–Sat 7.30am–8pm, Sun 7.30am–7pm

Established by the eponymous Frenchman in 1925, this firmly family enterprise is today run by grandson Dominic Pechon, who proudly stresses that it is still 'a specialised local business'. There have necessarily been changes over the years, in response to the area's shifting ethnic mix and to dietary fashion (egg-free and/or flour-free cakes and salt-free bread made to order). But largely it remains a resolutely French pâtisserie, with butter croissants, pains au chocolat, tartelettes au citron, madeleines, florentines, mirlitons among the daily output from the downstairs kitchens. Over 80 varieties of bread, from pain de campagne and baguette to focaccia and cholla, are baked daily in the bakery at Bridstow Place, using untreated flour and old-fashioned, slow processes of mixing and fermentation. They'll make novelty cakes to customers' own designs (a ball-and-chain wedding cake was one such; another was a 4-foot high birthday cake incorporating 200 icing roses to spell out the celebrant's name and 100 marzipan figurines – cost £1,100!), French profiterole wedding cakes, bread napkin rings, white-chocolate place-names. The back of the Queensway shop is given over to a busy restaurant, supplied by the on-site kitchens again. Also at 4 Chepstow Road, W2 (tel 0171 229 5289), and 27 Kensington Church Street, W8 (tel 0171 938 1547).

Coffee/Tea

Markus Coffee Company Ltd

13 Connaught Street W2. Tel: 0171 723 4020 (& fax) 0171 262 4630
Mon–Fri 8.30am–5.30pm, Sat 8.30am–1.30pm

Go early in the morning to catch the huge roasting and (possibly less exciting) packing machines in action, the combined bulks of which take up a fair amount of space in this small shop. Sacks of the green beans, which are more of a dingy beige colour and are only distinguishable one from the other to the expert eye, lie around elsewhere. A blend of Regent and Negresco is the popular house coffee. Beans come from all over the world and each type has its adherents. Even the fantastically expensive Jamaican Blue Mountain, which, at £26/500g, you'd have thought would be rarely bought and then only in small quantities: one customer, however, regularly buys 11 kilos at a time, and another wanted 200 kilos, an order which Mr Sarwar was sadly not able to fulfil. That amount of the fabled JBM just could not be found! (One of the reasons it is so scarce is that it is much appreciated by the Japanese – apparently dealers from Japan buy whole harvests in one go.)

Emporia

The Athenian Grocery

16a Moscow Road W2. Tel: 0171 229 6280
Mon–Sat 8.30am–7pm, Sun and Bank Holidays 9.30am–1.30pm

Before the Arabs, came the Greeks – to Bayswater, that is – and the Athenian has been catering to their needs for some 45 years, claiming, with some justification, to be one of the very first

Middle Eastern stores in London. Although owned by importers and distributors John Pascalis Ltd, this gorcery feels like a family business, with friendly, chatty staff and even chattier customers. There's everything you'd expect, plus some surprises such as green walnuts preserved in a syrup which blackens them – an expensive delicacy – Greek shortbread with almonds, Greek pasta (bought, according to manager Kimon, by Italians), and their own, very good brand of halva and tahini.

Noura Food Centre

71 Westbourne Grove W2. Tel: 0171 727 0729
Mon–Sun 9am–8.30pm

Mr Rifai runs a small, well ordered, predominantly Lebanese establishment, where the usual staples of the region's cuisine can be found. Attractively displayed in baskets along each side of the shop are three kinds of burghul wheat, sesame and pumpkin seeds, lentils, cardamoms, black beans, Sudanese beans, etc. The harissa is home-made, as are kafta and kibbeh to order. In the cold cabinet, there's a huge round of Roumy – Egyptian Cheddar, which is more highly prized, the older and drier it gets.

Tawana Oriental Supermarket

18–20 Chepstow Road W2. Tel: 0171 221 6316
Mon–Sun 9.30am–8pm all year round

Long known to residents of 'The Hill' (that's Notting Hill, of which it is on the edge) for its excellent exotic vegetables, Tawana is beginning to look a bit raggedy round the edges, but those who enter therein will be well rewarded. Everything you might need for South-East Asian cookery is here, including the hardware. Pickled catfish and salted water cockroaches may be above and beyond the call of culinary adventurousness, so head for the shelves of curry pastes – red and green, karee, panang, namya, kanokwan – and coconut cream/milk/extract, or the chill cabinet of freshly-flown-in produce – pak choi, lime leaves, curry leaves, lemon grass, morning glory leaves, garlic flowers, string beans, galangal (like ginger, but stronger), tamarind, Thai aubergines, etc. In March/April, they even have durian, the fruit which stinks like a sewer but, if you're brave enough to try, you'll discover tastes like nectar.

Zen

27 Moscow Road Bayswater W2. Tel: 0171 792 2058
Mon–Sat 8am–8pm

A friendly, clean and inviting establishment run by three Lebanese brothers, Michael, Ramiz and Mario. Meat is both halal and not – Ramiz, the butcher of the three, says he doesn't care either way as long as it's good quality (beef is all Scotch and grass-fed), so if you do (care, that is), ask. He makes his own Lebanese sausages (makanek and soujou) and pasturma (cured beef wrapped in a paste of garlic and spices), and kibbeh and kafta to order. Among the interesting dried preserved goods are kishk, a fermented cracked wheat and yoghurt powder for winter soups; dried strained yoghurt balls in oil; aubergines stuffed with walnuts, garlic and chilli in oil; pomegranate syrup for dressings or dips; and dried apricot paste, a Syrian speciality which can be sucked like a lollipop or used in com-potes or ice-creams. A lot of the veg and fruit comes direct from the Middle East and, while I was there, boxes of little green figs, Lebanese pears and grapes arrived straight from the airport – very tantalising.

Greengrocer

Archie Food Store

14 Moscow Road W2. Tel: 0171 229 2275
Mon–Sat 8am–8pm, Sun 8am–6pm

A rchie Dhoot has been on site for some 20 years, supplying the local Middle Easterners with excellent fruit, veg, breads, grains, beans etc. The last two are sold loose from huge, not very attractive plastic tubs (but don't let that put you off), and include lupin seeds (for chewing). There are the year-round familiars (pale green marrows, white courgettes, white onions, aubergines large and small, peppers, etc) as well as seasonal crops such as fresh m'lookhiyeh (Jew's mallow, from about April) and jujube fruit (Sept/Oct), Lebanese figs, wild endives, fresh butter beans (whose season lasts only about a month), desert truffles (kamah) and white figs.

Ice-Cream

Wintons'
58 Queensway Bayswater W2. Tel: 0171 243 2975
Mon–Sun 10am–midnight or later (summer), 10am–11pm (winter)

Wintons' Soda Fountain
Whiteley's Queensway Bayswater W2. Tel: 0171 229 8489
Mon–Sun 10am–10pm

Mike and Dee Seaton, vet and ex-nurse respectively, were once stuck in Marseilles Port waiting for their safari truck to make it over the Mediterranean from Africa. They twiddled their thumbs and slaked their thirst in a glacerie near the port, thinking how nice it would be if London had something similar. That thought eventually became Queensway's two Wintons', long before the Haagen-Dazs franchise arrived just a few doors down. Carlos, manager at no. 58, has a slogan: 'If Haagen-Dazs do it, we do it better'. You get bigger scoops, too. Marcia makes the ice-creams downstairs (up to 50 different flavours), although constrictions of space upstairs mean they can only display around 20 at any one time, of which one has to be Pooh Bear's Delight (vanilla and honey, drippingly gooey and yummy), another Dime Bar Crunch (vanilla with huge pieces of Fry's Dime Bar), these being the two hottest sellers, as it were. Another big seller is their Hot Chocolate Fudge Sauce, which receives fulsome accolades from Americans who have pronounced it the best in the capital. Jelly Beans, giant lollipops, Belgian chocolates and a very special frozen fruit yoghurt (the two are blended in the machine after freezing) are among other delights on offer. The Whiteley's branch, with its authentic 1950s American jukebox adapted to take CDs, is funky, noisy and busy, with a brisk turnover of sundaes, milkshakes and floats. You will find this place every bit as sensuous as Haagen-Dazs.

Natural Food

Planet Organic

42 Westbourne Grove W2. Tel: 0171 221 7171 Fax: 0171 221 1923
Mon–Sat 9am–8pm, Sun 11am–5pm

Opened in November 1995, this brash young addition to the capital's health food retailers aims to change the nut-loaf-and-lentils image of its predecessors – throwing down the gauntlet by locating just down the road from one of the very best (see Wild Oats). Co-founders Jonathan Dwek and Renee Elliott are part- and wholly American respectively and the store, from its all-embracing name to its large, bright white, modern interior, has something of that country's can-do, up-and-at-'em approach. The food emphasis, however, is on British organic produce, wherever possible. Like The Real Food Store in Maida Vale, its bottom line is that nothing contains artificial additives or preservatives, refined sugar, hydrogenated fats, 'E' numbers or nature-identical flavourings. In Dwek's words, 'we read the label so that you don't have to'. When I visited soon after it had opened its doors, it hadn't quite reached full throttle (bread suppliers had still to be satisfactorily sorted, for example), but what there was showed promise. The small fish counter had lovely dark red tuna and running-water salmon. Wines, beer and meat are 100 per cent organic, the last coming from Pure Suffolk Foods. Their home-made sausages (free tastings every Saturday) are even made with bottled water, and beef ones are encased in lamb-skins (for non-pork eaters). 'The biggest concentration of organic veg and fruit in Europe,' according to Jonathan, was also 100 per cent organic (they cannot guarantee this will always be the case) and was well stored in chill cabinets. Deli dishes were sparse, but when this department is established most of it will be supplied by Veronica's restaurant in Hereford Road. The choice of general groceries was wide, with lots of organic items. There's an espresso bar and, on Fridays, a delivery service (£3.50 charge on orders up to £50, free thereafter). A qualified nutritionist is on hand to give advice and eventually each department will have its own information leaflets for those interested. Ambitious, and why not?

Chiswick

Butcher

Macken Bros

44 Turnham Green Terrace W4. Tel: 0181 994 2646
Mon–Sat 6am–6pm. Deliveries.

K nown as 'the Lidgate of Chiswick', this is a long, narrow, bustling shop, with a lot of chat between staff and customers, who can be an exacting crowd. One actually went to Scotland to satisfy herself that treatment of the cattle from which her Sunday joints came met her high standards! Little fear of disappointment, as Rodney and Jimmy Macken (their father started the business 40 years ago) display the certificates attesting to their meat's quality – free-range pork from Natural Farms, Aberdeen Angus Cattle Society approved, Guild of Scotch Quality Meat Suppliers approved. Sausages are all home-made (except for game). There's game in season and free-range Norfolk Bronze turkeys at Christmas, and Home Farm pickles, mustards and jams.

Delicatessen

Mortimer & Bennett

33 Turnham Green Terrace W4. Tel: 0181 995 4145 Fax: 0181 742 3068
Mon–Fri 8.30am–7pm, Sat 8.30am–5.30pm

T his is what is sometimes disparagingly known as a 'designer deli', in other word, consciously up-market, and not cheap. It also happens to be very good, not least because owner Dan Mortimer is a self-confessed food-lover who travels the continent widely looking for things the supermarkets won't stock. You'll find up to 20 different vinegars; 30 different oils, including two (Lucca and Poggio Lamantano) that are exclusive; pure peanut and sesame oils; Dubernet foie gras; cassoulet; confit and pâté; some 70 cheeses; Bonnat chocolates; Sally Clarke's breads, biscuits and chocolates; and pastas of every hue and shape including some disguised as sombrero hats. Of special note are Frances Smith salad mixtures from Kent – each packet contains 11-15 different edible flower leaves, mixed by Daniel himself and a snip at £1.50 a packet – and hand-picked mushrooms. Depending on the season, there may be fresh blewits, orange birch boletus, beefsteak fungus, St George's mushrooms, honey fungus, puffballs. What isn't sold fresh Daniel dries and jars.

Emporium

T Adamou & Sons
126 Chiswick High Road W4. Tel: 0181 994 0752
Mon–Sat 8am–7pm Sun, and Bank Holidays 9am–2pm
(closed Christmas Day)

A sk how long the Adamou family have been trading here and son Nagi might well reply, 'too bloody long, and you can quote me on that'. But such truculence is largely put on and belies the essential good-naturedness of him, his father and cousin Serge Halasi (another cousin, Andrew Georghiou, runs Chiswick's premier greengrocer – see Macken & Collins). Greek Cypriots in origin, the Adamous cater to the world. The interior shop is wonderfully old-fashioned with lino flooring and white-painted wooden shelves, crammed with the ingredients for any imaginable cuisine – Indian, Thai, Arabic, Greek, Spanish, Italian, Central European. Outside are piled enticing fruit and vegetables, including such exotica as kologassi (otherwise known as taro) and butternut pumpkins from Cyprus. Serge is a walking-talking encyclopaedia when it comes to the origins of this and that and will happily make recipe suggestions. They always seem to have orange-fleshed sweet potatoes, when others only have the white-fleshed – a major plus.

Fishmongers

Covent Garden Fishmonger
37 Turnham Green Terrace W4. Tel: 0181 995 9273
Tues–Fri 8.30am–5.30pm, Sat 8.30am–5pm

T he ebullient Phil Diamond can talk fish till the seas run dry. Ex-taxi driver, PR for the National Federation of Fishmongers, author of *The Covent Garden Fish Book*, and self-taught sushi chef, Phil has spent 20 years proselytising in the cause of the greater consumption of fish, with 16 of them in Chiswick. Most of his fish comes direct from Cornwall, Scotland and Paris – soft-shelled crabs, oysters, green-lip mussels, turbot, mullet, wild salmon, baby crawfish, all immaculately displayed. He makes his own fish stock, as well as a limited amount of sushi daily (and stocks the Japanese ingredients for those customers skilled enough to do it themselves).

John Nicholson
46 Devonshire Road W4. Tel: 0181 994 0809
Tue–Fri 8am–5.30pm, Sat 8am–5pm

Confusingly, the windows of this shop have 'Kay's' etched on them. But it is still in the Nicholson family (his name appears modestly above the door). Kay is the daughter of one John (who with his wife Gloria runs the Wallington branch), and sister of the other (who has returned to the law, for which he originally trained). Kay ran a deli next to the other shop for six years, which accounts for the many surprises here other than the excellently fresh fish. Renowned for their home-smoked haddock and trout, the Nicholsons also bring whole Bries to maturity, only selling them when they are absolutely ready for eating to impatient customers in the know. There are frozen dinner-party dishes, such as stuffed duck and boneless cushion of lamb, game in season, ham-on-the-bone (no added water or preservatives), unpasteurised farm-house Cheddar. But it is primarily the fish that brings Chiswickians to this clean and friendly place. Also at 108a Manor Road, Wallington, Surrey, (tel: 0181 647 3922).

Greengrocer

Macken & Collins Ltd
35 Turnham Green Terrace Chiswick W4. Tel: 0181 995 0140
Mon–Thu 7am–6pm, Fri–Sat 6am–5.30pm. Deliveries.

Andrew Georghiou, nephew of T Adamou round the corner in the High Road (see entry), achieved the not inconsiderable feat of turning what had become a lack-lustre 'apples and pears' joint into a first-class greengrocer in less than a year. Queues during Christmas week start at four in the morning and are proof of Andrew's success, which, he says, is down to hard work and getting to know his market — that involved 'reading up' Jane Grigson ('very Chiswick'). He never has fewer than 17 different lettuces, stocks some 14 different fresh herbs, potato varieties galore, and is happy to find anything a customer might want. 'Something is always available from somewhere — someone wanted cranberries in mid-summer, and I found them.' Winning contracts to satisfy the caprices of tennis stars during Wimbledon fortnight can only have increased his resourcefulness. Cheery and helpful staff.

Ealing

Butchers

Richardson
88 Northfields Avenue W13. Tel: 0181 567 1064
Mon–Thu 8am–5.30pm, Fri 8am–6pm, Sat 8am–4.30pm. Local deliveries.

Richardson of Ealing
110 South Ealing Road South Ealing W5. Tel: 0181 567 4405
Mon–Thu 8am–5.30pm, Fri 8am–6pm, Sat 8am–4pm. Local deliveries.

With his two shops together totting up some 70 years of butchery, Mike Richardson is truly the meat baron of the area and the very picture of a Jolly Butcher. He guarantees that all his beef comes from grass–and–silage-fed herds (no animal-product feeds), his lambs gambol happily if briefly in the Forest of Dean or Herefordshire and his pigs are free-range (to ensure they are antibiotic-clean). Everything, apart from the raw meat itself, the salamis and corned beef, is made on one or other premises (pre-marinated cuts, prize-winning sausages, home-cured bacon, pressed brisket, German meatloaf, black pudding, pâtés, brawn). Both shops are bestrewn with award certificates. South Ealing is the 'showcase', having had a recent refit in smart green tiles and boasting a 100 per cent pork sausage called the 'Knightsbridge', fancy breads baked on site, and James White apple juices. West Ealing is more traditional, even though Mike has stopped hanging carcasses in the window, and has bags of chicken bones for stock-makers.

Thorogood's Real Meat

113 Northfields Avenue West Ealing W13. Tel: 0181 567 0339
Mon–Sat 7am–5pm. Deliveries and mail order.

Paul Thorogood is another Jolly Butcher who has responded to the challenge of the supermarkets (and of Richardson over the road – see entry) by going for the organic market, which he has steadily built up over the past 12 years. His beef comes from Welsh Black herds grazed on Soil Association-approved land. Welsh Black was very popular in the 18th century when thousands of them were walked to London, Corgis snapping at their heels. George III liked this meat so much he had his own herd at Windsor. It is tender, succulent and very, very tasty. Paul's carcasses arrive by more conventional means, one black ear still attached as proof). He has biltong, game in season, Martin Pitt and Mrs Woolley (organic) eggs, home-made pies and sausages (even made to customers' own recipes, especially if an allergy is involved) and free-range ducks boned and stuffed with various fruits (Paul mails these to a customer in Peterborough). At the other end of the scale, he does 'TV dinners' of BBQ'd chicken wings at 99p for six wings, which, according to a lady in the shop, are 'far better than Sainsbury's'.

Delicatessens

Au Gourmet Grec

124 Northfields Avenue West Ealing W13. Tel: 0181 579 2722
Mon 10am–5pm, Tue–Fri 9.30am–6pm (Wed 1.30pm), Sat 8.30am–5.30pm

Mr and Mrs Vengelis Gougoulis are a Greek-Polish team whose continental deli has a definite – surprise, surprise – Greek-Polish bias. Here are bigos (hunter's stew), golabki (stuffed cabbage leaves, pronounced 'golomki'), kotlety (beef and pork mince cutlets), zimne nózki (literally 'cold feet', actually shredded pigs' trotters in jelly), frozen uszka (ravioli-like parcels) and pierogi (dumplings with cheese, meat or mushrooms), as well as dolmades, Greek oils and breads, a variety of cheesecakes exclusively made for the shop, lightly salted young cucumbers (only three days old and from Norfolk), olives in home-made marinades. Among the more unusual cheeses is oscypek, a ewes' milk cheese from the Polish mountains.

Parade Delicatessen
8 Central Buildings The Broadway W5. Tel: 0181 567 9066
Mon–Fri 9.15am–6pm, Sat 9.15am–5pm

There has been a Polish deli here for 40 years, under various owners. Lidia Phillips has had it for two and a half years, and although it retains its ethnic identity, staff and customers speaking Polish most of the time, Lidia has expanded its range to include other cuisines. There is, for instance, a phenomenal range of pastas. She makes her own bigos, which no self-respecting Polish deli can be without, and other dishes are made by local cooks – nalesniki, a pancake with cabbage, wild mushrooms, curd cheese and meat, barszcz (aka borsch) and the uszka to put in it (ravioli-like parcels filled with mushrooms), pierogi (sauerkraut and mushroom dumplings). If you fancy a Polish Christmas, order your carp in good time from Lidia.

The Village Pantry
133 Pitshangar Lane W5. Tel: 0181 997 4776
Mon–Fri 9am–7pm, Sat 9am–6pm, Sun, and Bank Holidays 10am–2pm

Armenian partners Messrs Gregorians and Abrahamian set up shop four years ago to cater for the ethnic soup that is Ealing. All shapes and sizes of old loaves hang from the ceiling like bunting, and the shelves are well stocked with French preserves, Italian oils and pastas, Mrs H S Ball's chutney, pickles, soups etc. There are French and Danish pastries and bread, marinated olives, Polish sausages, French and Italian salamis, and cheeses from all over Europe.

Fishmonger

T H Carr
139 Pitshangar Lane W5. Tel: 0181 997 5639
Mon 9am–1pm, Tue–Fri 8am–5.30pm (Wed till 1pm), Sat 8am–4pm

In situ for 60 years, Carr's is now in the very capable hands of Mr Saunders who worked for the eponymous previous owner for decades. Chairman of the London Fishmonger Federation, Mr Saunders knows a thing or two about fish after 37 years in the business, and although his selection is small it is all fresh from either Billingsgate or direct from Cornwall and Scotland. He will order anything anyone wants given due notice. His regular stock includes sea bass, salmon, squid, sardines and lovely, fat, loose, barnacled mussels. They may take longer to clean and scrape but the throw-away ratio is minimal. A quirky sideline traditional to Carr's is the supply of pet food.

Greengrocer

Nicky's Fruit & Veg

98 South Ealing Road South Ealing W5. Tel: 0181 567 2659
Mon–Sat 6am–6pm

As Nicky has been supplying surrounding restaurants for some 16 years, his domestic customers benefit from out-of-season produce fresh from Western International Market, on top of the seasonal crops. Days were, he says, when he'd have had garden lettuces and cos – now he's always got radicchio, rosso, frisée and all the rest (if you don't see what you want, ask, as he keeps some of them refrigerated out of the back). Everything, from potatoes and apples to melons and mangoes, raspberries and redcurrants (in October) is beautifully displayed and glows with health.

Health Food

Cornucopia

64 St Mary's Road W5. Tel: 0181 579 9431
Mon–Sat 9am–5.30pm

A large, airy shop, suitably rustic-looking with wooden shelving and floor, and containing everything the health foodie could possibly desire. A huge cheese counter includes lots of organic varieties, interesting ones like Ribblesdale goats' (pale yellow and very subtle). There's bread from Cranks, Martin Pitt eggs, organic ale and milk, Rozbert goats' milk yoghurt (an acquired taste), organic grains and beans and nuts, dried fruits (mango and barberries among them), and lots of ready-to-eat snacks.

Hammersmith/ Brook Green

Butchers

Buckingham

63 Blythe Road Brook Green W14. Tel: 0171 603 5170
Mon–Fri 8am–5.30pm, Sat 8am–5pm

John Nevin has established himself as a butcher of local repute in the eight years since he took over this 50-year-old butchery. His are not large premises, and he tries to cater for the varying depths of his customers' pockets and consciences: not everything is organic or free-range, but what is, is clearly labelled. John is extremely obliging when it comes to quirky orders, such as wanting your leg of lamb boned and diced just so. Telephone in advance. He also stocks a small selection of wet fish, bought daily from Billingsgate, Martin Pitt eggs (never more than a week old – go on a Tuesday to be sure of the freshest), game in season (and he will dress customers' own, even when high as a lunar capsule), and makes his own home-made traditional English sausages.

Stenton

55 Aldensley Road W6. Tel: 0181 748 6121
Tue–Sat 8am–6.30pm (Thu till 1pm)

John Stenton could talk the hind legs off a herd of Welsh Blacks. Having said that, residents of 'Brackenbury Village' are lucky indeed to have him as their local butcher as he stocks, in addition to the organic Welsh Black, grass-fed Scotch (both of which he hangs for 'as long as possible'), Welsh and English lamb, free-range pork, Jewett's free-range eggs, home-made burgers, 15 types of home-made sausages and free-range Bronze turkeys. He'll do Continental cuts, dress game ('and they know the birds they get back are the very ones they brought in'), give you a full CV of the animal while dicing a bit of it for you, and generally pass the time of day – so don't go if you're in a rush.

Delicatessens

Adam & Agusia

258 King Street W6. Tel: 0181 741 8268
Mon–Fri 8am–10pm, Sat 10am–10pm, Sun 11am–8pm

Named after proprietor Mr Kubik's son and daughter, Adam and Agusia is a deli-cum-restaurant conveniently located next door to Hammersmith's Polish Institute, although after five years Mr Kubik says 80 per cent of his dining customers are British people who have discovered the joys of white borscht soup, golabki and bigos. The deli stocks a large range of Polish sausages – kabanos, dry krakowska, mysliwska, tuchowska, wiejeska, kaszanka (a kind of black pudding), traditional breads and cakes, doughnuts with plum spread, chocolate cheesecake, krupczatka flour, and famous chocolate plums.

Schillerstroms Butiken

369 King Street W6. Tel: 0181 563 9211 Fax: 0181 563 9811
Mon–Sat 8am–7pm

A mere six months old and the one and only specialist Swedish deli in town. Owner Claes Schillerstrom also runs a restaurant of the same name in Belgravia, but chose Hammersmith for his small shop for obvious economic reasons and because there is a Swedish school over the river in Barnes. This is a spotlessly clean, very Scandinavian joint, all stripped pine and blue paint. There are a couple of tables outside and large wooden ones inside for breakfasters, snackers and lunchers. Already established among ex-pat Swedes, it cannot be long before Brits discover the delights of cloudberry cheesecake (a cloudberry looks like a yellow raspberry/blackberry but tastes like neither), fruit soups, pytti panna (Swedish hash), salmon pudding, Jansson's Temptation (potatoes, cream, onions and anchovies), smorgastarta (a multi-layered sandwich-cake of bread, prawns, dill and gravadlax). Christmas, Easter and Midsummer are all celebrated with huge hams, and from around the second week in August for five or six weeks is the crayfish season. Among the products never before available are BOB cordials and preserves and Spendrups beer. Cloudberry preserve goes wonderfully with deep-fried camembert.

Sutherland's

140 Shepherd's Bush Road Brook Green. W6 Tel: 0171 603 5717
Mon-Fri 8.30am-7.30pm, Sat 8.30am-5pm, Sun 8.30am-3pm
Local deliveries

Owner John Sutherland feels a bit embattled — a Tesco's recently opened nearby and a Sainsbury's is due to open in Shepherd's Bush soon. But he's not rolling over just yet. After seven years he has built up a loyal customer base which he hopes to keep by continuing to offer a selection of things you can't get in superstores – Neal's Yard British cheeses, ham and bacon from Dorset Farms' free-range porkers, his own-brand cooked ham, roast beef and sausages, ravioli and other pastas from Mauro of Muswell Hill (see entry), Cotswold meringue bases and gleaming gold tins of Valette produce (confit, lapin aux deux moutardes, graisse d'oie, etc). Beverages include organic wines, Dunkerton and French cider. Lots of oils, other deli staples and, possibly uniquely, an oil from a customer's own olive grove in Provence – fill your own container for £6 a half-litre

Health Food

Bushwacker Wholefoods

132 King Street W6. Tel: 0181 748 2061
Mon-Thu 10am-6.30pm, Fri-Sat 9.30am-6.30pm

Chris and Sunita Shipton have been catering to West London's vegans and vegetarians for 13 years, moving from Shepherd's Bush to larger premises in Hammersmith three years ago. They stock everything that can be organically grown, from medicinal and culinary herbs to pasta and rice to fruit and veg. If it's not organic the Shiptons guarantee that it is at least additive- and preservative-free. There's a large range of grains, seeds, nuts, mueslis, wheat-free and gluten-free products, non-dairy milks, such as Rice Dream (made from brown rice), macrobiotic and vegan-friendly products. They also stock the wonderful Tropical Wholefoods' sun-dried fruits – mango, pineapple, chewy banana: buy these and you are not only getting a healthy delicious snack, but are contributing to a worthwhile fair-trading partnership between two English persons and farmers in Uganda and Burkina Faso. For details of new projects, contact Kate Sebag, Rear of 83 Brixton Hill, SW2 1JE (tel: 0181 671 1300).

Holland Park

Butcher/Charcutier

C Lidgate

110 Holland Park Avenue W11. Tel: 0171 727 8243
Mon–Fri 7am–6pm, Sat 7am–5pm
Delivery within 5 miles if order telephoned before 10am

If you see a queue of Third-World length, albeit better dressed, stretching down Holland Park Avenue and round the corner, you will undoubtedly be passing C Lidgate on a Friday or Saturday. It is probably true that you won't find better meat in the capital – possibly as good, but never better. Opened in 1850 by one Alexander Lidgate, it is now run by his great-grandson David who knows a thing or two when it comes to butchery. Henrietta Green, food writer and broadcaster, has called him 'a man of vision'. And certainly he is an enthusiastic and dedicated advocate of quality meat, founding Chairman of the National Q Guild of Butchers, set up to fight declining standards. He has a firmly held theory about how good meat is achieved: breed, feed, age of animal, method of slaughter, conditions and length of hanging, and, last but by no means least, skill of butchery – all these are of equal importance in producing that prime beef sirloin or leg of lamb: 'Meat from badly reared animals will never improve however long you hang it for. Even organic meat will be as tough as old boots if it's not hung for long enough'. Beef and lamb come exclusively from grass-fed or organic herds in Scotland, the West Country, brother Lidgate's farm in Buckinghamshire and the royal herds at Highgrove; pigs are outdoor-reared and fed; veal is from humanely reared English calves (he does sell Dutch and French veal, but only from 'group-fed' herds, never from crate-confined beasts). David Lidgate regularly visits and inspects his suppliers' herds to ensure standards are kept up. Butchery covers the familiar British cuts, as well as Continental and American ones. There are lots of prepared cuts, and a splendid range of award-winning pies, including game, steak and kidney, boeuf en croûte, and lamb and leek. Made to order, these can accommodate any number of portions up to 16, and you get a ceramic pie dish into the bargain. In season, you'll find game, ducks' and gulls' eggs, in addition to the chickens' eggs from Martin Pitt's Wiltshire flock – the only egg-producer in the country who annually and voluntarily submits his birds for salmonella testing. Finally, there's a good selection of farmhouse British, French and Spanish cheeses, a range of bottled condiments and preserves, and those delicious root vegetable crisps that are all the rage these days.

Cheesemonger

Jeroboams

6 Clarendon Road W11. Tel: 0171 727 9359 Fax: 0171 792 3672
Mon–Fri 9am–7.30pm, Sat 9am–6pm, Sun 10am–3pm

The newest, biggest and therefore main link in the 11-year-old cheese-chain (hardly a chain: the only other two are at 24 Bute Street, SW7, and 51 Elizabeth Street, SW1). Good cheeses have always been available around here, but Jeroboams, being a specialist, adds considerably to the expertise and selection on offer. Particularly enticing in the window display are those small waxed-paper parcels of delicious moist goats' cheeses, more usually seen in French markets. All the Continental varieties come weekly direct from Rungis market in Paris. Livarot and Vacherin drip and ooze, Reblochon walks out of its own accord (because it's so popular), Manchego and Mimolette sit solid and mature, the latter positively glowing orange. The ever-expanding range of British and Irish cheeses, which have been enjoying a long-overdue renaissance in the past decade, include richly coloured Cheddars from as far afield as the Isle of Mull; stately blues, such as Dorset Vinny, St Dunsyre (from Lanarkshire) and Stilton from Colston Bassett; Welsh goats'; hard ewes' Ballindalloch from Scotland; Cooleeney, the Irish answer to Camembert, and Gubeens, with its 'taste of fresh-mown hay', from County Cork. All the native cheeses come from traditional farmhouse producers, so don't be put off by the appearance of a bluish mould on the cut surface – this is entirely natural and proof of the untinkered-with manufacturing process. Manager Matthew Rosser 'cleans' them every morning, but by the end of the day there's that tell-tale sign of a living, breathing food. British cheeses are matured and ripened in Jeroboams's own cellars, thus ensuring they are sold in peak condition. If you and he have the time, Matthew will talk you through his shop and you'll doubtless come away with more than a wedge of Brie and just the half of Cheddar. He'll advise on how to store and for how long, what to drink with what, and anything else you could conceivably want to know. Alternatively, pick up (for £1.50) one of his informative leaflets, which covers everything. You can get all the latest tackle here too — cheese larders, boards, slicers, knives etc, as well as books, and French wines. If you're too busy to visit the shop itself, they will 'design' a cheeseboard for you. And if you live too far away ever to call in, join the Cheese Club — for £20 per month you'll be sent a selection of four cheeses.

Delicatessen

Speck
2 Portland Road W11. Tel: 0171 229 7005
Mon–Fri 9am–8.30pm, Sat 9am–7pm

Giovanni Renzo is a relative newcomer to Holland Park's haut-produit block, but has made his mark in three and a half short years. He stocks 20 or so different hams and salamis, including the eponymous one from the South Tyrolean Alps (cured), various Italian cheeses (two-year-old Parmigiano Reggiano, Provolone Anticchio, an extra-mature goats', and the nutty Pecorino Sardo, young and matured versions, among them), fancy estate-bottled oils (those from Frantoio di Sante Tea actually specify the date of pressing, Dec–Jan giving a 'smooth and delicate' oil, November a 'fruity and intense' one). There's a generous 'gastronomia' counter (the Italian equivalent of traiteur) of home-made dishes — Involtinidi di Bresaola, Rucola and Mozzarella, speck and beans in balsamic vinegar, aubergines parmigiano, stuffed peppers, pesto, salsas and the like.

Greengrocer

Michanicou Brothers
2 Clarendon Road W11. Tel: 0171 727 5191
Mon–Fri 9am–6.30pm, Sat 9am–5.30pm. Deliveries.

A joy of a shop. You are enticed in by its near-vertical pavement display and by the cheery grins of Michanicou brothers Chris and Andy. Once inside, a kind of slow shoe-shuffle takes place as packed customers wait their turn in the small space. There's also the most wonderful earthy smell of really fresh produce brought daily from Spitalfields market (NB: the van doesn't get back to the shop until 10.30am, so if you go in the first hour and a half you'll only have a choice of what was left over from the day before). Sometimes referred to as the 'French veg shop' for obscure reasons (the family is Greek by origin), this is where to come for mini Queens pineapples (sweet beyond compare), shiny green salad leaves, royally purple baby artichokes, custard apples; fresh herbs, sorrel, juniper berries, seaweed; chanterelles, shitake, morels and ceps. Yes, they also sell potatoes, carrots, sprouts, apples, oranges, pears... But nothing is here because of competitive pricing; only quality counts with the Michanicou brothers and you get, as they say, what you pay for.

Pâtisserie

Maison Blanc

102 Holland Park Avenue W11. Tel: 0171 221 2494 Fax: 0171 221 7794
*Mon, Tue 8am–7pm, Wed–Fri 8am–7.30pm, Sat 7.30am–7pm,
Sun 8.30am–6pm*

With five branches in London, this Oxford-born company no longer hauls its wares up the M40 every morning – it's all made in their new bakery at Park Royal, or as manageress Natalie Vernier charmingly says 'Parc Royale', a pronunciation far better befitting the quality of the goods, if rather aggrandising the west London suburb. Their breads are famously good – campaillou (a holey soda bread), pain de campagne, pain au levain (yeast-free), pain paysan, pain parisien, boule de meule (stoneground) – all have that authentic French look and taste. An American friend swears theirs is the best tarte au citron she's ever had outside Paris, and she's almost decided the same of the tartelette au chocolat. There are madeleines and florentines, and a full range of 'Viennoiserie' – the generic name for croissants (plain, almond, almond and currants), pain chocolat, brioche, etc. Party catering consists of 'petits salés' (miniature savouries), as they are not traiteurs. Coffee is good and, in true French style, has to be drunk standing up at a chest-high plinth. Tastings of new lines often happen during the week, but depend entirely on 'our mood'!

Kensington

Butchers

Mark's in Kensington

17 Kensington Court Place, W8. Tel: 0171 937 0630 Fax: 0171 376 2096
Mon-Fri 8.30am-5.30pm, Sat 8.30am-12.30pm

New Zealander Mark Wormald has in three years transformed this long-established butchery into a small one-stop shop – about the only thing he doesn't have is greens. Otherwise there is free-range English and Scottish beef, lamb pork and poultry (organic to order only), wet fish, farmhouse British cheeses, biltong, 22 types of home-made sausages and various oils, vinegars and condiments.

W J Miller

14 Stratford Road, W8. Tel: 0171 937 1777
Mon & Sat 8am-1pm, Tue-Fri 8am-6pm

Although assured that organic halal meat is not that unusual, I have not come across another halal butcher whose meat is produced from animals reared to Organic Farmers' and Growers' standards, as the beef lamb and poultry are here. There are also various delicious-looking Middle-eastern prepared dishes – spicy kebabs and sausages, marinaded lamb and chicken.

Delicatessens/Ready-Made Foods

Hamlins of Kensington

3 Abingdon Road W8. Tel: 0171 376 2191
Mon-Fri 9.30am-6pm, Sat 9.30am-4pm

Siblings Stephen and Kelda Anderson took over this deli 18 months ago and are making a good fist of turning it into something special. Ninety per cent of what's on offer is made on the premises, including speciality breads (baking days are Mondays, Wednesdays and Fridays), hand-made truffles, light crumbly biscuits and shortbreads, lots of salads, terrines, mousses and pâtés, pasta dishes and casseroles. Many of the hot dishes are also available frozen, and they'll cater for any-sized party or dinner. British cheeses come from Neal's Yard, French from The Cheese Cellar. The deli side is small but impressively selective – Duchy Originals, Orkney Herrings, Womersley jams, good oils.

The Pie Man Food Company
20 Stratford Road W8. Tel: 0171 937 3385
Mon–Fri 8.30am–6.30pm, Sat 8.30am–5pm

This is now the biggest of the Pie Man shops, because Andrew Price has added a deli section which sports various quality brands, some familiar, others unusual – Cotswold Meringues, Joubère soups (such as Bajan Jug Jug – chicken and coconut curry, and jolly good, too), O'Hagan sausages, pastas, Tropical Wholefoods sun-dried fruits (see Bushwacker Wholefoods in Hammersmith), and lots of the famed Pie Man freezer meals. The catering arm of Pie Man can be reached on 0171 627 5232. Other shops at 16 Cale Street, SW3 (tel: 0171 225 0587 – see entry) and 75 High Street, SW19 (tel: 0181 944 1200).

Emporia

Crackers
272 Kensington High Street W8. Tel: 0171 603 7071
Mon–Sat 9am–8pm

This is the latest of the clutch of Middle Eastern shops that have set-tled at the western end of Kensington High Street. Vincent Danil is one of those suave men-of-the-world – born in Jaffa, brought up in Dar es Salaam, then Beirut, now London. Perhaps a better recommendation is that of Lebanese cookery writer Anissa Helou, who praises the muhummara (a coarse purée of walnuts and pine nuts mixed with burghul and spiced with chilli). They make a mean shankleesh as well (dried cheese mixed with thyme and spices, which should be chopped up with tomatoes, parsley and oil), kafteh (mince, parsley and onions), babaghamouj (aubergine dip), hoummus, makanek (sausages), etc. Rice and some beans are sold loose. Lebanese wines and arak are a welcome extra.

Reza Pâtisserie/Reza Meats

345-7 Kensington High Street W8. Tel: 0171 602 3674 Fax: 0171 610 4221
Mon-Sun 9am-9pm

I have been treating myself to Mr Reza's amazingly reasonable (in price, that is; the taste is sublime) Iranian caviar for years, thinking that I was one of a select few who knew about it – stupidly, as he advertises it on his window – when all along most of my friends were doing (and thinking) the same thing. The caviar is not as plentiful as it once was (nor as reasonable, though still cheaper than most other places), but there are plenty of other reasons to explore his shops. Everything in the pâtisserie is made on the premises (you can watch the baker at work through a doorway at the back) and although much may look familiar if you know Greek and Turkish pastries, these are the Persian versions – baclava, biscuits, ice-cream, cream cakes, all sweet and gooey. Next door, the first things you notice are the huge sprays, all year round, of coriander, flat-leaf parsley, mint, dill, tarragon, thyme, toreh (Iranian chive). These come from Cyprus in the winter; in the summer from Mr Reza's farm near Oxford (where he also grows his own garlic). Huge oblong, yellow Iranian melons are a treat (they only come from Iran, and are imported only by Reza). The interior is crammed with all things Middle Eastern, though the emphasis is Iranian. Lavash and barberi naans and other Arab breads, red barberries for mixing with rice, pomegranate and sour grape juices, saffron, dried plums and shallots, dried smoked salmon (which is rehydrated and then cooked under rice), frozen Iranian meals, Turkish, Lebanese and Iranian halva, and myriad other things. The 'Meats' bit is at the back – lambs' tongue, testicles, brain, liver, heart, whole heads and feet and, unexpectedly, free-range poussin.

Super Bahar

349a Kensington High Street W8. Tel: 0171 603 5083
Mon-Sun 9am-9pm

M r Hamid claims his shop, nostalgically named after a popular shopping district in his native Tehran, was the first Iranian supermarket in London, 'if not in Europe' – a record that Mr Reza (see above) next door might dispute! The rival shops stock almost identical produce, down to the same make of dried herbs and naans, so if one shop has run out, try the other. Super Bahar also deals in Iranian caviar, but will nowadays only get it to order; it arrives within 24 hours.

Pâtisserie

Cannelle

221 Kensington High Street W8. Tel: 0171 938 1547
Mon–Sat 8am–7pm, Sun 9am–6pm

One of three in a superior cake-and-chocs chain. All ingredients come from France and go to 'somewhere near Wembley' to be made into tartelettes (try the soufflé au framboise – it is absolutely delicious), sponge cakes, madeleines, sablés, éclairs, etc. Bread sells out quickly and sandwiches are made daily, the truffles are home-made, though other chocolate on sale is Valrhona. There's gourmet rock candy, and orders can be taken for profiterole wedding-cakes (and others), St Valentine cakes and party canapés. Other branches at 166 Fulham Road, SW10 (tel: 0171 370 5573) and 26 North Audley Street, W1 (tel: 0171 409 0500).

North Kensington

Baker

Joe's Bakery

5 All Saints Road W11. Tel: 0171 221 1083
Mon–Sat 8am–6pm

Joe's Caribbean hard-dough bread is well established among the West Indian community London-wide, but he also makes cholla and bagels, and the occasional wholemeal. He's a wholesaler as well, so you'll find his bread around and about. Foodwriter Charles Campion of ES Magazine is a big fan.

Delicatessen

Lisboa Delicatessen
54 Golborne Road W10. Tel: 0181 969 1052
Mon–Sat 9.30am–7.30pm, Sun and Bank Holidays 10am–1pm

The front area of this 25-year-old shop (the first Portuguese deli in London) seems familiarly deli-like, if with a decided Portuguese bias – heavy breads, tinned sardines, anchovies and other fish, olive oils from Portugal (which owner Carlos Gomes controversially claims are 'the best in the world'), a counter stuffed with cured meats (paio – smoked pork loin) and sausages (torresmos, choricos, cozidos) – but the back room is a world apart and not for the faint-hearted. Here, piled high on the wooden tables, are all the raw ingredients for those hefty Portuguese stews which can defeat the healthiest appetite. 'Raw' is a misnomer, since it is all salt-cured – pigs' ears, trotters, snouts, ribs, tails and belly, and of course the essential bacalhau – salt cod – in enormous pieces which Señor Gomes will cut to requested size with his bandsaw. Cheap (about £3.30/500g – 1lb) and nourishing, salt cod is an under-used basis for many a delicious dish, particularly when cooked with potatoes and tomatoes to make winter fillers – but Carlos says there's a way to cook it for every day of the year. A peculiar sideline is boxes and boxes of Portuguese knitting cotton – linha de crochet e tricotar – now mostly bought by West Indian ladies.

Emporium

R Garcia & Sons
248–250 Portobello Road Notting Hill W11 . Tel/Fax: 0171 221 6119
Mon–Wed & Fri–Sat 9am–6pm, Thu 9am–1.30pm

For nearly 40 years Raphael Garcia and family have been satisfying local Spanish appetites with the tastes of Iberia. Mr Garcia is justly famous for his Serrano hams which swing darkly and enticingly from the ceiling. Not only are they delicious, being matured year-old hams, but at about £7 per 500g/1lb must be one of the capital's best bargains. In the run-up to Christmas, the exquisitely flavoursome 'patanegra' ham (from acorn-fed pigs) sells briskly despite a price tag of around £20 per 500g (1lb) – and 50 per cent of purchasers are British, which, Mr Garcia confesses, surprised him at first. The shop is also crammed with tins of Spanish staples – chorizo in lard, with lentils, with tripe, with bacon, black pudding and beans; tripe with beef trotters, bacon and shoulder of pork; snails in hot sauce; mussels in their shells. Cheeses include the familiar Manchego, as well as Tetilla, a smooth-tasting yellow cone-shaped cow's milk cheese from Galicia.

Fishmonger

Golborne Fisheries

75 Golborne Road W10. Tel: 0181 960 3100
Mon–Wed 7.30am–6pm, Thu–Sat 7.30am–8pm

If you want something fishily exotic, look no further than George's shop. If he hasn't got it, it probably isn't edible or remains undiscovered in the bathysphere. He claims to have 160 varieties of sea creature at any one time (I didn't stop to count), mostly from Portugal, Morocco and the West Indies, delivered daily, and indeed his display of fish has to be one of the more spectacular around. Nothing is labelled so you have to ask what those long, ugly sharp-toothed things are – white or black deep-water spiderfish from Madeira. Parrot fish, bourgeois, dolphin fish, spotted grouper, red grouper, catch the eye among the more familiar turbot, halibut, cod, and flat fish. Lord knows what you do with some of them, but George will help if possible. He also stocks piles of salt cod. The size of some specimens might upset those concerned about the state of the sea-larder.

Pâtisserie /Café

Lisboa Pâtisserie

57 Golborne Road W10. Tel: 0181 968 5242
Mon–Sat 8am–8pm

After 12 years on the block and despite its popularity with young local Brits, Lisboa has lost none of its Continental atmosphere. Portuguese and other Mediterranean languages still dominate in the tiled room, packed tight with small metal tables, around which customers squeeze, steaming hot mugs of coffee, fags and newspapers in hand. There's often a two-deep row of chattering counter-proppers, discussing Lord-knows-what over picas of very strong black coffee and a nip of something even stronger. The hustle and bustle is contained with admirable equanimity by Celia Gomes, wife of Carlos across the road (see Lisboa Delicatessen). All the coffee comes from Brazil via Portugal, where it is roasted. All the scrummy pastries, cakes, bread and snacks on display are made in the downstairs bakery on a daily basis. Try the pasteis de nata, a melt-in-the-mouth custard tart which is the speciality of the house, the pasteis camarão (prawn tart), the almond or coconut cakes, the pão de deus (God's bread). In fact, try anything, just be prepared to wait – it's worth it.

West Kensington

Baker

Maison du Moulin

27 North End Parade, North End Road W14. Tel: 0171 603 0385
Mon–Fri 7.30am-6pm, Sat 7am-4pm

A small, friendly bakery, but not so small that it cannot rise to an order of 100 ham-and-cheese croissants for a birthday party. Everything is made on the premises by manager and chief baker Mohsen. The speciality seems to be savoury pastries, from ham-and-cheese croissants to spinach quiche, chicken puffs, mushroom slices, individual pies and tarts (the doll-sized pecan tartlets are delightful), sausage rolls, pretzels and pizzas (an interesting miscegenated variation is the 'bagel pizza' – a half of the famous Jewish roll topped with the familiar Italian mixture). Breads range from French sticks to bloomers and wholemeal loaves. A few flamboyant French-style gateaux.

Delicatessen

Prima

192 North End Road W14. Tel: 0171 385 2070
Mon-Thu, Sat 9.30am-6pm, Fri 9.30am-7pm

A 20-year-old store selling basic Polish goods – various cured meats and herring preparations, fresh carp for Christmas (to order), poppy seed and yeast cakes, frozen pierogi (dumplings), lots of flavoured vodkas, and Jovan products from John & Sons in Shepherd's Bush (see entry).

Emporium

Super Masoud

9a Hammersmith Road W14. Tel: 0171 602 1090
Mon-Sun 9am-11pm

A 'pure Persian' shop, according to its proprietor, the waggish Mr 'Super' Masoud Yasini. There are the many different Arab breads, all excellent for soaking up stews or folding round salady stuffings (my favourite is probably the one-and-a-half-foot-long oval Barbaree which doubles as a plate); lots of nuts, fresh and dried, for mixing with rice; sheets of dried apricot paste for diluting and drinking; dried orange peel, again for rice-flavouring; pomegranate syrup; limoo (dried limes); pulses and rices. Outside is a good selection of fruit and veg, most of it rather more European than Persian, which 'Super' fetches daily from Western International.

Market

North End Road

SW6
Mon-Sat 8am-5pm approx.

S trictly speaking we are in Fulham, but for some reason this market has always been associated with West Kensington. It cheers up considerably what is otherwise a dreary street of cut-price stores, dubious looking butchers, and burger bars. There are 74 pitches of which a good half are still dedicated to foodstuffs. One of the longest-serving costermongering families is the Johnson clan, a 100 years in the trade and still going strong with two brothers and two sisters: Michael, at pitch 68, always has a long queue snaking round his stall, which reassuringly announces that he sells 'Fruit from the World' – these include unseasonal and huge American strawberries ('leave in a warm place for a couple of hours to bring out the flavour') and apricots, nectarines and Gaviota plums from South Africa; at pitch 60, sister Vera, trading under her nickname of 'Tubby', peddles figure-reducing salad ingredients, pitch 35 finds brother and nephew Peter and Peter Junior and firm seasonal veg; at the far end (nearest Fulham Broadway), sister Marie sells her free-range ducks' and 'dead-ordinary' eggs at competitive prices. Another name to note for fruit and veg is Woodward, at 33, 34 and 35 (mates of the Johnson's). Reg Curtis at pitch 41 is the last remaining fishmonger, 80 per cent of whose stock is fresh, from sprats to Dover sole – tilapia, trevally, snappers tend to be frozen. He'll get 'anything that swims' given 24 hours' notice. At No. 31, 'Bridget' provides dried fruits, nuts, herbs and spices, the last freshly ground in her shop at No. 1 Blenheim Crescent, W11 and mixed by her into Thai 7 Spice or Korean Red Curry Mix – no salt or anything else ever added. She only pitches up on Fridays and Saturdays. Afro-Caribbean and Asian veg is, perhaps surprisingly thin on the stalls, but across the pavement from Tubby's is an Asian grocer/butcher which has fresh herbs, plantains, bonnet peppers, little aubergines, dhudi, tinda etc. in boxes outside.

Maida Vale

Pâtisserie

Mimma
414 Harrow Road Maida Hill W9. Tel: 0171 266 4224
Mon–Sun 8am–7pm

Iraqi Dean Sumaiday took over this establishment a year and a half ago, but has kept the Portuguese bias — why destabilise a good customer base? His one concession to his own regional cuisine are Arab breads, pitta and the small Lebanese flat bread, mostly used for the sandwich trade. Portuguese breads and pâtisserie nowadays come from Funchal in Stockwell) and are therefore guaranteed good: pasteis de nata, que ques (fairy cakes), feijao (coconut custard), pão de leite, pão de deus, xadres, maca and palmieres, fruit tarts, éclairs etc. The bakery downstairs is out of commission at the moment, but Dean plans to get it going again soon.

Delicatessen

Carlton Deli
344 Harrow Road W9. Tel: 0171 266 2890
Mon–Sat 8am–9pm

Owned by the Dean Sumaiday of Mimma (see above), this deli sells a wide variety of Mediterranean (with a markedly Italian emphasis) and Middle Eastern foods, as well as a selection of freshly-made sandwiches, and has rapidly established itself since opening in January this year with the deli-starved locals.

Fishmonger

Jefferson's Seafoods
17 Clifton Road W9. Tel: 0171 266 0811 0171 266 1724
(24hr answerphone) Fax: 0171 266 3166
Mon–Sat 9am–6pm. Deliveries.

Touchingly named after owner Peter Grosvenor's dog (RIP), the cool, black interior of this three-year-old shop lures you in past the old lobster pots standing guard at the entrance. Peter was in the fashion industry until he decided to up sticks to Cornwall, where he got a job in the 'seafood business', learnt it and returned to London to open up shop. He deals direct with fleets in Newlyn and Looe, getting whatever's best on the day. And to prove his credentials as an expert judge of the catch, displayed on his walls (next to the picture of Jefferson) are the cards of those smart London restaurants supplied by him – among them Daphne's, The Cow and Zafferano. He was about to expand into prepared fish dishes when I visited, so expect top-notch fare made from his yellow-tail bream, John Dory, squid, sole (various), tuna and sword-fish. Martin Pitt eggs, French crab and fish soups, Orkney marinaded herrings, free-range chickens are also on sale.

Greengrocer

Roy's Greengrocers
5 Formosa Street W9. Tel: 0171 286 2408
Mon–Sat 8.30am–6pm, Sun 9.30am–1pm

Roy worked here for over 20 years before becoming the owner at the end of the eighties. He hopes his son, also Roy, will take over 'soon'. Until then, he presides jovially over the daily deliveries of top-quality produce. He has a good range of less usual stuff – persimmons, Chinese gooseberries, various squashes, orange-flesh sweet potatoes (these are not really unusual but it's worth noting that you are more likely to find them in a 'European' greengrocer than a Caribbean/African establishment which all seem to prefer the white-flesh varieties) and seasonals like wet walnuts, cob nuts and fresh dates. But what strikes the eye are the luscious displays of good old English veg, like rich green cabbages, one halved to reveal the perfect yellowy-green interior (you immediately want to sink your teeth into it). At the back is a chill cabinet holding salad necessities, including wild rocket, so they are always fresh and crisp.

Natural Food

The Realfood Store
14 Clifton Road W9. Tel: 0171 266 1162 0171 266 1550 (deliveries)
Mon–Fri 8.30am–7.45pm, Sat 8.30am–6pm

Kevin Gould may be a man with a mission – to bring 'real food' to the people – but he is not a proselytiser, wanting the discovery to be fun. By real food, he means 'food that is made with integrity – no artificial preservatives, no additives, no hydrogenated fats, no refined sugar'. And judging by his success over the past five years, the message is getting across. There are 7,000 lines in all, and all 'real'. Green & Black's 'fairly traded' organic chocolate, De Rit honeys from

Holland, 100 per cent buffalo milk Mozarella from Aversa (most buffalo milk mozarella has a percentage of cows' milk), Sally Clarke, Innes and Neal's Yard breads, cheeses from Neal's Yard, unpasteurised olives from the South of France, ravioli and linguine made by Franco di Lombardi (who supplies 'the top five Italian restaurants in London'), loose, paper-thin sun-dried tomatoes, persechelle (baby green peaches in truffle oil, a delicacy supplied by a few farmers of Abruzzo 'as a result of climatic changes which meant the fruit rotted before ripening') and so on. Everything is organic only if it is 'as good as or better than' the non-organic equivalent. Most of this is pricey but, it has to be said, it's worth it. As for the sandwiches, Kevin says 'we are not constrained by normal sandwich-making philosophy'. And he's right. The vermilion-haired Sam stacks anything she fancies between two slices of the above-named breads – leek, fennel, French bean and cos lettuce was one example of her innovative way with the humble sarnie, a snip at £1.25. Fruit and veg, some organic, are stacked outside, and include seasonal home-grown wild mushrooms.

Notting Hill

Baker

Clarke's
122 Kensington Church Street W8. Tel: 0171 229 2190
Mon–Fri 8am–8pm, Sat 9am–4pm

Slap next to Clarke's restaurant, this is strictly speaking called '&
Clarke's', but it is universally known just as Clarke's. Chef Sally's breads are now available in many other stores, mostly delis, around the capital, but for greatest choice (and perhaps the best of the batch) come here and have a cup of Monmouth Coffee Co coffee and a croissant while you think about which of the many loaves appeals: apricot crescent, fougasse (olive oil and herbs), corn ears, campagnard (lovely thick and floury), buttermilk, brioche, honey wholewheat, pane toscano, pumpkin, olive and sun-dried tomato. Why stop at breads? There are

Neal's Yard and Innes cheeses, tarts, truffles (just the one deeply choc-olately plain variety), English apple juices, coffees and teas. Staff could be friendlier, but you can't have everything. Unhurried locals use it as a breakfast café (only two tables).

Delicatessens

Applewold Farm Shop
206 Portobello Road W11. Tel: 0171 229 5282
Mon-Sat 8am-6pm

This small deli is eye-catching, even in the hurly-burly of Porto-bello Market on a Saturday, because of the vast number of eggs piled up outside the door. Indeed, it was eggs that got Mr and Mrs Burton started eight years ago. Although not all truly free-range, the eggs come from various suppliers in the West Country), are delivered three times a week and their manner of production is clearly marked. Apart from chicken eggs, you'll usually find ducks', often geese, and pheasants' and gulls' in season. Inside the shop, Mrs Burton keeps a small cheese counter and some of the better brands of preserves and condiments, among them Wiltshire Tracklements. But eggs are really the point here.

Mr Christian's
11 Elgin Crescent W11. Tel: 0171 229 0501 Fax: 0171 727 6980
Mon–Fri 6am–7pm, Sat 5am–7pm, Sun 7am–2pm (approx)

For much of its 21-year existence (it came of age in September last year), Mr Christian's had no competition in the area at all; if you commented adversely on the price of something, you were confi-dently told to go somewhere else. But there wasn't anywhere else to go. Sainsbury's (in Ladbroke Grove), Tom's and Applewold Farm Shop may have encroached slightly on its patch, but Mr Christian's is still the best up-market corner-shop around this area. On Saturdays Mr Christian's sets up a trestle table outside the shop which creaks and groans with the weight of loaves, bagels and delicious ciabatta sandwiches. Along with the steaming cups of coffee, these are snapped up by stall-holders and punters alike. Inside, it's a traditional-style deli, ceiling-high shelves stacked with fancy oils and vinegars, jars of haricots à la graisse d'oie, poulet Basquaise, salmis de pintade, various olive pastes, fresh liquid stocks, a large choice of French, Italian and German salamis, French and British farmhouse cheeses, chutneys, chocolate Olivers, and more. Breads come from various suppliers, and include the famed sourdough from Innes, Ukrainian and Estonian rye from Bradford, ciabatta, baguettes, olive, sun-dried tomato, farmhouse white. What really pulls the punters in throughout the week, however, is the lunchtime fodder. Made in the kitchens downstairs every day, this features ciabatta sandwiches, pizzas, lasagne, chicken dishes, hoummos, pasta salads, cottage pie, cauliflower cheese, and soups. Mr Christian's is also one of the few places to stock a beef consommé, sadly, good though it is, not the jellied kind, but in these beggared times we have to take what we can get.

Tom's

226 Westbourne Grove W11. Tel: 0171 221 8818 Fax: 0171 221 7717
Mon–Sat 8am–8pm, Sun 10am–2pm

Established in 1990 by Tom Conran, son of design guru and foodie Sir Terence, Tom's got off to a sticky start. Now under the management of Alistair Cameron, it seems to be surer of what it's about. The deli has lots of oils and vinegars, pâtés and pastes, dips and sauces, clamato juice, risotto rices and pastas, excellent breads from Bagatelle, among others. The fridges are packed with Duskin Farm single-variety apple juices – Cox, Crispin, James Grieve, Bramley, Ida Red and Worcester; lots of different Continental beers (including Belgian Trappist), Pete's Wicked Lager and strong French cider; and trendy stuff like Mountain Iced Tea. The traiteur counter boasts an array of food-to-go: grilled vegetables, Puy lentil salad, grilled chicken with garlic and coriander; charcuterie (from Merrivale Charcuterie in Cornwall). Cheeses include imports such as Vieux Comté, Mimolette, buffalo Mozzarella and others, flown in weekly from Lille, and British ones from Neal's Yard and Innes). There's a small selection of fresh fruit and veg, and a coffee counter at which you can pass the time of day with a steaming cappuccino, get a take-away or buy beans of various strength and guaranteed quality — they all come from the Algerian Coffee Store in Soho. A recent refit has seen the addition of an upstairs café, and the al fresco area is about to be redesigned for the summer.

Fishmonger

Chalmers & Gray

67 Notting Hill Gate W11. 0171 221 6177
Mon–Fri 8am–6pm, Sat 8am–5pm. Deliveries Central London.

When local resident John Gray decided to open a wet-fish shop in 1983, predictions of its success were very gloomy. Such establishments had, after all, been going out of business as if there were no more fish in the sea (which our Cornish fishermen think there well may not be soon if certain Europeans have their way). Twelve years on and the gloom-mongers have been proved irrefutably wrong. True, competition has been limited to what's available in Portobello Market and nearby supermarkets, but Chalmers & Gray is not cheap, so its success is clearly a result not of price, but of quality. Manager Mike Lear buys direct from ports, liaising every afternoon with his men-on-the-spot in Aberdeen, Newlyn, Grimsby, North Shields and Brighton, who give him the low-down on what's in the catches. Familiarity with customers' preferences is vital as tired fish is junked, and Mr Lear is not averse to fiddling prices — bunging 10p per 500g/1lb on quick-sellers such as mackerel — in order to keep down the lower-turnover species, such as turbot, which he believes everyone should have a chance to try. I can safely say I have never had a dud buy from this ace fish shop. Tuna is fresh enough to eat raw with ginger, oil and soya sauce, 95 per cent of a bag of mussels open (and they are almost clean, needing only a bit of de-bearding and a couple of rinses), scallops (on and off the shell) shine wetly, salmon is wild and succulent (out of season they sell only 'running loch' farmed fish), sole melts in the mouth, crustacea are a healthy size and cooked to perfection, monkfish is firm and white (left out too long it can turn a most unappetising greyish-yellow). He also sells selected game in season (will pluck and draw customers' own birds), Norfolk squabs, duckling, haggis (from Macsweens of Edinburgh), free-range and quails' eggs, and a variety of condiments made by small firms (including Wiltshire Tracklements) that do not supply the big supermarket chains.

Health Food

Wild Oats

210 Westbourne Grove W11. Tel: 0171 229 1063 Fax: 0171 221 1995
Mon-Fri 9am-7pm (Tue 10am), Sat 9am-6pm, Sun 10am-4pm

One of London's premier health food stores, this is justly well known for quality. Owner Stephen Mosbacher believes that 'you are what you eat' means a great deal more than that you'll get fat if you eat too much or get spots from sweets. His asthma, he says, is largely cured by a macrobiotic diet. Therefore expect a sympathetic hearing if you suffer from any food-related ailments, or just think that the unknowns used in food production might be the cause of aches and pains. Pasta here is likely to be made from any grain other than durum wheat – rye, corn, rice, barley. Rice Dream is a non-dairy drink made from organic brown rice, which Stephen says is not only delicious but absolutely non-mucus forming (soya milk can have this effect). There isn't an E number, additive or preservative in sight. Organic is very much the rule rather than the exception, there's a huge range of beans and grains, and about 25 different breads. Brands to go for include Duskin's (apple juices), Whole Earth (spaghetti sauces and baked beans), De Rit (organic honey and preserves made from 'biodynamically' grown vegetables), Mr Bean's (tasty soups, nothing at all to do with Rowan Atkinson's character, perhaps thankfully), Rocombe Farm (ice-cream). Staff are knowledgeable and friendly.

Market

Portobello Road W11

Mon-Sat 8am-7pm (Thurs 1pm)

Those are the official times – in practice, stallholders can come and go as they please and few are likely to be around by seven o'clock; and while it is a daily market, there are more food vendors on Fridays and Saturdays when the antiques and distressed-items stalls and arcades are fleecing the tourists. The food stalls start about half-way down, by Elgin Crescent. Quality and price vary, as do the tempers of the stallholders – beware of notices saying 'lovely ripe ready-to-eat plums' over a pile of what looks like exactly that: when you get home you may well find you've got a bag of purple bullets taken from the vendor's side of the stall. Others let you choose, feel and smell. The later you go, the more bargains you'll hear being called out. Produce is mixed: everything from seasonal British to non-seasonal imported stuff; this market is not as good as Shepherd's Bush Market for Afro-Caribbean stuff, but there are stalls dedicated to salady things which therefore have a wide choice of leaves. On the corner of Blenheim Crescent there's an excellent coffee stall whose aromas and prices are quite irresistible. On Thursday afternoons (2pm–6pm), at the far end of Portobello Road underneath the West-way flyover, you will find organic produce, home-made jams, pickles and chutneys, and organic meat and poultry from Longwood Farm in Suffolk.

Sausages

Mrs O'Keeffe's

217 Kensington Church Street W8. Tel: 0171 229 6652
Mon–Sat 8.30am–7pm

Simon O'Keeffe is an ex-submariner and the Man Who Leaked the Diaries About the Sinking of the *Belgrano*. Life is lower-profile nowadays, though probably more hectic as Simon's sausages (some made to his grandmother's recipes, hence the 'Mrs') are incredibly popular. You may well have eaten them without realising in pubs around London and the country. They are all additive- and preservative-free, made from dairy-fed pork, Scotch beef or lamb in natural skins (gut), and come in a huge range from the traditional English, such as Oxford and Lincoln, to swarthy European types like Merguez, Toulouse and spicy Spanish. My personal favourite is the Windie, so hotly powerful it truly is a banger!

Paddington

Delicatessen

La Tienda
81 Praed Street W2.Tel: 0171 706 4695
Mon–Fri 9.30am–6pm, Sat 10.30am–6pm

Señor Ruben Ruiz and family have been running this small life-saver for expatriate South Americans for five years. Ninety per cent of the packets and tins come from Columbia, the rest from Venezuela and Spain, and feature staples that the natives presumably cannot do without – Bogota potatoes in brine, mangoes in syrup, 'ajiaco' soup (yellow potatoes and guascas herbs), 100 per cent sugar cane, maize flour, Knorr Camarones (prawns) Soup. A tooth-aching fudge-like dessert made from milk and sugar ('arequipe' in Columbia, generally 'dulce de leche') and a guava cheese (like quince cheese) are worthy of particular note.

Shepherd's Bush

Bakers

Forrest the Baker
75 Uxbridge Road W12. Tel: 0181 743 2675
Mon–Sat 7am–6pm

Local independent selling a good selection of straightforward breads, rolls, buns, croissants, sausage rolls, pasties, filled croissants, rolls and sarnies for lunchers, all baked on the premises, as are the scones, rock cakes, jam and custard tarts, sponge slices and cakes, doughnuts and cream cakes, for those who take tea.

Halim's Bakery & Pâtisserie
182 Uxbridge Road W12. Tel: 0181 740 9477
Mon–Fri 8am–7pm, Sat 8am–6.30pm

This is the western outpost of Haringey's renowned bakery, and its arrival in October '93 greatly cheered Bush commuters' walk home from the tube station. Mr Halim is a Turkish Cypriot and his shops consequently stock anything but pre-sliced white. Corek, a staple of the Greek table, sits next to huge flat adana, a Turkish bread made with milk rather than water, which in turn shares shelf-space with long, thin, crisp French sticks and caraway seed loaves. As well as the ultra-sweet honey-coated cakes which go so well with a really strong cup of Turkish coffee, such as baklava and kadayife, samigo and samali (all variations of honey, almonds, filo pastry or sweet noodles), there are croissants, Danish pastries, cheese pastries, French pâtisserie, whole apple pies, sandwiches, carrot cake, gingerbread men. Orders are readily accepted for wedding, christening (two weeks' notice) and birthday cakes (one day's notice) of any kind.

Butcher/Delicatessen

The Lebanese Butchery
348 Uxbridge Road W12. Tel: 0181 743 9226
Mon–Sat 9am–9pm, Sun 9am–7pm

A delightful year-old newcomer and a real boost to the area. Its owners, Mr and Mrs Bitar, are the daughter and son-in-law of Michael Yazbek, the chef at Fakhreldine, one of London's top Lebanese restaurants, and everything home-made is made by him. Painted an eye-catching bright orange outside, inside it's cool and white, with nose-tickling smells of coriander and mint. The deli counter holds houmous, babaghamouj (aubergine dip, subtly smoky in flavour) and garlic sauce (which, if you love the pure taste of garlic as I do, is wonderful with bread and tomatoes, but is more usually eaten with grilled chicken; it also works well added to tomato pasta sauces); meat and vegetable kebbeh, spinach pies, falafel and shankleesh (a dried cheese ball with thyme and hot spices: chop it up with a diced tomato, oil and parsley and stuff a pitta bread with the mixture). The butchery is at the rear – fat testicles, brains and tongue, succulent marinated dishes of shawarma (diced lamb with spices) and sheesh taouk (spice-marinated chicken), hot Lebanese sausages, all made downstairs in the early hours of each morning by Mr Yazbek. Oils, pickled vegetables and vine leaves, and syrup drinks line the shelves.

Delicatessen

John & Sons

103 Uxbridge Road W12. Tel: 0181 743 9224
Mon–Fri 8.15am–7.30pm, Sat 8.15am–6pm

This is the sort of deli that rewards repeat visits – the more you go, the more you discover. Albert and Armen Banian are Iranian-born Armenians, here because Ayatollah Khomeini's revolution relieved the family of a successful business overnight. They started John & Sons as a general delicatessen with their father in 1980, but were soon being persistently asked by the local Yugoslavian community for products from home. The result is possibly London's only 'Yugoslavian' deli, whose various products are well worth investigating, especially their own 'Jovan' brand (named in memory of Dad who died five years ago, and which they distribute to over 200 outlets nationwide). This line includes pindjur, a delicious, piquant, coarse-cut red pepper relish, scrummy with feta cheese (buy their wonderfully wet Bulgarian feta) on rounds of French bread or ciabatta; ajvar, a milder, smooth pepper relish for adding to sauces; fried peppers in oil; applepears in oil; tins of sarma, a favourite dish with local Serbs consisting of stuffed pickled cabbage leaves which are simmered in water or broth (they also sell the whole pickled cabbage heads if you feel brave enough to make your own). The Banian brothers are the sole importers for Podravka products, a Croatian firm whose reputation for quality transcends recent political differences – items include chicken and beef pâtés, rose-hip jam, and the apparently magical Vegeta, a special dried seasoning of vegetables, spices and salt, without which Yugoslavians cannot cook anything. It can be made into soup or added to paellas, pastas, stews – you name it, Vegeta improves it – they say! (There's an accompanying recipe booklet for beginners.) Salamis and hams come from all over Europe – particularly good is the English boiled ham-on-the-bone; German Blacky smoked ham; and boczek, Polish cured and smoked belly of pork which is then boiled to give it a subtler but still smoky flavour. There's a small range of good, pricey wines and Polish flavoured vodkas. Sally Clarke breads at weekends.

Emporia

Damas Gate
81–85 Uxbridge Road W12. Tel: 0181 743 5116 Fax: 0181 749 0235
Mon–Sun 7am–10pm

Named after the entrance to Damascus, this temple to all things Middle-Eastern opened its doors in 1989, is signposted by piles of giant watermelons on the pavement and is presided over by Syrian Apdolfettah Ekrayem. It seems to have a staff of hundreds (the 'family'), and there is never a moment when boxes aren't being unpacked, shelves stacked, cans priced, freezers rearranged. Row upon orderly row of herbs and spices, beans and pulses, nuts and seeds will keep a browser happy for hours and are an inspiration to expand one's kitchen repertoire. Some things will be familiar, but many are peculiar to Middle-Eastern dishes, such as ready-mixed spices for shawarma or kebbeh. Huge jars of pickled veg march across the floor. Washing-up bowls contain tons of different olives. Then there are bags of unmarked and unidentifiable hard objects which turn out to be slices of a large kind of shallot which gets bunged into stews and the like, or dried limes. The packets of m'lookiyeh look like nothing so much as wacky baccy; it is in fact a glutinous leaf largely used in an eponymous Egyptian soup.

Moon Foods Cash & Carry
183 Railway Approach Shepherd's Bush Market W12. Tel: 0181 749 1412
Mon–Sat 9am–6pm

How to describe a store that stocks West African ogbono and egusi (the inner kernel of the African bush mango and pumpkin seeds respectively), dried fish, Jamaican hard-dough bread, Asian spices, English corned beef, Italian pastas, yam-, bean-, rice- and wheat-flours, West Indian syrups and other curious drinks, many pulses and dals, rices and grains, except as 'international'?

Sri Thai

56 Shepherd's Bush Road W6. Tel: 0171 602 0621
Mon–Sun 9am–8.30pm

Go on Tuesdays for the freshest choice of the very best Thai vegetables in town. They are collected from the airport on Monday evenings, and include those that anyone interested in Thai cuisine will know about – little Thai aubergines, lemon grass, sweet basil, pak choi, galanga, green papaya, galanga – plus some that might be new even to them, such as water mimosa leaves, cha-om, a samphire-like plant of which only the fronds are used so needs careful preparation, patai, a kind of bean, and whole kaffir limes (the leaves are more usually seen), which according to the charming Mr Thepprasits, who set up shop 10 years ago, is very good for hair loss! The shelves are stacked with curry pastes, noodles, chilli sauces, rice, coconut extracts, and everything else you need to recreate the taste of that summer on the beach... There are even fresh green coconuts, prepared in that fetching way which makes them look like little huts, and just waiting to slake your thirst.

Fishmonger

W H Roe & Sons

12 Railway Approach Shepherd's Bush Market W12.
Tel (answering machine only) 01268 583415
Tue–Sat 9am–5pm, Thurs 9am–2pm

Has ever a fishmonger been so aptly named? An incredibly busy, noisy place, always surrounded by shoppers, so be prepared to queue – well, wait in the crowd – and to shout when it's your turn, although the chaps behind the counter always seem to know who's next. The ubiquitous snapper (usually frozen) is here in quantity, grouper, redfish, as well as cod, haddock, trout, mackerel, salmon (heads sold separately at 50-60p/500g (1lb) for fish stock – or cats). Whiting, cod, mackerel, salmon and trout are always fresh, collected from Billingsgate by Darren on his way into London; other things may well be frozen, so ask.

Greengrocer

Strawberry Hill Fruiterers

163 Railway Approach Shepherd's Bush Market. Tel: 0181 749 9351
Mon–Sat 8am–6.30pm

This is an excellent fruit and veg shop, in which it is possible to get your British staples to go with the Sunday roast – but its real attraction is the many different kinds of yam (yellow, soft, hard, coco, sweet), sweet potatoes, plantains, tinda, drum stick, Ghanaian garden eggs (a little yellow aubergine-type veg), kologassi (otherwise known as taro and essential for 'Pacific Rim' cuisine), tinda, dhudi, golden apples (aka June plums), sugar plums, loose curry leaves, fresh herbs, etc. The produce comes from all over the world – the Indian subcontinent, West Indies, Africa, and is enough to make you vow never to roast a potato or boil a cabbage again.

Market

Railway Approaches

Uxbridge/Goldhawk Roads W12
Mon–Sat 8am–5pm (Thurs 1pm)

Largely given over to cheap clothes and household goods, Shepherd's Bush Market still has a few fruit and veg stalls, particularly one at the Uxbridge Road end – good seasonal British veg, with surprises like fresh tamarinds and quinces. About half-way down, hard by Strawberry Hill Fruiterers, is Steve Hill's Afro-Caribbean stall (units 20 and 21), where you'll find yams, avocados, plantains, and juicy yellow limes for about 60p for ten, making them second only to plucking them from the tree in cheapness. Farther down still, stalls 44 and 45 have a huge choice of European and Afro-Caribbean produce. On the west side of the railway line, there are tiny stalls selling only yams and plantains, or 'garden eggs' and dried fish, but this area is being redeveloped at the time of writing, so they may all disappear. Moon Foods and W H Roe & Sons are also within the market (see entries).

Southall

I have listed only a few of the many shops to be found in this Asian stronghold. Exploring is fun and shopkeepers are invariably helpful. Sunday is the busiest day: although some of the best restaurants are closed, it's not possible to go hungry – samosas and bhajis abound. Avoid the run-up to Diwali (October) – it's the equivalent to Oxford Street before Christmas.

Emporia

Dokal & Sons Cash & Carry
133 The Broadway. Tel: 0181 574 1647
Mon–Sun 9am–8pm

Sira Cash & Carry
128 The Broadway SW13. Tel: 0181 574 2280
Mon–Sun 8am–9pm

Toto Grocers
44 The Broadway SW13. Tel: 0181 574 7669
Mon–Sun 9am–8pm

The industrial-sized tins of ghee or sacks of rice and flour should not deter the Dinky (double-income-no-kids) couple or single person from entering this shop: everything is also sold in smaller quantities. If you're a pickle/chutney fan, you'd probably find a different one for every week of the year. Herbs and spices abound, flour comes from potatoes, rice, lentils, beans, breads from all over India and Arabia. Dokal stocks the Bikaji range of 'snack foods', which to the uninitiated may all look like 'Bombay Mix' but are actually very varied and come with great names and descriptions – chhote-chhote 'tiny titillating titbits set your tongue tripping', khaz-cheez 'special delight at every bite', gup-shup 'dainty relishes to flatter the palate', and so on; Sira has fresh vegetables as well; Toto is the smallest but has long queues (they're all busy).

Greengrocers

Best Fruit Fare
77 The Broadway. Tel: 0181 574 6596
Mon–Sun 7am–8pm

Fruits of Paradise
79 The Broadway. Tel: 0181 574 3032
Mon–Sun 8am–8pm

Rana Brothers
145 The Broadway. Tel: 0181 574 4481
Mon–Sun 9am–9pm

Sunnyway
143 The Broadway. Tel: 0181 571 9459
Mon–Sun 7am–8.30pm

Four shops which between them stock every conceivable Asian fruit and vegetable. Some are labelled (although this won't necessarily help you), some aren't, presumably on the same grounds that English greengrocers don't put up signs saying simply 'apples' or 'pears'. Staff are keen to help when asked, and will suggest cooking methods. (With all due respect to the menfolk who predominate in these shops, such advice is usually more reliable coming from a member of the distaff, as it were, Asian males are not that different from the majority of their European counterparts when it comes to culinary savvy.) Here are huge bunches of methi (fenugreek) and dhiyani (coriander), baby aubergines (rayia), long dhudi and round dhudi, tindori and tinda, karela and kantola, pomegranates, nasi pears, bullet and bird's eye chillies, fresh dates, and more.

Indian Sweets

A Sweet
106 The Broadway SW13. Tel: 0181 574 8814
Mon closed, Tues–Sat 9am–7pm, Sun, and Bank Holidays 10am–6pm

This is the Harrods of the Indian sweet world. A 26-year-old family concern, which is also an excellent vegetarian café, it is run by Mr Khanna, his brothers and his son Bobby (and around Diwali by every other member of the family who can be roped in to cope with the queues). Everything is made in the large kitchens at the back, from natural ingredients. Milk, butter ghee and sugar form the basic barfi, a dry fudge-like sweet, which can also be flavoured with pistachios or almonds. Jalebi, the extremely popular orange rings you'll see being deep-fried on the pavements, is here made with honey and without the food colouring that is known to bring on sore throats. Faluda is a cooling summer rose-flavoured milk-shake with vermicelli and kufti, topped with crushed ice (though often that is dispensed with in England!). During Diwali the café is closed completely as demand for sweets rockets — they have a particular significance as offerings during the Festival of Light. If you're unsure about Indian sweets, this is the place to start (but go early, as they make only as much as is expected to shift in a day, so that by the afternoon choice is limited).

South West

North of the River

The neighbourhood names here reek of wealth and standing – Knightsbridge, Belgravia, Chelsea – so a fair showing of the best food shops is only to be expected: Harrods and Harvey Nichols, Bagatelle for real French breads and pâtisserie; Curnick's for superlative meat; Luigi's for anything Italian, The House of Albert Roux for Gallic indulgences; Rococo in King's Road for exquisite chocolates. Don't look for ethnic stores – there aren't any.

Belgravia

Butcher/Fishmonger

Charles

46 Elizabeth Street SW1. Tel: 0171 730 3321
Mon-Fri 8am-5.30pm, Sat 8.am-1.pm Deliveries

All the beef here is naturally-reared Scotch, lambs are Welsh and English, chickens free-range. Organic meat can be supplied to order, as can free-range pork, foie gras, and perle noire truffles. There's game in season, and hares will be properly jugged. On the fish side, deliveries come every afternoon, even Mondays, direct from Suffolk, so although the selection is not enormous it is very fresh. Iranian caviar also stocked.

Cheesemonger

Jeroboams

51 Elizabeth Street SW1. Tel: 0171 823 5623
Mon-Fri 9am-6pm, Sat 9am-2pm

This is the branch at which all Jeroboams' bloomy-rind and washed-rind cheeses are brought to mature perfection by Karine, buyer and affineur. She took me below to show me a newly arrived St Andrew's, for example, and one that she had been nurturing in the wonderfully pungent, temperature- and humidity-controlled 'finishing' room – and the difference is startling. To the uninitiated the 'ready' cheese might look almost unappetising, wizened and shrunken like an old shoe, but what aroma! The unripe specimen was twice the size, lacked any discernible nose, and looked just like supermarket cheese. Upstairs all is as you'd expect in a Jeroboams – well-arranged cheeses of all textures, shapes and sizes. They are expanding their range of British cheeses and new on the list was a delicious, tangy but not sharp goats' from the New Forest. Apply here to join the monthly Cheese Club. See also entries in Holland Park and South Kensington.

Delicatessen/Ready-Meals

The House of Albert Roux
229 Ebury Street SW1. Tel: 0171 730 3037
Mon-Fri 7am-8.30pm, Sat-Sun 8.30am-3pm

Cher Albert has been dispensing advice to the capital's amateur cooks through his column in ES for several years. However, there are still many aspirants out there who would rather leave the success of their dinner party to him than risk their reputations as hosts. This is the place for them. Whether they give credit where it's due or risk nose-lengthening prevarication will not affect the sublime taste of the salmis of pheasant, stuffed quails, chicken in foie gras sauce, goats' cheese provençal in filo pastry, mini puff-pastry game pies, tartelettes niçoises, etc. Everything is made in the Wandsworth Road kitchens, as are the Viennoiserie and breads (from imported French flour and yeast). What's not made in London comes from 'artisan' producers in France, such as charcuterie from small producers in the Pyrenees, farmhouse apple juices and cheeses, flavoured vinegars (Champagne and truffles is one of ten) and oils. There are seasonal wild mushrooms, a 'spit shop' (a rotisserie, in other words) at the back, poulets de Bresse, risotto rice, and around Christmas lots of gift items and hampers. The whole caboodle is smoothly managed by Pierre-Michel Manni, an ex-butler who 'has worked in some demanding celebrity households' and, if requested, will butle at customers' parties.

Brompton Cross

Baker

Baker and Spice
46 Walton Street SW3. Tel: 0171 589 4734
Mon-Sat 7am-7pm, Sun 8.30am-2pm

The redoubtable Gail Stephenson (she who as Gailforce hurtles bread around London's better outlets each morning) has taken over Justin de Blanc's premises with partner, French masterbaker

Philippe Dade, transformed it into an exceptionally pretty shop and, since September last year, produced a wonderful range of home-baked goods from Viennoiserie to Chelsea buns (good and spicy). There are English and Continental loaves, her pride and joy being the sour-dough; brownies, treacle tart, Venetian rolls (a sort of enclosed pizza); giant meringues, croque monsieurs, fishcakes in brioche crumbs, biscuits; fresh pasta dishes, quiches and more. They'll do canapés for cocktail parties, lunch snacks, pain surprise (take one large loaf, slice the top off, carefully cut the bread from inside, slice it and make sandwiches, replace in empty loaf and put lid on – et voilà!). Gail also keeps a small selection of 'artisan' farmhouse cheeses, mostly unpasteurised.

Delicatessens

La Picena
5 Walton Street SW3. Tel: 0171 584 6573
Mon- Fri 9am-7.30pm, Sat 9am-5.30pm

Lina di Angelis runs a hugely popular, old-fashioned neighbourhood grocery (the only other one for years was Harrods, though now there is also Harvey Nichols!) which, while the emphasis is undoubtedly on Italian fare, also has Twining's tea and lots of other staples of the English larder. There's a good home-made gastronomia counter, home-made ravioli and gnocchi, a small selection of good fresh veg (including vine tomatoes and salad leaves in a chill cabinet), and shelf upon shelf of eye-catching cans, tins and packets of top brand-name Italian groceries. The prioisciutto comes highly recommended by a gourmet friend.

Les Spécialités St Quentin
256 Brompton Road SW3. Tel: 0171 225 1664
Tue-Sat 9am-7pm, Sun 9am-4pm

Sumptuous-looking fruit tarts and a goodly selection of Viennoiserie are on obvious not-to-be-missed display here. A notice on the wall announces the presence of fresh foie gras. At the back there's a discreet-to-the-point-of-invisibility cheese room (chill and dark), an extensive selection of wines and some olive oils. Dotted around are goods like Minoix du Périgord (roasted nut kernels coated in dark chocolate). Everything is made in the downstairs kitchens, but that 'everything' seems rather limited these days. Still, I am reliably informed that the foie gras is excellent. The shop is particularly busy on Sunday mornings following the end of church services at the nearby Brompton Oratory.

B's

167 Draycott Avenue SW3. Tel: 0171 581 0676 Fax: 0171 591 0996
Answerphone: 0171 591 0985
Mon-Fri 7am-7pm, Sat 7am-4pm

The apostrophe that appears in the name should really be a button mushroom, this three-year-old oddity being owned by one Mr Button. It's an oddity because from the outside it looks like an upmarket greengrocer's, with its wooden pottles piled high with herbs, vine tomatoes and other shiny veg. Inside there's organic pastas and sauces; Frank Cooper's Oxford marmalade, and French and Italian jams; Tradition Gasconne haute-cuisine foie gras d'oie, cassoulet au porc, salmis de pintade, etc; fresh herbs and salads; homemade ricotta cheesecake; daily-made sandwiches (arranged on platters for local businesses); and whole top shelves full of Andrex loo paper! As I said, an oddity, but great fun.

Emporium

Jerry's Homestore

163-167 Fulham Road SW3. Tel: 0171 581 0909 Fax: 0171 584 3749
Mon-Fri 10am-6pm, Sat 10am-6.30pm, Sun 12pm-5.30pm

This is really an American version of the Conran shop, with an amazing array of glassware, chinaware, kitchen utensils, cutlery, etc. It's included here because it also has a small but selective range of US brand names – Dean & Deluca beans, Stubb's Legendary Chilli Fixin's, Silver Palate Good Old Apricot Mustard Sauce and other condiments, Uncle Dave's Pure Vermont Honey and pasta sauces, Buddy

Boy's Boss BBQ sauce, Ass Kicking Salsa, Habañero from Hell Bloody Mary mix, organic maple syrup. All excellent, fun and not so cheap... but what the heck!

Fishmonger

Bibendum Crustacea
The Michelin Building 81 Fulham Road SW3. Tel: 0171 589 0864
Mon-Fri 10am-8pm, Sat 9am-8pm, Sun 11am-5pm

Simon Thomas and James Baird-Murray run the oyster, caviar and crustacea counter in the forecourt of the stunning Michelin Building. If you can't afford the Restaurant and haven't got time for the Oyster Bar (which is always crowded around lunchtimes) you can be sure of the quality of anything you buy to eat at home, since it all comes down from above. This is also where food for the Oyster Bar is prepared. Caviar is Iranian and is no pricier than usual (£20 for 50g of Sevruga, larger quantities must be ordered), oysters from Ireland, Scotland and France, lobsters from Scotland and Dorset. Wet fish was introduced at the end of last year. The fish looks wonderfully fresh, is attractively displayed and decorated with plump lemons. (The flower stall next to it is worth drooling over too.)

La Marée
76 Sloane Avenue SW3. Tel: 0171 589 8067
Mon-Sat 9am-6pm

Another wetfish-and-shellfish joint with a quality-guarantee by virtue of its attachment to a respected restaurant (see Bibendum Crustacea, above). This one's warrant comes from La Poissonnerie de l'Avenue next door. Staffed by an Englishman, a Spaniard and a Portuguese, and stuffed with the produce of French, Irish, Belgian, Canadian, English and Scottish waters. Rumour had it that the fishcakes came from La Poissonnerie's kitchens - they don't, but are home-made and very good; the fish soup and lobster bisque do, however. They will poach large fish for customers if ordered through the shop.

Chelsea

Butcher

Curnick

170 Fulham Road SW3. Tel: 0171 370 1191
Mon-Fri 8am-5.30pm, Sat 8am-4pm

If you want to know what the steer fed on before you feed on it, this is the place to come – they can actually give you a leaflet from Old Springfield Farm (whose farmer is brother to the butcher) which lists the ingredients of the cattle's supplementary feed. And there's not a suspect item in there. The beasts are Angus and Hereford, and graze on organic pastures green in Sussex. Everything else is free-range – chickens and eggs, lamb and pork. Continental and American cuts present no problem, sausages are home-made in natural skins, there's black pudding and offal, seasonal game, and they'll jug a hare for you.

Novelty Cakes

Jane Asher Cakes

24 Cale Street SW3. Tel: 0171 584 6177 Fax: 0171 584 6179
Mon-Sat 9.30am-5.30pm

When is a cake not a cake? When it's a roast chicken, four-and-twenty blackbirds baked in a pie, man-buried-in sand, Gucci handbag, a caviar tin (lid off)... these are just some of the thousands of witty designs from probably the country's most famous cake-maker. She is assisted by two baker/decorators, the odd art student, and manageress Ruth Clark, who shows customers photographs of cakes-we-made-earlier, or talks through their own designs. The shop is really just an order point, though there are a few fruit-cakes which can be personalised while-u-wait (in the adjoining tearoom) and basic essentials for the home-decorator on sale. Cakes are chocolate, vanilla or lemon sponges, or fruit-cake (special dietary needs are accommodated). A minimum of one week's notice is required for orders.

Chocolates

Rococo

321 King's Road SW3. Tel: 0171 352 5857 Fax: 0171 352 7360
Mon-Sat 10am-6.30pm, Sun 11am-4pm Mail order

Chantal Coady is serious about chocolate. She talks about it with the same inspirational enthusiasm that oenophiles do about wine, even borrowing some of the less fanciful descriptions (thankfully none of her chocolates gives off, in Jilly Goulden's immortal phrase, 'the smell of wet gumboots drying in front of the Aga'), and explains that the criterion for a good chocolate bar is not simply a matter of the percentage of cocoa solids ('that would be like choosing wine on the basis of its proof percentage'). She does three Grand Cru bars (Valrhona) of which No. 1, made from the rare Criollo cocoa bean, is pure heaven and, as if to prove her point, has the lowest percentage of cocoa solids; Artisan Bars made exclusively for her in a Belgian farmhouse kitchen and naturally flavoured, unusually and magically, with such things as cardamom, Earl Grey Tea, juniper, pink peppercorn and others (Nigel Slater has memorably described these as 'Bounty, Caramac, Toblerone and peppermint Aero for grown-ups'); a range of Swiss chocolates (from Ackermans – see entry); traditional English hand-dipped creams; and her own sublime Criollo-bean truffles. But the shop also lives up to the frivolity of its name – there are snowballs and holly berries for Christmas, hearts galore for Valentine's Day, white asparagus spears, almond 'olives', gawdy packaging, jewellery and animals. I have a cousin who, used to decorate his dining table with long swirls of dark blue and silver sugar-coated almonds in true 'rococo' style. A great place.

Delicatessen/Rosticceria

Luigi's Delicatessen

349 Fulham Road SW10. Tel: 0171 352 7739 Fax: 0171 351 9551
Mon-Fri 9am-9.30pm, Sat 9am-7pm

Luigi's 2

359-361 Fulham Road SW10. Tel: 0171 351 7825 Fax: 0171 351 9551
Mon-Fri 8am-8pm, Sat 9am-6pm

L uigi has become something of a Chelsea institution, serving the great and the good of the borough (and everybody else, of course) with Mediterranean friendliness for the past 21 years. Everything on the gastronomia counter is made on the premises - pesto and other sauces, fresh pasta, grilled vegetables, roast garlic (not a staple of many Italian delis), and lots more - and comes highly praised by everyone I know who lives around here. A home-made tiramisu looked good enough to cheer up Eeyore. There's an excellent selection of cheeses, including 14 different Pecorini, loads of pasta, gallons of Santal juices (the Italians' favourite drink after wine and espresso, apparently), over 50 different oils and some 400 wines. There isn't a millimetre of empty shelf-space. The ceiling is thickly hung with panettone, which are sold all year round here, but the week before Christmas Luigi gets fresh panettone direct from a small bakery in Italy. It arrives around December 18 and, if you've only ever tried the long-life version, is a revelation. In 1990 Luigi took over what had been Wainwright & Daughter of silly-hats fame a few doors down the road. After a time as a one-stop shop, it is now a brilliant rosticceria. Again everything is made on site, and the choice is wide: four or five pizzas, many pasta, chicken and veal dishes, stews and casseroles, tortillas, arancini, spinach soufflé, grilled ciabatta and veg, papaya/mango/grape/melon fruit salad... I could go on, but duty calls and I must return to the shop to try a couple more dishes.

Emporium

Partridge's

132-134 Sloane Street SW1. Tel: 0171 730 0651
Mon-Sun 8am-10pm

A sound, old-fashioned store, much loved by regulars, who tend towards the female and elderly. I have to say there is nothing particularly exciting about it, but perhaps that is its point - it is reliable on all counts, from fresh fruit and veg to dry goods. It had the Prince of Wales's new cheeses the day they were launched last November, which is no more than should be expected in this area. It belongs to The Guild of Fine Food retailers.

Fishmongers

The Chelsea Fishery

10 Cale Street SW3. Tel: 0171 589 9432
Tue-Sat 8.30am-4pm approx (Thu till 3pm)

The husky-voiced proprietor of this old-fashioned shop is known affectionately by other 'Chelsea Green' retailers as 'Bill the Fish', for reasons that none of them could quite explain, but he is clearly 'a bit of a character'. He doesn't seem to go in for display much, and was too behind with his numerous telephoned orders to talk, but what better recommendation could you have than to meet cookery writer Arabella Boxer in the queue: 'There's never a great deal of choice, but what there is, is the best.'

La Poissonnerie

405 King's Road SW10. Tel: 0171 349 9317
Mon-Sat 9am-6pm

A newcomer to World's End (opened in November last year), which has nothing to do with the restaurant of the same name in Sloane Avenue, but everything to do with Goldbourne Fish (see entry) in North Kensington: they are owned by the same company. Like George's gaff, some things are obviously frozen, others not. There was a good display of John Dory, lobster tails, sea bass, dourade, bourgeois, Shetland salmon, whelks and cockles, monkfish, halibut, turbot and more. Time will tell.

Greengrocers

The Chelsea Fruiterer

206 Fulham Road SW10. Tel: 0171 352 5164
Mon-Sat 7am-7pm, Sun 7am-5pm

It makes a welcome change to find a greengrocer who puts all his produce out of reach of the smut and grit of passing traffic. Stanley Polydorou crams everything inside his small premises so that you have to walk sideways, point and stretch to reach things. But that doesn't deter his customers who come for the choice and quality – everything from apples and pears, potatoes and cabbage to pok choi, baby artichokes and fresh wild mushrooms.

Fry's of Chelsea

14 Cale Street SW3. Tel: 0171 589 0342
Mon-Fri 5.30am-5pm, Sat 5.30am-1pm. Local deliveries.

Paul Fry gets up at midnight to get the best out of Covent Garden market for his customers, many of whom have remained loyal to his onions for some 14 years. He and wife Maureen once won a 'Greengrocer of the Year Award' and would undoubtedly still be in the running for first place were such a competition held again. Renowned for their exotic fruit, they have 'summer' fruits all year round, luscious fresh dates (the soft brown kind as opposed to the hard yellow ones) and something called a 'kiwi grape' from Canada – a small green hairless object that looks like an olive and bursts in the mouth like... well, a small kiwi. Made-up baskets of exotica start at around £15. They have a wide choice of salad leaves, at least 10 varieties of potatoes, herbs packed by them, and will order wild mushrooms (and anything else customers ask for) for the following day. There are also fresh English loaves, yoghurts, apple juices, olive oils and four-year-old balsamic vinegar, which the Frys put on their kippers of a Sunday – delicious, says Maureen. The shops in Cake Street have a village feel to them, and to stop at Fry's of Chelsea, close to the fish shop, cake shop and deli, is really a great time-dawdling pleasure.

The Italian Fruit Company

423 King's Road SW3. Tel: 0171 354 5841
Mon-Sat 8.30am-6pm

Franco Loi's six-year-old shop is spacious and tidy, the plump fruit and veg beckoning you in. There are baby pineapples and prickly pears, strawberries and papayas, potted and loose fresh herbs, fat vine tomatoes, baby white onions, strings of garlic, and everything else. Fresh porcini in season, and truffles to order.

Ready-Made Meals/Catering

Finns

4 Elystan Street SW3. Tel: 0171 225 0733/4
Mon-Fri 8am-7pm, Sat 8am-2pm

It is hard to believe that only two cooks produce the quantity of prepared dishes that Finns turns over every day – though the broth might definitely be spoiled if any more crammed into the tiny rear kitchen. This is unpretentious, top-notch fare for stressed hosts – manageress Beth Stuart-Findlay says they specialise in quantities for two to 20, but obviously can cater for more. The range is extensive – soups, from mixed veg to gazpacho or borscht; dozens of salads; chicken in 20 different guises, hot or cold; pheasant; venison; pork; beef (pied, stewed, en croute); poussin in honey and soy sauce; a dozen or so fish dishes and lashings of puddings. There are special menus throughout the year (Christmas, Summer Picnics, Thanksgiving, etc) and they are happy to make customers' own favourite dishes. Anything that isn't made on the premises, such as jams and chutneys, or lime and lemon cordial, probably comes from owner Julia Bannister's family's estate in Yorkshire.

The Pie Man Food Company

16 Cale Street SW3. Tel: 0171 225 0587
Mon-Fri 9am-6.30pm, Sat 9am-5pm

This tiny shop is the original Pie Man outlet. Its freezer is full of the dishes that the company has built its reputation on – pies, curries, casseroles, vegetables – all of which can also be ordered in larger quantities for dinners or lunches. Ready-to-eat foods centre around sandwiches, filled brioches and the like, and more substantial hot dishes and soups. Be prepared to queue. Everything is made in the catering kitchens in Battersea (0171 627 5232) which offer a big choice of menus to suit directors' lunches, dances, cocker-p's, dinners, weddings, etc. Also at 20 Stratford Road, W8 (see entry) and 75 High Street, SW19 (tel: 0181 944 1200).

Tea & Coffee

Whittard

184 Kings Road SW3. Tel: 0171 351 3381
Mail order and general enquiries: 0171 924 1888
Mon-Sat 10am-6pm, Sun 10pm-5pm

This 110-year-old tea and coffee merchant goes from strength to strength, with some 17 shops in London, the newest of which was opened at 65 Regent Street last year. Whittard's success rests on its bright, youthful and cheerful image, quite at odds with that which is usually attached to tea and coffee sellers. There are some 60 different types of tea on offer, from fruit varieties to the prized single-estates of Sri Lanka and India. A new source is Vietnam. There are 20 different coffees (any beans not sold after four weeks are binned or given to charity), numerous tea and coffee related gadgets, and some great china, cheap and colourful plates, cups and saucers from Italy and Portugal which are sometimes in stock and sometimes not. Not all branches carry the full range, so call General Enquiries.

Earl's Court

Emporium

Manila Supermarket

11 Hogarth Place SW5. Tel: 0171 373 8305
Mon-Sun 9am-9pm

One of the first places to be besieged by returning travellers hungry for the cheap, nourishing and delicious food they'd lapped up over there — although back home, of course, it is not so cheap. Still, with ingredients bought here it is possible to dream you are still in that beach restaurant under the palm trees... There's lots of fresh veg, pak choi, various chillies, lemon grass, curry leaves, kaffir lime leaves, dasheen leaves, dhudi, karela, chow-chow, fresh tamarind, even dried chrysanthemum leaves, etc, salted and frozen fish.

Knightsbridge

Emporia

Harrods

Knightsbridge SW1. Tel: 0171 730 1234 Fax: 0171 581 0470
Mon-Tue, Sat 10am-6pm, Wed-Fri 10am-7pm. London-wide deliveries.

Harrods, the most famous store in the world, whose telegraphic address is 'Everything London SW1', through whose doors pass some 35,000 people every day, and which is the capital's third most popular tourist attraction, is for many of the area's residents simply the local grocery shop. And in the basement 'Pantry' (what most people would call a supermarket) you can indeed get your baked beans and cornflakes, and even have your groceries gathered for you, but the point of shopping here, given the crowds and the premium prices, has to be the famous Food Halls. Not only are they magnificent rooms in their own right, with their Doulton-made wall and ceiling tiles, but they hold an astonishing amount of edibles, all stunningly displayed. It is almost impossible not to talk statistics – on offer are some 350 cheeses, 200 tea varieties, 50 different salamis, 180 different breads, 300 kinds of choc-olates, 50 species of wet fish, 25 varieties of smoked, and so on - and it is all too easy to be overwhelmed. But a little fortitude is well rewarded. The cheese counter has to be one of the best: 95 per cent are unpas-teurised, there's an excellent showing of British cheeses, from the well-known (Kirkham's Lancashire, Keens' and Montgomery's Cheddar, Har-bourne Blue goats') to those not often found outside specialist shops: organic Loch Arthur 'Cheddar' and Lanark Blue from Scotland, Anne Wigmore's Waterloo and Wellington, made with milk from the Duke of Wellington's Guernsey cows. Among the huge range of Continental cheeses is Boule de Truffes, a scrummy lemony goats' with an earthy flavour of truffles. This Hall also houses the pies/cooked and cured meats counter, and the excellent traiteur department, which includes exquisitely arranged boxes of sushi. Next door, the fruit and veg boasts something from almost every country in the world – pitihayas from Vietnam, purple potatoes from France, custard apples from Thailand,

Snow Pink apples from New Zealand (a new sweet variety of which Harrods took the whole harvest in 1995), white raspberries, strawberries all year round, huge cherries at £3 each (one female customer bought ten every morning while they were in stock), wild and water asparagus, yellow watermelons, as well as turnips, swedes and parsnips. The fish displays are so artfully created, featuring spun-sugar sculptures of leaping salmon or whatever, that getting entangled with a tourist throng is almost inevitable. In addition to all the staples there are red-spotted grouper (the spots remain after cooking), West African sea bream, the little-seen black bream, parrot-fish, carp rouge from the Middle East. In season, salmon is wild exclusively from the illustrious River Tay, but year-round demand is such that there is no question of not stocking farmed fish. At £13.50/lb, you'd think fillet steak might be a slow mover - in fact, it's the Meat Hall's bestseller. All the beef is naturally reared and fed in Scotland, lamb comes from the Northumbrian hills, pork is all free-range. In season, there's always a wonderful hanging display of game birds, so prettily feathered that the sentimental could easily be dissuaded from ever again enjoying the delights of partridge, quail, woodcock, teal and widgeon. Bacon comes in two county cures, traditional Wiltshire and Suffolk sweetcure, both extremely good. Then there are the chocolate, pâtisserie, coffee and tea departments, details of which I have no room to explore, although of course they are well worth exploration. Food shopping at Harrods is what you make of it – a nightmare or a delight: to ensure the latter, go with a list or at least some idea of what you want, in off-peak hours and with a wallet that won't be bruised by the experience.

Harvey Nichols

Knightsbridge SW1. Tel: 0171 235 5000
Mon-Fri 10am-8pm, Sat 10am-6pm, Sun 12pm-5pm. London deliveries.

The 'other' Knightsbridge store has sensibly not tried to compete with its older more established neighbour (although it sells many of the same things). Its Sunday opening attests to greater concessions to modern times, as does its whole appearance, from the smart metal shelving to the HN own-brand packaging, trendy and award-winning (even if you can't make sense of it). This is a supermarket, if you can afford it (no problem spending £50 on half a dozen items), stocking everything from fresh fruit and veg to dried Tuscan soup mixes. There's no doubt that everything is of a very high quality: the fish counter features cuckoo wrasse, lumpsucker, black-banded bream and mojama (air-dried tuna – shave over scrambled eggs) among the more usual flat fish from Cornwall and 'round' fish from Scotland. British farm-producers are well represented in the meat department, Eldon Wild Blue pork and Goodman's geese alongside poulet de Bresse (over £4/lb) and capons at £160 each (they do sell). Britain also makes a good showing in the cheeses, where the emphasis is on the unpasteurised; charcuterie features the more obvious salamis as well as the well-aged Serrano and Bayonne hams; that much-prized Spanish delicacy, ham from acorn-fed pigs; and wild venison from Rannoch Smokery in Tayside. Undoubtedly excellent as all this is, for me the point of this heavily designed one-stop shop is the deli/dry-goods department – shelf upon metal shelf of bottles, jars, tins and packets of deliciousness, including a small section of Japanese and Thai ingredients (five-and-a-half-pound bags of sushi rice don't hang around). Exclusive to HN are Knorr porcini stock cubes (for risotto); not necessarily exclusive, but wonderful, are chestnut/ basil/artichoke pasta, lemon pasta, Swedish potato chips, and a sublime pesto with cashews, peanuts and walnuts in addition to the pine kernels. If you are really interested in food, as opposed simply to scoffing it, the Food Market runs weekly promotional tastings and workshops in the evenings which are well worth attending (further details on 0171 581 7562).

Parson's Green

Delicatessen

Salumeria Estense

837 Fulham Road SW6 Tel: 0171 731 7643

Mon-Fri 10am-7.30pm, Sat 10am-5pm

The presence of the Brie de Meaux, Vacherin Mont d'Or and Montgomery's Cheddar among the Pecorini, Fontina, Parmigiano reggiano and Taleggio lets you know at once that Signor Gorinis no food-chauvinist, but is definitely a food-élitist. Further investigation of his seven-year-old shop reveals stacks of other delights: artisan-produced pasta; loose Puy lentils, carnaroli rice, Camargue red rice, and pulses; estate-bottled oils, including what he calls 'the gentleman of oils', exclusive to his establishment, Castellare di Castellino; and moistly dense white and dark panforte, the latter properly made with cinnamon as opposed to the travesty of chocolate. Signora Gorini makes fresh pasta daily (try the scrummy smoked salmon ravioli) and a fine selection of dishes for the gastronomia counter. Fresh white truffles in season (Oct-Nov approximately).

Emporia

A A King

30-34 New King's Road SW6. Tel: 0171 736 4004

Mon-Fri 7am-5.30pm, Sat 7am-4pm

Elizabeth King

address as above Tel: 0171 736 2826

Mon-Fri 7am-7pm, Sat 7am-6pm

It's all a bit confusing: A A King has been here for 'yonks', as the locals might say, and the two shops are still known collectively as that. However, since Mr King Senior's retirement the empire has been divided between two sons, Colin and Michael, the former keeping the name over the butcher/fishmonger, the latter restyling the deli/greengrocer 'Elizabeth King'. Happily, there is no such confusion over the quality of their produce, both sons continuing the tradition of excellence. All meat is free-range, sausages are home-made; hams, beef and salmon home-cooked. The fish selection is perhaps smaller than before, but fresh and bright. Next door is a good choice of fruit and veg, including yellow courgettes, wild mushrooms, wild rocket and fresh herbs; tins of coconut milk (among other essentials for currently trendy cuisines) and graisse d'oie (half the price of French shops); and fresh orange juice every morning. The deli bakes its own bread, some 20 different English and Continental loaves, every morning and makes an array of ready-meals (pastas, pizzas, baked potatoes, salads) and sandwiches. Cheeses come from all over Europe, with British making a good showing. Sheila presides over the deli with motherly Northern good-humour, as much 'part of the furniture' (her phrase) as the old-fashioned black delivery-boy's bicycle on the pavement outside.

Fishmonger

The Catch

760 Fulham Road SW6. Tel: 0171 736 1523

Tue-Fri 8.30am-5.30pm, Sat 8.30am-4pm

Dave and Luke took over The Catch about 18 months ago. They buy mostly through Billingsgate but aim to stock only what's freshest, rather than what's expected. When I stopped by, choice was limited to Dover sole, salmon, monkfish, sea bass, a few others from the top-bracket, and lobsters and crabs which they cook themselves, but I was assured that later in the week they have more.

Greengrocer

F C Jones

764 Fulham Road SW6. Tel: 0171 736 1643

Mon 9am-1pm, Tue-Fri 9am-5.30pm, Sat 8am-4pm

A greengrocer in the same family for 60 odd years is quite a rarity these days, particularly one that has resisted all temptation to 'add value' for the customer, such as a little deli or small grocery section. About the only concession to modern demands is a greater variety and year-round availability of salad leaves. Otherwise, it's a good, sensible, seasonal costermonger, much-loved by its regular customers, some of whom are as old as the century.

Pimlico

Butcher

Harts (Victoria) Ltd

39 Tachbrook Street SW1. Tel: 0171 821 6341
Mon-Sat 8am-5.30pm

An elderly lady on a recent television programme about food rationing during and after the war asked, not unreasonably: 'Whatever happened to all those fillets? I mean, all the animals had fillets, didn't they?' The original owners of this old-fashioned butcher's might have been able to help her out: Harts, a large concern (which explains the geographical exactitude of the name although there is no other branch today), was done for black-marketeering and forced to sell off its various shops, most of which changed names. The current owner, Douglas Quin, has worked here for 15 years and owned it for four. He tries to appeal to the varied elements of his catchment area, to which end he carries organic beef, lamb and pork, as well as lots of offal and cheaper cuts, such as shin of beef. His lamb and pork sausages are made from organic meat, pies are bought in. Finally, he comes highly recommended by chef and broadcaster Jennifer Patterson, who knows her offal from her onions.

Cheesemonger

Rippon Cheese Stores

26 Upper Tachbrook Street SW1. Tel: 0171 931 0628 Fax: 0171 828 2368
Mon-Fri 9am-6.30pm, Sat 9am-5pm

This charming old-fashioned-looking store was opened by Philip Rippon in September 1990, since when it has built up a loyal customer base on word-of-mouth recommendations (my dental hygienist, who lives in Clapham, will get her cheese nowhere else). There are usually some 500 cheeses in stock, from all over Europe, including some little-seen ones from Sweden. Britain is well represented across the range. Great truckles of Cheddar (normally six or seven different ones) stand about the shop just like elephants' feet, smaller Stiltons (Colston Basset and Cropwell Bishop among them) march along the shelves. They recently made over some cellar space to maturing rooms (James Aldridge, Britain's premier cheesemaker and affineur, matured them before). Staff are keen and helpful.

Delicatessen

Gastronomia Italia

8 Upper Tachbrook Street SW1. Tel: 0171 834 2767
Mon-Fri 9am-6pm Sat 9am-5pm

B ritish deli-owners are, more often than not, ex-something else: actors, management consultants, estate agents, but Italian ones are seemingly born to the job. Italo-Scottish Mario d'Annunzio is an ex-skiing instructor but after 12 years on the shop-floor you'd never guess he wasn't born on it. He has a good range of estate-bottled olive oils from different regions – from Sicily to Tuscany – lots of salamis and hams, cheeses, pastas, jars of preserved veg, country Italian breads, etc, all of which he'll talk you through in his lilting Scottish accent.

Greengrocer/Ready-Meals

Ivano

38 Tachbrook Street SW1. Tel: 0171 630 6977
44 Tachbrook Street SW1. Tel: 0171 834 1857
Mon-Sat 8am-6pm

A n extremely popular source of nourishing and tasty dishes for the area's workers, all made downstairs by Maria in the night-marishly hours of the morning. If a dish runs out (and they do with frequency), that's it: there are no repeat orders, as the kitchens are scrubbed down by mid-morning to make way for preparation of the next day's corporate orders, such as lunches for Westminster Council officers and perhaps an MP or two. There's a huge array of dishes – pastas, paella, lasagne, tortillas, salads ('fantasia' is particularly popular, consisting of asparagus tips, artichoke hearts and other delicacies tartly dressed). Vegetables come from number 44, where Ivano's missus presides over an excellent selection of roots and leaves (if it can be Italian, it will be). Among these were the brilliant green chard, turnip tops, raddichio trevisiano and fresh pods of borlotti beans from the motherland (only available between October and December).

Market

Tachbrook Street SW1

A small busy market of about half a dozen fruit and veg stalls, and a clean-smelling wet-fish stall belonging to one R E Wright – scallops on the shell and sea bass looked lovely.

Pasta (Fresh)

Ciaccio
5 Warwick Way SW1. Tel: 0171 828 1342
Mon-Fri 10am-6pm, Sat 9.30am-5pm

This tiny 11-year-old shop sells nothing but fresh pasta. It's really the retail arm of a wholesale operation in Battersea. The choice is not enormous (about ten kinds a day), but special orders can be phoned through the day before. A restaurant and take-away has recently opened a spaghetti-length away at 17 Strutton Ground (tel: 0171 233 1701).

Sand's End

Butcher

Randall's
113 Wandsworth Bridge Road SW6. Tel: 0171 736 3426
Mon-Fri 7am-5.40pm, Sat 7am-3pm

Everything here is free-range, additive-free or organic. Beef and lamb come from Highgrove. Sausages, pies and chicken liver pâté are home-made; pork pies and pasties are made for them – but they supply the meat, so these too are guaranteed top quality. There's also smoked chicken, French duck, game in season, free-range Bronze turkeys, Continental cuts, and a selection of prepared dishes. Innes' organic sour-dough bread is a stock item, perhaps because the Boss loves it so much!

South Kensington

Butcher

Bute Street Boucherie
19 Bute Street SW7. Tel: 0171 589 5739
Mon-Fri 7.30am-6pm, Sat 7.30am-5pm

Many moons ago this was the renowned Arthur's who played to the French gallery provided by the Lycée Française round the corner. New owner Martin Croucher also nods in that direction with French ducks and chickens (free-range), boudin noir and blanc and fresh foie gras on Thursdays, French cuts, Fauchon products, and tins of confit d'oie and graisse d'oie. However, his lamb has gambolled in Devon or Wiltshire, and his beef has been organically reared by Pure Suffolk Foods. A tactful compromise, you might say.

Cheesemonger

Jeroboams
24 Bute Street SW7. Tel: 0171 225 2232
Mon-Sat 9am-6pm

The smallest of the three Jeroboams (see entries in Holland Park and Belgravia) is run by Beth Jeanes whose parents make the sublime unpasteurised Keen's Cheddar (which is of course much in evidence). Otherwise the variety is much the same, but considerations of space mean there may be slightly less actual quantity and because of the Lycée Française's proximity a higher turnover of French cheeses. However it's a wonderfully tempting, fragrant shop.

Delicatessen

Michel Montignac Food Boutique
160 Old Brompton Road SW5. Tel: 0171 370 2010
Mon-Sat 8.30am-7.30pm

Monsieur Montignac's 'method of eating' (diet is not a word he uses) is all the rage over the Channel and is said to be healthy, pleasurable and slimming. Like the Hay Diet, the Montignac plan only restricts combinations of foods and time of eating, not what you eat. This shop-cum-café is a franchise held by an American, Mr Hilton, who was favourably impressed by the results of following the Montignac regimen. All the prepared foods – the salads, pastas, rice dishes, mousses – are made in the downstairs kitchens to the Master's recipes. Ingredients are organic and whole (i.e., brown rice and flour). There are oils and vinegars, natural sea salts, organic breads from La Boulangerie Savoyarde in France, luscious-looking fruit spreads ('jam' is another word frowned upon) without any added sugar. Of particular novelty is Le Pain Kamut, a loaf made from an ancient Egyptian variety of wheat, a seed of which was found in a sarcophagus where it had lain dormant for 3,000 years. Now reintroduced, it makes a heavily textured, flavoursome loaf, but one which may struggle to achieve daily bread status at over £3 a throw. In fact, nothing in this shop is cheap – a tin of graisse d'oie, for example, costs twice as much as the same brand in Harvey Nichols even! Monsieur Montignac's book is also on sale.

Pâtisserie

Bagatelle Boutique
44 Harrington Road SW7. Tel: 0171 581 1551
Mon-Sat 8am-8pm, Sun 8am-6pm

When I visited in November, one of the large windows boasted the customary works of cake-art, such as tarte tatin, truffoise, Fontainebleau (which looks like a hat worthy of the races), while the other rather incongruously displayed a stuffed fox, crow and pheasant. Had it become a taxidermist on the side? *Bah non*! They were merely celebrating the tricentenary of French author Jean de la Fontaine, and apart from the stuffed characters had pretty cakes iced with illustrations from his fables. They do several such promotions throughout the year, so there's often a chance of bumping into a bit of fun on top of the excellent daily fare which has made Bagatelle's reputation. Breads are made with imported French flour, milled in Jacky Lesellier's (managing director) family mill; the dough is kneaded and shaped by hand in traditional style, and is left to prove in its own good time (the pain de campagne takes 16 hours). They do over 30 types, including an old-fashioned baguette, a 'Brioche' one (softer and whiter), canaillou (stone-ground wheat flour with added malt), a carrot and thyme loaf and 'Naturvie', a 'genuine organic bread' with natural yeast and Guérande coarse sea-salt. The range of Viennoiserie, pâtisserie, and pâtés is enormous and simply delicious. Fresh foie gras is available at Christmas. The traiteur counter features fortnightly menus of gourmet dishes and the full-scale catering menus range from buffet to '*carte gastronomie*' (beef fillet in puff pastry stuffed with foie gras, for example). A splendid shop all round.

Filéric

57 Old Brompton Road SW7. Tel: 0171 584 2967
Mon-Sat 8am-8pm, Sun 9am-8pm

Another life-line for South Kensington's French community, this one with a small café at the rear. The emphasis is on breads and Viennoiserie, baked on site, and sumptuous cakes and tarts which all come from the kitchens of sister restaurant La Madeleine in Vigo Street. Ham, cheese, pâté and terrines are imported from France once a week.

South West

South of the River

There are many delights to be discovered in this sprawling area — Italian, Portuguese and Caribbean bakeries; old- and new-style delicatessens; superior butchers and fishmongers; old-fashioned cakes and pies (Maids of Honour in Kew). Brixton Market stands out as a source of fish and Afro-Caribbean produce. Among the curiosities are Emory St Marcus' biltong-bestrewn shop, and The Hive and Devonia, both in Clapham, respectively a honey-shop and a West Country 'real food' specialist — talk about pinpointing your market.

Balham

Butcher

M L Ware

204 Trinity Road SW17. Tel: 0181 672 3498
Mon-Fri 8am-5.30pm (Wed until 1pm, Sat until 4pm)

Catch this good old-fashioned butcher while you can: Harry Lisle and Geoff Phillips are retiring in 18 months, and Geoff's son had not yet decided to take it over when I visited. There's nothing fancy about Ware's, but you can rely on top-quality meat, be it Scotch grass-fed beef, Scotch or Welsh lamb (they belong to the Guild of Scotch Quality Meat Suppliers), free-range chickens, turkeys (from Norfolk) and eggs, home-made pies (supplied by Bryce Sargent of Henry Read). Wet smoked fish and seasonal veg also stocked. Free delivery.

Delicatessens

Bon Vivant

59 Nightingale Lane SW12. Tel: 0181 675 6314
Mon-Fri 8.30am-8pm, Sat 8.30am-7pm, Sun 9.30am-12.30pm

An aptly named shop, since owner Simon Robertson obviously loves the good things in life. Here are Sally Clarke and Innes breads, Valrhona chocolate, top names in relishes and dips, chutneys and pickles, estate-bottled oils, various vinegars, a wide range of French cheeses, Duskin's single-variety apple juices, good brands of pasta sauces and pastas. As if to confirm that Simon's eye is on Clapham's City-working single men, the rear room has meals-for-one: fresh, as in organically-produced fillet steak, pork leg-steak, lamb leg steaks, pheasant sausages, or frozen ready-mades. Organic sausages come from Eastbrook Farm, eggs from Martin Pitt (whose hens must be the most prolific free-rangers in the country). Smoked chicken and smoked duck breasts are two delicacies not always easy to find.

Fox's of Wandsworth Common

14 Bellevue Road SW17. Tel: 0181 672 0987
Mon-Fri 8.30am-8pm, Sat 8.30am-7pm, Sun 10am-4pm

The well-connected Bruce Parris, ex-design consultant and cousin of the more famous Matthew, lived in New York for many years and has modelled his shop on Zabar's, Manhattan's premier deli. You could be forgiven for not immediately recognising this, even though there's a helpful hint in the form of one of their distinctive carrier bags on the wall in homage. Having said that carpily, it must be owned that Bruce has filled his shop with delectables. Most of the breads come from Elizabeth King every day, but baguettes and ciabatta are baked on the premises. Small local firms supply pies, filled mini-brioches and mini-quiches. There are many top brands – Paul Newman for sauces, Rana and De Cecco for, respectively, fresh and packet pasta, Duskin's (apple juice), Quick's and Gedi for cheeses (among many others), Fudge's (scrummy cheese biscuits not widely available – Stephen Fudge is another family connection), Sarah Jayne (the mail-order-only chocolate-maker, and Bruce swears he is the only retail supplier), Rocombe Farm (ice-cream), Martin Pitt (eggs). There's also a selection of wines and French ciders, and Sporting Spirits, which are rum- or brandy-based fruit-flavoured liqueurs, the king of them uncompromisingly called Director's Bollux! There's also a very pretty range of chinaware made by Anna Timlett. Fruit and veg adorn the pavement outside.

Panadam Delicatessen

2 Marius Road SW17. Tel: 0181 673 4062
Tue-Sat 9.30am-5.45pm, Sun 10am-2pm

Zbigniew Brzeski does a mean cheesecake. Or rather his wife's bakery does, based on his mother's and grandmother's recipes. These are emphatically not the American-style cheesecakes which have ruined the very name, but a Polish/East European version (and probably the original). The one I tried was out of this world – a light, creamy, non-cloying cheesecake on a layer of poppy-seed/almond/honey paste, both on a rich, crunchy pastry base. This is just one of five or six always on offer. Zbigniew has been here for 15 years, catering to those Poles who chose South rather than West London, and although he styles himself 'Continental' his emphasis is definitely Polish: there are good rye breads (from the famed Kolos bakery in Bradford and a Greek baker in Brixton); lots of beetroot juice (concentrated for borscht and the potable diluted version); pickled mushrooms (a meat accompaniment); a solid selection of salamis; jars of bigos (Hunter's stew) and golabki (stuffed cabbage); Knorr soup mixes ('not like British ones at all'), biscotti, pastas, oils, etc.

Market

Hildreth Street SW12

A short street linking Balham High Road and Bedford Hill, with a high standard of fruit and veg on its few stalls, both British and Afro-Caribbean. There are shops down each side, of which 43-year-old Broadway Fisheries (8 Hildreth Street, 0181 673 1999; Monday-Thursday & Friday 7am-5.30pm, Sat till 6.15pm) and the much younger M. & M. Bakery (11 Hildreth Street, 0181 673 1989; Monday-Friday 8.30am-10.30pm, Saturday till 6pm) are worth noting.

Barnes

Butcher

J Seal
7 Barnes High Street SW13. Tel: 0181 876 5118
Mon-Fri 6.30am-5.30pm, Wed to 1.30pm, Sat 6.30am-4pm

A straight-up family butcher without any fancy ready-prepared dishes to distract attention from the grass-fed Scotch beef, English lamb, Bramble Farm free-range chickens, Derek Kelly turkeys and Martin Pitt eggs. Pies, burgers and sausages are home-made, the last with natural skins. They roast their own chickens, beef, ham (there's a boiled version, too) and turkey (all year round). McSween's haggis and proper black pudding are proudly displayed. There are a few 'foreign' sausages. Service is friendly and efficient.

Cheesemonger

The Real Cheese Shop
62 Barnes High Street SW13. Tel: 0181 878 6676
Tue-Thu 9.30am-5pm (closed for lunch 1-2pm), Fri-Sat 9am-5pm

96a High Street Wimbledon SW19. Tel: 0181 947 0564
Tue-Sat 9am-5pm (closed Wed, Thu 1-2pm), Sun 11am-4pm

Robert Handyside and his wife used to close on Saturday, dash down to the cheesemakers in the south west and load up the Golf with the following week's stock. Now the cheese comes to them, from all over Britain and the Continent. There are interesting Swedish cheeses, mature Pecorino from Italy, excellent French staples, but the real point is the British farm cheeses, many unpasteurised, from cow, sheep and goat. Creamy, lemony Hereford Hops, Harbourne Blue and Ticklemore (both goats' milk cheeses made by Robin Congdon in Devon), Cashel Blue and Gubbeen from Ireland, Swaledale cows', Elsdon goats' from Northumberland, Worcestershire Gold (a pure unpasteurised Jersey milk with a pungent flavour), Torville (unpasteurised, cider-washed from Somerset) are just a few to get your teeth into from the large choice. Tasting is encouraged (and irresistible, as the smells are so enticing). After 11 years in the cheese-selling business and with some 180 different cheeses in stock at any one time, Robert's choice of 'Desert Island Cheese' would still be a mature farmhouse cheddar: 'It can't be beaten for depth of flavour. I just never tire of it'. Nor, it seems, do the customers of his two South London shops, as it is the best-seller of both (except, predictably, at Christmas, when Stilton takes over). Staff are knowledgeable and helpful – Judy Bell manages in Barnes, and Harry Lovestone in Wimbledon (where opening times vary in the summer, as Harry is a keen bowls competitor).

Delicatessen/Traiteur

Sonny's Food Shop
92 Church Road SW13. Tel: 0181 741 8451
Mon-Fri 10am-4pm, Sat 9am-5pm

The home-made dishes here (the deli has its own chef, so don't expect a take-away version of the restaurant's menu) are extremely popular with local residents and workers – when I visited at 11am one day there was only one portion left of the dish of the day. Others included bean and lentil salad, pequillo peppers, couscous, pasta salad and chicken salads. Other than that, Sonny's is a smart, designer-deli – estate-bottled oils, pasta, risotto rice, char-grilled artichokes, Duskin's single-variety apple juices, etc, Carluccio's own-label produce, Monmouth Coffee Co. coffee and Neal's Yard cheeses – a godsend to the area's food-lovers.

Greengrocer

Two Peas in a Pod
85 Church Road SW13. Tel: 0181 748 0232
Mon-Sat 7am-5.30pm, Sun 10am-1pm

Malcolm Louis left a job as supermarket manager to set up on his own 12 years ago because it 'was too impersonal', a reason often cited by ex-chainstore employees without much subsequent evidence that they enjoy or are graced with the personal touch. Malcolm does and is. Every year, October sees his small shop frontage obliterated by local children's drawings of pumpkins, supposedly a competition for the best. But, as he says, it's impossible to choose and he ends up giving prizes to almost everyone. Malcolm goes to Western International Market every day to get seasonal and non-seasonal produce (he also supplies restaurants, which makes the latter viable), and always gets available organic fruit 'n' veg – organic curly cale among the usual potatoes, carrots and onions. In October he had still-sweet raspberries and strawberries, as well as the more timely blackberries, cobnuts and green Crown Prince pumpkins, which he swears are the real thing to eat: 'Those orange ones are commercially produced, only good for faces.'

Battersea

Baker

Rae-Ra-El Bakery
64 Northcote Road SW11. Tel: 0171 228 4537
Mon-Fri 8.30am-5pm, Sat 7.30am-5pm

L en and Burgel Walters, a Jamaican/German husband-and-wife team, started out five years ago and in that time have established themselves as *the* local bakery. Ninety-eight per cent of the goods are made on the premises by Len and his staff – Jamaican patties, hard-dough breads and buns, five varieties of rye bread, ciabatta, pesto bread, their own French sticks (which are hot-sellers on Saturdays), white, granary, wholemeal and stoneground loaves. Len's previous employment in a Polish bakery means there are also scrummy Continental cheesecakes and poppy stollen. Some are sort of 'seasonal' in that Len does not necessarily make everything every day. Sponge cakes also feature, including the wonderfully named 'Hummingbird cake' – pineapple, coconut and nuts.

Butcher

Dove
71 Northcote Road SW11. Tel: 0171 223 5191 (24hr answerphone)
Mon 8am-1pm, Tue-Sat 8am-6pm

A s recently as the 1980s, when Bob Dove's father was still running the shop, this was a traditional English butcher, the bulk of whose business was scrag end of neck, stewing steak and the like. Momentous changes have taken place under the hard-living Bob and his wife. Freezer cabinets contain Linda's pies, which differ greatly from those of her more famous namesake – these are stuffed with meat and wine ('She's a bit of a Floyd when it comes to cooking,' says Bob) and are much in demand among locals, toffs and market stall-holders alike. She also makes hamburgers, fish pies and cooks hams. Cool cabinets contain a good range of British and French farmhouse cheeses. But first and foremost Bob is a quality butcher – Welsh Black beef, Welsh and English lamb, free-range pork, all properly hung as required. Certificates of humane rearing methods are produced on request. The smart new tiled floor is still sprinkled with sawdust and the original wooden chopping blocks, dating back to his grandfather's day, have been granted stay of incineration by the hygiene police. Bob also stocks Wiltshire Tracklements and jars of preserved lemons for those following the latest culinary craze for Moroccan stews.

Henry Read Butchers

45 Tyneham Road SW11. Tel:0171 223 5680
Tue, Thu & Fri 8.15am-5.30pm, Wed 8am-1pm, Sat 8am-3.30pm

Tucked away down this residential street off Lavender Hill, with ne'er another shop in sight, is a delightful small butcher, which owes its continuing existence to the dedication of Bryce Sargent and his wife. He is one of only seven London stockists of Real Meat Company produce (the area's residents are spoilt – another is M. Meon of Clapham), but also deals direct with other reputable suppliers, such as Pure Suffolk Foods. His beef, uncommonly, is English, as are lambs (he does still get some New Zealand for elderly customers), his pork free-range and organic. He'll order special requests, such as beef sausages for non-pork eaters. Between serving and answering the telephone, Bryce makes mouth-watering pies.

Cheesemonger

Hamish Johnston

48 Northcote Road SW11. Tel: 0171 738 0741
Mon-Fri-9am-7pm, Sat 9am-6pm, Sun 9am-1pm

Hamish Johnston once worked with Vivian Martin (of Vivian's in Richmond), and his elegant shop reflects this. There are robinets dispensing classy olive oils and a small range of quality dry goods, but Hamish consciously chose not to travel too far down the designer-deli route and to concentrate on cheese instead. There are two large counters, one for British and Irish, the other for Continental cheeses, all farm-produced. He runs charity cheese-tasting evenings once every two months, ring for details.

Delicatessens

Mise-en-Place
21 Battersea Rise SW11. Tel: 0171 228 4392 Fax: 0171 924 1911

Guy Wolley, owner of La Bouffe restaurant up the road, started this pretty modern deli a mere 16 months ago, putting it in the capable hands of ex-Michelin inspector Nick Smallwood. With its stylish lighting, curved shelves, terracotta paintwork and murals, it feels very *à la mode*, and this is continued in the selection of foodstuffs which ranges from milk to miso paste. Guy and Nick try to search out the best from world cuisines, and consequently stock British, French, Spanish, Italian, Japanese, Chinese, Thai and Tex-Mex produce. There are over 100 cheeses from all over Europe, a large range of charcuterie, Sally Clarke breads, olives and ready-meals from La Bouffe's menu.

Salumeria Napoli
69 Northcote Road SW11. Tel: 0171 228 2445
Mon-Sat 9am-6pm, Sun 10am-2pm

Salvatore and Marcello keep a well-stocked larder, the ceiling festooned with hanging cakes (panettone and colomba), the shelves neatly displaying the immense variety that is the basis of any good Italian deli - pastas galore, sauces to go with them, sun-dried this-and-that in oil, olive oils and vinegars, etc. Olives are home-marinated, red and green pesto home-made. There's lots of cheese (five different Pecorini, Stracchino, a soft and sourish type) and salami and ham, including Speck from the South Tyrol. They also have an Italian roast ham with herbs which is delicious, and Rana fresh pasta.

Wainwright & Neill
284 Battersea Park Road SW11. Tel: 0171 350 2035
Mon-Fri 9.30am-7.30pm, Sat 9am-6pm, Sun 10am-7pm

This is the sort of store where Ryvita nestles up to Duchy Originals, tomato ketchup to Paul Newman's hot sauces. The breads, baked on the premises, seem to be the main point – grand rustique, pain rustique, cylindrical sourdoughs, wholemeal, etc, all made with unbleached flour and vegetable fats There are home-made frozen meals, various cheeses and cold cuts, French cider, L'Ile de Noirmoutier salt and other miscellany.

Fishmonger

Lyons Fisheries
14 Northcote Road SW11. Tel: 0171 978 4428
Tue-Sat 7am-6pm

Jim and Tony Lyons get 99 per cent of their fish fresh from Billingsgate or direct from fleets (ask if you're in doubt or want to freeze it yourself – some of the more exotic varieties, such as tilapia, snapper, parrot-fish and grouper, arrive here already frozen). They usually have about 80 different species, from British standards – sole, salmon, brill, monkfish, mackerel, etc – to the above-mentioned foreigners. Ask for off-cuts (heads and skeletons, etc) for cats or fish stock. They also sell Caribbean veg which comes direct from a school-mate's Jamaican plantation. Tony reckons they beat Brixton Market on choice (fish) and price (fish and veg).

Health Food

Dandelion
120 Northcote Road SW11. Tel: 0171 350 0902
Mon-Sat 9.30am-6pm

An extremely popular source of nourishing lunchtime food, cooked by co-owner Jo Risley and including daily a soup such as onion and watercress or mixed veg and herbs, a cheese-based main course and a vegan main, plus excellent salads of leaves and beans (seven in summer, three in winter). There's the usual range of healthy grains, seeds, rices, pulses, gluten-free mueslis, some organic, and Tivall frozen meals, James White single-variety apple juices, Whole Earth juices, organic veg in a chill cabinet, soya yoghurts and milk, huge Kilner jars of herbs and spices. Partner Hillel Friedman used to be in 'senior management', but after four years here you'd never have guessed it – he's more likely now to offer to do the washing up than plan a business flow-chart. Free home-delivery service available.

Honey

The Hive
53 Webbs Road SW11. Tel/Fax: 0171 924 6233
Mon-Sat 10am-6pm

Ex-pat American James Hammill, like his grand-father and father before him, is a fanatical apiarist, and his shop is given over to all things apiarian. There are 50-60 honeys, many single-blossom, painstakingly collected at various times of the year by James and his wife from their hives in Wimbledon, Tooting and the Home Counties. They refine the honey on site, using a traditional 'spinning' method, and keeping some of it aside for their much-in-demand honey/rum/raisin fudge sauce. The shop doubles as James's 'bee museum' - there's a living wall of bees in glass going about their buzziness, several types of hives (one delightful example carved in the shape of a man's face, through whose open mouth the bees fly), some ancient, apiarist's tools, and bee-related products such as soap and candles. Schoolchildren flock to watch and listen (James gives 'honey lectures').

Market

Northcote Road SW11
Mon-Sat 7am-5pm (half-day Wed)

Probably the only market to boast an ex-popstar as costermonger: at stall 151 (opposite Whittard) you'll find street-cred Tony who between 1979 and '82 was a member of New Musik ('Living by Numbers' was their biggest hit). He still does the 'occasional session', but his heart is now in fruit and veg and he runs, a stall more interesting by half than the current charts – salad leaves, fresh herbs, Spanish saffron and lots of good, healthy, ordinary veg. On the corner of Shelgate Road is an excellent fish stall, E. Dunbar, manned by the grandson of the 1928 founder — they still have their own smoke-house just up Shelgate Road where they cold-smoke haddock and cod. You don't find a market fish stall like this too often, even in Brixton.

Brixton

Bakers

Cecil's Bakery
411a Brixton Road SW9. Tel: 0171 737 0885
Mon-Sat 8.30am-5.30pm

A complete range of Caribbean breads, dumplings, patties, cakes and sweets, some luridly dressed in technicolour icing. There are saltfish/plantain dumplings, banana fritters, hard-dough breads, casava pone, coconut buns. On Fridays and Saturdays the ovens are given over to the very sweet Guyanese breads and sweets, such as salava (coconut and food colouring) and casava pone. Everything is made on the premises, and ordinary old English breads are available during the week.

Thompson's Bread Shop
14d Market Row SW9. Tel: 0171 673 2249
Mon-Sat 9am-5pm (Wed until 1pm)

368 Norwood Road West Norwood SE27. Tel: 0181 766 7288
Mon-Sat 9am-5.30pm

Started by James Thompson's father seven years ago, the bakery (which is actually in Balham) now supplies most of the rest of London, South Wales and Luton with its hard-dough requirements. Hard-dough bread is very dense and made without animal fats. The loaves come in various shapes and sizes — duck, high-top, crown, heart, buns — and can be white, wholemeal or granary. Some are sweetened with currants and dark cane sugar, giving them a rich dark hue. Buns packed with cherries and other fruits are popular at Christmas and Easter. Large quantities or huge loaves can be ordered for weddings, parties, business functions.

Emporium

A & C Co. Continental Grocers

3 Atlantic Road SW9. Tel: 0171 733 3766
Mon-Sat 8am-8pm

It's hard to pin a nationality to this pleasant little shop. The original Greek-Turkish Cypriot basics are still much in evidence – breads, baklava, shamali, taramasalata, hoummos, a solid range of pulses, etc – but Portuguese Francisco, who has presided over it for five years, has added cheeses and hams from Spain, Portuguese black and white puddings, tiny, fresh salt-cod fishcakes, Italian pastas (there had always been Greek brands). Fresh veg, fruit and herbs come from wherever Francisco can get what he wants – Cyprus, Egypt, the Lebanon, Spain.

Fishmonger

L S Mash & Sons

11 Atlantic Road SW9 Tel: 0171 274 6423
Mon-Sat 7am-6.30pm

Known locally (they say) as 'Grant' and 'Phil' after *EastEnders*' Mitchell brothers, the Mash sons run a friendlier establishment than the Queen Vic, where the only fishy smells come from the day's delivery from Billingsgate and Cornish fleets. Beautifully displayed on beds of ice are rows of silvery salmon, red mullet, parrotfish, octopus, squid, plaice, sole, cod, etc. Special requests welcomed.

Health Food

Brixton Wholefoods

56-58 Atlantic Road SW9. Tel: 0171 737 2210
Mon, Fri 9.30am-6pm, Tue-Thu, Sat 9.30am-5.30pm

This charming, ramshackle shop feels like a throwback to 'hippier' times, and indeed it evolved some 15 years ago out of a campaign to raise funds for Bangladesh. Huge jars of herbs and spices from which you weigh and bag as much as you want suggest a trust between shopkeeper and customer not often found nowadays. There are organic veg, some, like the pumpkins, locally grown, masses of rices, cereals and beans (some organic), a good selection of wholemeal breads and the usual range of brand-name health foods. Eggs are Jewett's free-range and Mrs Wooley's organic. They also have an Aquathin pure-water filter which produces liquid containing less than 100ppm of foreign matter, as against the EU's recommended limit of 400ppm! Take your own container. Incidentally, if the shop appears not be there, look across the road at no. 59 – the 'Trans-Atlantic' branch, while renovations are being carried out at no. 56 (whose front is happily protected by a preservation order).

Market

Brixton
Mon-Sat 8am- 5.30pm (Wed 1pm, Fri 7pm)

Sprawling either side of Atlantic Road in the covered areas (Market Rows and Granville Arcade), down Atlantic Road itself and Electric Avenue and Lane, this is what a market should be: noisy, busy and fun, with competing sound systems adding to the general din. There are British costermongers among the exotica, but the latter is the real point – it is arguably the best place to buy Afro-Caribbean raw ingredients and dry goods. And because it features so strongly in West Indian cuisine, fish is everywhere. Butchers tend towards the sheep's-head-and-cow's-feet type, but don't go looking for 'naturally reared' signs. Here are some pointers, but it's best just to dive into the melee and explore.

Fish: The Original Fisherman, 23 Electric Avenue; Dagon's, 1st Avenue, Granville Arcade; Harry Otto & Son, 1st Avenue, Granville Arcade; Jeffries of Brixton, 5 Market Row. A lot of the fish like the red snappers which seem to be eaten in copious quantities, is frozen, so ask if in doubt.

Greengrocers/Grocers: Kashmiri Grocers, 45 Electric Avenue; Ghana House, 3rd Avenue, Granville Arcade; Sierra Leone, 3rd Avenue, Granville Arcade; Tina's Tropical Fruits, South Avenue, Granville Arcade; Robinson's, 3rd Avenue, Granville Arcade; Back Home Foods, 1st Avenue, Granville Arcade; R P Tropical Foods, 1st Avenue, Granville Arcade.

Clapham

Butcher

M Moen & Sons
17 The Pavement SW4. Tel/fax: 0171 622 1624
Mon-Fri-8am-6.30pm, Sat 8am-5pm

The Moen family have moved with the times over the past 25 years. One of only seven butchers in the Greater London area supplied by the Real Meat Company, everything here is free-range from beef to eggs. Organic meat can be ordered. Game in season is plentiful, customers' own birds are dressed, 10-12 different sausages are made on the premises, gammon and ham are home-cooked. There is a selection of continental salamis (chorizo piccante, often difficult to get outside Spain), MacSween's haggis and mutton pies (anyone who has ever lived in Scotland will be glad of these pies — I love them). Wicker baskets of wild mushrooms (trompettes de mort, chanterelles, shinogi) line up along the counter and there's a modest but top-quality range of cheeses. A thoroughly classy, modern butcher.

Delicatessens

Devonia
53a Old Town SW4. Tel/fax: 0171 622 7033
Mon-Sat 8am-9pm, Sun 10am-2pm

This must have one of the narrowest briefs of any deli in London — only real food from the West Country (give or take the odd stray from Suffolk or Kent). Still very much in its infancy when I went (it opened in September 1994), it is owned and run by two youngbloods, Will Dennis and Olly Dickinson. Will produces his own mineral water which he distributed to London outlets until he thought it would be a better wheeze to sell it himself, along with other lines. These include Fudge's delectable cheese biscuits, Rose Farm pickles, mustards and jams (sole distributors), Browne's chocolate truffles, Clive's pies from Buckfastleigh, Cobley Farm free-range eggs, Dunster flour, 25-30 cheeses, including an exceedingly creamy but tangy Exmoor Jersey Blue, and pies and pasties made by a locally renowned butcher in Bampton. Fresh sarnies every day. Will's sister Flora runs Truffles Kitchens from the same address (tel: 0171 622 7017), which caters for parties and dinners and makes freezer pies for the shop. Definitely a new enterprise that deserves to succeed.

Pamela Price
26 The Pavement SW4. Tel: 0171 622 4051
Mon-Sun 7am-10pm (inc. Christmas Day)

Pamela Price's shop is crammed with goodies to tempt even the most jaded palate. She is a magpie buyer, getting supplies from all over the country on a fairly *ad hoc* basis, but if she hasn't got her usual stock of a particular brand, she'll certainly have another just as good. Breads are gathered from London's best bakeries by Gail Stephens (see Baker and Spice) and include Sally Clarke's, and also come from an organic German baker round the corner (the fig fruit loaf is highly recommended). Quiche, apple pies and cherry pies are all locally made, Rocombe Farm ice-cream, Bridge Farm cakes and preserves, Langage Farm flavoured oils and dressings, Womersley Hall jams, Fiona Dickson's Windsor Great Park honey, Mrs Gill's Indian Kitchen frozen curries, oils, vinegars, All Things Nice mini Christmas cakes... And probably lots more that has caught Pamela's eye or palate (she's keen on aesthetically pleasing things – a Spanish bouquet garni of twiggy herbs wrapped in a bayleaf, for instance: 'I just smell it or look at it – at 45p I'd never use it!').

Kew

Baker

The Original Maids of Honour
288 Kew Road Surrey. Tel: 0181 940 2752
Mon 9.30am-1pm, Tue-Sat 9.30am-6pm

Many shops which have retained the name of the original founder over the decades have in fact changed ownership several times. Maids of Honour, perversely, did the reverse: in the hands of the same family since 1863 it was for years called Newen's, until John N., great-great-grandson of the founder, changed the name in honour of the Maids for which it is most famous. (Maids of Honour are tartlets of puff pastry filled with curd cheese, said to be so named because Henry VIII once spied Ann Boleyn and other Maids of Honour eating them and was so taken by the maids and the tarts that they were for ever linked. They are delicious warmed, particularly with a dollop of vanilla ice-cream dropped on top of the hot curd.) Everything here is baked on the premises (except bread). Three bakers produce daily a wonderful range of scones, macaroons, Danish pastries, cream horns, eclairs, cakes, pasties, quiches, sausage rolls, stupendous pies – steak and kidney is sublime, the veal and ham so perfect to behold it is almost a shame to eat it (but temptation is irresistible). All the meat used is organic. At Christmas, puddings, fruit cakes and mince pies (their own mincemeat mixture) walk out of the door. Coffee, luncheon (sittings at 12.30 and 13.30) and teas can be 'taken' in the adjoining restaurant. To call Maids of Honour old-fashioned is, for once, accurate and nothing if not very complimentary.

Nine Elms

Baker

Ewings Classic American Bakers
Unit 12 Sleaford Road. SW8 Tel: 0171 498 0550
Orders by telephone only

Ex-food writer Scott Ewing describes his wares as 'bespoke sweets', but they are in fact luscious, tasty cakes and pies, made with unbleached flour and vegetable fats, real fresh flavourings (no mixes or pre-packed things for Scott). And they're big, each 'loaf' providing 10-12 generous slices. He makes brownies, cinnamon cake, chocolate/lime, chocolate/rum/pineapple gateaux, pecan and pumpkin pies, and something he calls 'Demise by Chocolate', which contains three different real chocolates and offers, he says, an altogether more sensuous experience than the more usual 'Death'.

Norbiton/Kingston

Butcher

Jefferies

42 Coombe Road Norbiton. Tel: 0181 546 0453
*Mon 7am-3pm, Tue 7am-4pm, Wed 7am-1pm, Thu-Fri 7am-5pm,
Sat 6.30am-4pm*

S adly, there is no longer an organic-meat counter here, but it's still all top-quality meat – Aberdeen Angus Cattle Society approved beef, additive-free lamb and pork, Norfolk Bronze turkeys, home-made sausages. There's a refreshing lack of prepared dishes, but will 'coat on request' – i.e., if you can't be bothered to make your own marinade, they'll do it for you in the catering department next door which supplies restaurants and clubs. Wiltshire Tracklements are among the many delicious accessories on sale.

Cheesemonger/Delicatessen

La Sienne

54 Coombe Road Norbiton. Tel: 0181 546 3767
Mon-Sat 9am-5.30pm (Wed until 1pm)

R asik Chuahan is one of Britain's few Chevaliers de Fromage and the only Asian member of the Guilde de Fromagers. When he opened his shop 23 years ago he thought cheese meant Cheddar and Edam. Then customers began asking for things like Dolcelatte and Brie. It took him ten years to educate his palate and to be invited to join the distinguished ranks of Fromagers. And Surrey cheese fans are the beneficiaries. His selection is not large, but always offers something of interest, such as semi-soft Livarot, Vacherin Mont d'Or (seasonal) and Munster (with cumin seed), or the washed-rind Cuvée de Brochon and Epoisse, both from Burgundy, Mimolette, Crottin de Chavignol. Most come from Jacques Hennart in Saquedin. Apart from the cheeses, there's Russian beluga caviar in winter months, jars or tins of truffles, an extensive range of coffees and teas, and other basic deli stuffs.

Delicatessen

Fratelli
57 Park Road Norbiton. Tel: 0181 549 8021
Mon-Fri 8.30am-6pm, Sat 8.30am-5pm (closed last two weeks in August)

The name of this shop, meaning 'brothers and sisters', is the equivalent to 'siblings', but the English doesn't have quite the same ring to it. Franco Vitiello, his sister Rita and her husband Bob Simmons run a truly Italian joint, the window stuffed with home-made dishes – meat balls, peppers, aubergines, seafood salad, fresh pasta – the king of which, says Franco, is his fried squid in ink on Saturdays. There's every imaginable shape and size of pasta, including the traditional handmade-with-eggs strozzapreti, which means 'chokepriest', something that many might like to do! Lots of cheeses, salamis and bread. At the back of the shop is the wine, all Italian and unusual (none of your straw-covered chianti), and some, at 16 per cent by volume, heady stuff indeed.

Emporium

Miura Foods
40 Coombe Road Norbiton. Tel: 0181 549 8076
Tue-Sat 9am-6pm, Sun 10am-6pm

Everything you need for Japanese cookery can be found in this friendly, busy store, including the excellent fresh fish for sashimi and sushi (they make their own to take away, the former all week, the latter at weekends only). The shelves are packed with dried goods – seaweeds, gourd strips, aubergine, radish, shitake; various noodles, among them buckwheat, yam and rice; tofu mixes; saifun for sukiyaki and salads; pickled veg; miso and other soup bases; wasabi powder and pastes; mirin (a sweet sake for teriyaki marinade); sushi vinegar and brown rice vinegar, which Keiko, the manageress, says is very good for diabetes, high blood pressure and general aches and pains – mix with honey and water. If in doubt about anything at all, ask Keiko.

Fishmonger

Jarvis & Sons

56 Coombe Road Norbiton. Tel: 0181 546 0989
Mon-Sat 8am-5pm (Mon until 3pm, Wed until 4pm)

Although ownership has moved from the family to a fish wholesaler, the quality and service have been upheld. It still has one of the best and largest piscine displays, artfully arranged on and behind the long counter. A third of the customers are Japanese and Korean, so sushi and sashimi filleting methods are well understood. Carp can be ordered for Christmas and New Year (in fact, anything can be ordered anytime, including Japanese delicacies such as sea urchin and samma). There's all the usual species, plus more unusual items like smoked sprats from Devon (an excellent lunctime snack), marinated French anchovies (if your only experience of this maligned little fish is the salty tinned version, be prepared for a revelation), palourde clams, dorade royale, and monkfish cheeks, which are almost half the price of the tail but every bit as good in the eating. At weekends there are live crabs and langoustines direct from Scotland. There's an expanded non-piscatorial range which includes fresh wild mushrooms (some from local pickers), game, herb parcels, and Puy lentils. Upstairs are the old smoking ovens where salmon and haddock are still treated. Staff are extremely friendly and helpful, and will put together specials, such as a fish soup mix of gurnard, rascasse and other kinds not much good for anything else.

Putney

Emporium

Talad Thai
320 Upper Richmond Road SW15. Tel: 0181 789 8084
Mon-Sat 9am-10.30pm, Sun 10am-8pm

Try to hit this excellent Thai store on a Thursday or Friday – the new supplies are collected from Heathrow on Wednesday afternoons and are therefore at their freshest. Not only that, but leave it until Sunday, or worse, Monday, and you could find stocks of fresh produce severely depleted. Demand in the upstairs café, where there's always a huddle of young Thais eating, reading and writing, might have been heavy, but husband-and-wife owners Piak and Pranee have a perfectly credible theory that if there's been a television programme on Thai cuisine, or an article about it in 'a certain supermarket's magazine', then the necessary ingredients are snapped up by Londoners trying a 'new thing'. Downstairs are fresh tamarind, sweet basil, lime leaves, curry leaves, lemon grass, krachai, small aubergine, galingale, bird's-eye chillies, kaffir lime, fresh turmeric, green papaya, and red and green curry pastes, all of which will be familiar to anyone who's been to Thailand. The dry-goods shelves present most of the above in preserved form, plus all sorts of eyebrow-raisers, like pickled mudfish. Thai and other Oriental cookbooks can guide a willing beginner, or ask Pranee herself, who is always happy to offer her advice.

Richmond

Delicatessen

Vivian's
2 Worple Way Richmond Surrey. Tel: 0181 940 3600
Mon-Fri 9am-7pm, Sat 8.30am-6pm, Sun 8.30-midday

Vivian Martin has come a long way from his days as a professional bridge-player and stagehand. Recent expansion behind the elegant Art Nouveau frontage bears testimony to the success of his eclectic taste (marrons glacés) from Spain – 'just as good and half the price'; egg pastas from Alsace – 'they've been making it there for festivals for centuries') over the past five years. Famous for his olive oils sold on tap (bring your own container), he now has twelve robinets dispensing the stuff, all of which can be tasted beforehand (empty robinets are also on sale). These come from Greece, Italy and Spain, and range from the mild and smooth to those 'packed with tropical fruit flavours completely unexpected in an olive oil'. Otherwise, Vivian stocks whatever takes his fancy, and swears he has tasted everything he sells – baby onions in balsamic vinegar, Iranian cornichons, bitter lemon pickle, Womersley Hall (a range that includes apache jelly, coriander jelly and geranium jelly) and Rosebud Farm jams and chutneys (all excellent). The traiteur counter boasts, along with the French and Italian salamis, hams from Cumbria (cooked with cider and juniper berries) and Hampshire (Eldon Wild Blue, a dry cure, dense and dark), dishes from the kitchens of master-restaurateur Stephen Bull – tapenade parfait, fish terrine, chicken livers wrapped in orange and herb butter, foie gras with lentils, black pudding and boudin blanc, pecan tart. This is something of a coup on Vivian's part ('we're friends'), since short of spending a fortune in one of his restaurants you can't get to savour the Bull flavour anywhere else. All in all, a fun deli, well worth making a detour for, which promises and delivers surprises and deserves more support from conservative Richmondites.

Roehampton/Sheen

Chocolates

Sandrine

233 Upper Richmond Road West SW14. Tel: 0181 878 8168
Mon-Sat 10am-5.30pm

Jean Bradley is cagey about where exactly she goes in Belgium to get her chocolates, competition for the products of that country's chocolate craftsmen being what it is. Suffice to say that the small firm which supplies her shop (named after her daughter) is somewhere near Ghent and that its hand-made creations are delicious. You can tell they really are hand-made as the decorative touches – whirls, squirls, and squiggles – are sometimes endearingly off-centre or lopsided. The English, it seems, are particularly fond of soft-centred creams and fondants, in which Jean does brisk business. I was astonished, being a hard-centre fan myself, to discover that the rose-cream and the ginger fondant (both English made) were scrummy, the advocaat cream (Belgian) out of this world, and the marzipan liqueur so delicate that even an inveterate loather of the stuff like me found it more than palatable. Jean also designs her own delightfully gaudy packaging.

Delicatessens

Valentina

210 Upper Richmond Road West SW14. Tel: 0181 392 9127
Mon-Fri 9am-8pm, Sat 8.30am-6pm, Sun 9.30am-3pm

The residents of these environs are lucky indeed – when, around mid-October, the white truffle season comes upon us (or rather them in Italy and France) Sergio Borfecchia takes orders for this delicacy from his customers. Other shops stock fresh truffles (Carluccio's, Harrods, Luigi's, to name three), but not to order (guaranteeing earthy freshness) and certainly not at Sergio's prices – £105-£120 per $100g/3\frac{1}{2}$oz may make them sound illegal, but it's actually a sort of bargain-basement rate. Apart from this seasonal joy, Sergei and his wife Anna provide home-made pasta in all its lengths and breadths, home-made dishes such as melanzane Parmigiana (aubergines), suppli di riso (a Roman speciality of Mozzarella and Bolognese sauce rolled in a ball of egged breadcrumbs), cannelloni, lasagne, etc. He has 'the Rolls-Royces' of oils, home-marinated olives, fresh basil all year round, Italian vine tomatoes, loose pulses and rice, lots of fresh Italian bread daily, six or seven different Pecorino, selected wines and baccala (salt cod).

St Marcus Fine Foods
1 Rockingham Close Priory Lane SW15. Tel: 0181 878 1898
Mon-Sun 8am-6pm

The first thing you notice on entering this peculiar shop is the curtains of biltong, those sticks of salted dried beef beloved of South Africans, hanging from the ceiling. It is all made on the premises, using Aberdeen Angus meat (owner Emory St Marcus is a member of the AA Cattle Society), as are other South African specialities like landjager (smoked beef/pork sausages), boerewors (fresh beef sausages), droewors (the air-dried version) and sosaties (spiced fillets of lamb or beef with apricots). More familiar bangers include Oxford, Lincoln and Toulouse; among oddities from other parts of the world are Russian, Hungarian, Thai, Hawaiian, Gurkha (lamb with spices), Cajun (hot). If you're feeling adventurous, try the ostrich biltong or sausages, crocodile or kangaroo steaks. Or chew some beef jerky. The 'deli' side mostly consists of South African brand-names, some, like Mrs H S Ball's Original chutney, quite commonplace in London nowadays, others new. An excellent place to stop at for summer barbecue essentials after a stroll in nearby Richmond Park.

South Lambeth

Baker/Delicatessen

Di Lieto
175 South Lambeth Road SW8. Tel: 0171 735 1997
Mon-Sat 9.30am-7pm, Sun 11am-3pm

A spacious shop pervaded by lovely warm floury smells which emanate from the baking ovens at the back. There are croissants and currant buns, huge round Italian loaves like plates, ciabattas that would fit a giant (ciabatta means 'slipper'), small country-style rolls, and many more. The deli side is your basic Italian – lots of pasta, Provolone, Pecorino etc. Go promptly in the morning for the best choice of fresh bread, and in the afternoon (around three o'clock) for the olive-oil ciabatta.

Fishmonger

Condon

363 Wandsworth Road South Lambeth. SW8. Tel: 0171 622 2934
Mon-Sat 8.45am-5.30pm (half-day Thu)

One of the few remaining wet-fish providers left in the immediate area (apart from Brixton Market), Ken Condon still smokes his own salmon (the 'best in London', according to a customer), haddock, cod, trout, sprats and herring. And the herring don't just become kippers, but the rarely found bloaters (smoked with guts intact) and buckling (gutted, headless, hot-smoked). Also of delectable interest are smoked halibut and fillets of Jamaican tilapia. All the smoked goods are lovely and pale – no dyes. Wet fish includes all that you would expect, and whelks, winkles and cockles, all cooked by Ken, so very fresh. Oysters come from Galway, mussels from Norfolk. Ken also keeps fish kettles which he lends for big fish like salmon or sea trout, and arranges taxi deliveries all over London.

Greengrocer

Hyams & Cockerton

41-44 Southville SW8. Tel: 0171 622 1167 Fax: 0171 622 8458
Mon-Sat 8.30am-midday

Just round the corner from Condon Fishmonger, the Cockerton family (Hyams is no more) are really wholesalers, but what wholesalers! They supply many of London's top hot-headed chefs and the Royals (three Warrants from the Queen, two from Prince Charles, all proudly framed and displayed), and are called upon frequently by the magazine and advertising industries. All this means that their produce is top-notch, so don't go for looking for bargains. Between the times given, retail customers are welcomed by a smiley Blair Cockerton, who will escort you in and out of three huge cold rooms (one is for salads, another for sensitive veg, yet another for fruits) and two warm rooms (where avocados, bananas and the like are ripened). And they have everything – from ordinary spuds to truffle potatoes, vine tomatoes, black radish, fresh herbs, wild mushrooms, little gem artichokes. It is a most pleasurable way to shop, but go when you need a lot – cash is not encouraged as they don't keep change. Best to telephone beforehand.

Southfields

Butcher

S A Elliott

261 Wimbledon Park Road SW18. Tel: 0181 788 0678
Mon-Fri 7am-5pm, Sat 6.30am-1.30pm

A no-frills butcher, approved by the Guild of Scotch Quality Meat Suppliers (beef and lamb). They roast their own beef, turkey and leg of pork, sausages are made by 'a millionaire who supplies Selfridges'. Gammon and hams are from naturally-reared pigs, eggs free-range from Orchard Farm in Surrey. Christmas brings pheasants and whole French Barbary ducks. Don't ask for any cheap cuts – they don't do 'em: 'Nothing frozen and nothing gristly'. There is also an astonishing collection of ceramic pigs built up over the years by owner and staff.

Delicatessen

Brotherhood's

38 Replingham Road SW18. Tel: 0181 874 2138
Mon-Fri 8.30am-8pm, Sat 9am-6pm, Sun 9am-3pm

Ex-actors Chris Connah and Simon Brotherhood took over this shop two and a half years ago, renovated and expanded it, and filled it with all manner of goodies. There's an impressive range of breads - at least ten when I visited – all baked daily (the success of this side of the business took them rather by surprise, but they responded manfully). They have home-roast ham and beef, all from free-range or grass-fed animals, Neal's Yard cheeses, estate-bottled oils, lots of jams, chutneys and pickles. Madame Josephine's banana chutney made to a traditional St Lucian recipe proved to be a special delight.

Greengrocer

Southfield Fruiterers

253 Wimbledon Park Road SW18. Tel: 0181 870 3076
Mon-Fri 6am-5.30pm, Sat 6am-5pm

In the early hours of the morning, dog-walkers and shift-workers stop for a chat and an apple as Jean Grigor and her merry band of women build the splendid displays which spill on to the pavement from her shop. After 15 years on the spot, Jean can probably set her clock by the comings and goings of the street. In fact, her stretch of pavement seems to be a regular gossip-stop for locals. She always aims to have English seasonal produce (in October there were handsome sweetcorn, wet walnuts, blackberries and cob nuts) as well as the best of the unseasonal. She believes in customer service and if someone should want a dozen ripe mangoes for a weekend dinner party she'll do her damnedest to get them.

Pâtisserie/Novelty Cakes

Suzelle's Celebration Cakes

10 Replingham Road SW18. Tel: 0181 874 4616 Fax: 0181 877 1173
Mon-Sat 8.30am-10pm, Sun 9am-5pm

Want a 1936 Harley-Davidson that you can eat? Or a fairy-story character, or a musical instrument, or tennis racquets? Your wish is Suzelle's signal to get her team of five bakers and decorators on the job. Nothing, it seems, is beyond them, from giant telephones to Ninja turtles. Susan Flatau, a barrister by training, has seen her business expand from cottage-industry (she started with her mother Estelle by making wedding and birthday cakes from home) to a small shop plus a bar-counter with five stools, to a large shop plus fully licensed café-restaurant, which serves snacks and four or five daily specials including pasta, fish, duck breasts and a vegetarian dish. Everything is made on the premises, bar bread. The range of pâtisserie is extensive, cakes can be made of almost anything – carrot, chocolate, orange, banana and cashew nuts (very popular as a wedding cake with those who can't eat eggs). In the summer there are tables outside. During Wimbledon Fortnight, they run an open-ended day starting at 6am, and the place is packed. While excellent for business, it can have its drawbacks — the mother of one dark-haired racquet-wielding beauty brought her own food and insisted on eating it on the premises, an insult to any food-purveyor but particularly to one of Susan's calibre. Since she lacked a common language with the perpetrator, Susan resorted to easily comprehensible gestures.

Stockwell

Bakers/Pâtisseries

Funchal Pâtisserie

141 Stockwell Road SW9. Tel: 0171 733 3134
Mon-Sun 8am-8pm

A bleak stretch of busy thoroughfare is cheered up by this two-year-old bakery which sells alentejano, rosquilha, bolo do cato, palmieres, pasteis de nata, pão de deus and lots of other Portuguese breads, pastries and cakes. It's all made on the premises and their breads and patisserie can also be found at Mimma in Harrow Road.

Pâtisserie Floridia

224 Brixton Road SW9. Tel: 0171 737 3371
Mon-Sat 9am-5pm, Sun 9am-2pm

A nother pastry shop which seems to have alighted on a most unpromising main road (see Funchal above), but which has nevertheless been in business and the same family for 16 years. Now run by Sandro Floridia and his partner Isaac, it is a tiny space supplied by a larger rear kitchen where everything is made on a daily basis. There's only so much you can eat in the interests of research, but I can vouch for the sfogliatella here, a sort of pasta-wrapped cake with Ricotta which was delicious. Croquembouches are made to order.

Delicatessen

Sintra Delicatessen

146 Stockwell Road SW9. Tel: 0171 733 3134
Mon-Sun 9am-8pm

Maria Coelho has been running this deli-café for nine years, providing her compatriots with bacalhau fishcakes, Portuguese cheeses and hams such as tipo de Serra (a hard, strong mountain cheese) and bresunto (like Parma), black and white puddings, chorizo, and larder staples such as quince marmalade, oils and cereals. Slabs of salt cod are piled under a table. Pastries come from Lisboa in Golborne Road and, like them, Senora Coelho also stocks boxes and boxes of the cotton thread for knitting which seems almost as important to the Portuguese as their food!

Streatham

Delicatessens

Rosticceria Roma

152 Streatham Hill SW2. Tel: 0181 674 1901
Mon-Fri 10am-7pm, Sat 10am-6pm, Sun 10.30am-1pm

After eight years, Gianni and Caroline Mascolo have become something of a fixture on 'the Hill', and well-nigh a necessity for lunchers. Their freshly-made dishes are famed in the region, and range from pizzas (you can design your own topping) through various pastas to turkey breast with peppers and artichokes, or chicken and mushrooms in a creamy sauce, or arancini, those delightful balls of vegetables, Parmesan and Mozzarella rolled in breadcrumbs that put the Scotch egg firmly in its lowly place. There's an Italian chicken Kiev which, according to Gianni, is subtly different from and infinitely superior to the French version. They roast their own pork, beef and free-range chickens, stock nothing younger than two-year-old Parmesan, have oils from Sardinia, Tuscany, Umbria and Puglia. The mature farmhouse Cheddar nestling among the Provalone and Pecorino has to be Gianni's single concession to our native cuisine. Among the goods without which Italians cannot survive are panettone Virginia (hand-made with almonds), Santal fruit juices, Rachelli ice-creams and sorbets, and first-division grappa. Home-made tiramisu and Torta della Nonna are sorely resisted temptations indeed.

Korona
30 Streatham High Road SW16. Tel: 0181 769 6647
Mon-Sat 9am-7pm, Sun 9am-1pm

Peter and Elonora Wicinska have recently moved down the road to smart new, parquet-floored premises, but regular customers, among whom are many elderly Poles now retired to the South Coast, can be assured of service as usual. This includes wild mushrooms gathered on Wimbledon Common which, if not sold fresh on the day of picking, are threaded on strings to dry or are pickled to Elonora's own authentic Polish recipe. She also makes pierogi and krokiety (sauerkraut and mush-room dumplings) and golabki (stuffed cabbage). The orderly shelves are packed with Polish jars and tins and cartons, including labour-saving beetroot juice for borscht, and quite a wide range of kosher products. There are over 20 different breads of all nationalities, poppyseed cakes, babkas, Continental-style cheesecakes (lemon-flavoured is delicious), apple cakes, Polish honeys and spreads (thicker and less sweet than jams), chocolate-covered praline wafers and plums – indeed, everything the homesick Eastern European heart could desire.

Tooting

Butcher

J R's Superstore
163 Upper Tooting Road SW17. Tel: 0181 682 3949
Mon-Sat 8am-7pm, Sun 9am-6pm

Not really a superstore, but definitely a super butcher, run so successfully for the past 15 years by the Rashid brothers ('JR' is one of them) that they have customers from as far afield as Brighton and Belgium (a captain in the Air Force). An unsolicited testimonial was offered by a customer from Beckenham: 'I wouldn't go anywhere else, they're the best in South London'. All the beef is from naturally-reared Scotch herds, the mutton is beautifully trimmed of fat (and made an excellent stew with haricot beans), there's goat galore, and Zahid will get kid to order. All meat is halal.

Emporia

Deepak's Cash & Carry
953-959 Garratt Lane SW17. Tel: 0181 767 7810
Mon-Sat 9am-7pm, Sun 10am-3.30pm

You don't have to have an extended family to shop here, but it helps. Goods are sold in industrial quantities – vast tubs of ghee, sacks of rice and flour, etc – although they do also come in single-parent sizes. If you're seriously into Indian food, you'll find everything you need in this cavern of a place, from spices, pickles and chutneys, rice flours, bean flours, lentil flours, to valiary (sugar-coated fennel seeds), aritha, gugar, alkonet root, sopari (betel nuts) and snack foods such as 'far far' which looks like technicoloured pasta but is made of uncooked potato and rice.

Mehta Fruit & Veg
111-113 Upper Tooting Road SW17. Tel: 0181 767 8214
Mon-Sun 8.30am-7.30pm

Mr Mehta started as a plain greengrocer three years ago, but competition (see Everfresh and Nature Fresh below) being as tough as old banana leaves he expanded into dry goods. He still keeps a goodly selection of imported fruit and veg, among which you would find the necessary ingredients for cuisines from the eastern Mediterranean to Thailand. Shelves of rice, beans, spices, etc line the walls.

Greengrocers

Everfresh Ltd

204-208 Upper Tooting Road SW17. Tel: 0181 672 7396
Mon-Sun 8am-7pm

The biggest, and possibly the best, of the exotic-fruit-and-veg shops on this very subcontinental stretch of road, is airy and tidy, with lots of space for strolling between the island counters piled high with gravity-defying mounds of ginger, garlic, yellow limes and green limes. Of course, there are apples and pears, potatoes and carrots, but the real attractions are the eddoes, cassava, chow chow, amba hali, round dudhi, tinda, tindoori, paraval, snake cord (long paraval), fresh tamarind, turia, ash plantain, banana flower, onion flower, patra, arbi (root of patra), bird's-eye chillies, chickoo, nasi pears, Bangladeshi guava... Even in comparatively ordinary categories, such as onions and aubergines, one is spoilt for choice, the former coming in white, green, red varieties and baby to huge sizes, the latter in pale pink through striped to purple-black, round, long, small, very long, large. Most of the labels say nothing more than 'veg £x/lb' or 'all veg £x/lb', but don't be put off – Mr John and his staff are always somewhere around ready to advise and explain. Taped Indian music plays quietly in the background.

Nature Fresh

126 Upper Tooting Road SW17. Tel: 0181 682 4988
Mon-Sun (inc. Christmas Day) 8am-7pm

Smaller and less varied than Everfresh, this is none the less a good source of fresh produce from home and abroad, with an impressive pavement display, on which a mound of small, brilliant-red tomatoes caught my eye. At 19p/lb they were a snip, and juicy and flavoursome. It is always worth sniffing around the different stores here.

Vauxhall

Delicatessen

Delicatessen Piacenza
2 Brixton Road SW9. Tel: 0171 735 2121
Mon-Sun 9am-6.30pm

Edward and Carmen Coda run a packed shop full of up-market Italian tins and packets, jars and bottles, as well as making their own pasta (favourites include Sicilian ravioli - Ricotta, orange peel and saffron – and walnut, Ricotta and Parmesan ravioli), gnocchi di patate and 'four cheeses' pies – these each have a different vegetable emphasis, be it leek, courgette, french bean, pumpkin or whatever, but share the Emmental/Camembert/Cheddar/Mozzarella mix that gives them their wonderful aroma. Carmen also makes bruschetta and focaccia to order. There are lots of cheeses (Asiago, Fontina and Taleggio among the Pecorini), and salamis and hams.

Wimbledon

Butchers

Robert Edwards
19 Leopold Road Wimbledon SW19. Tel: 0181 946 5834
Mon-Fri 7am-5pm, Sun 7am-1.30pm

Young Robert Edwards has taken over and changed the name of the last remaining shop in his father's once-extensive empire (which traded as H J Grimes and at its peak had four shops in the Wimbledon area). He is Approved by the Aberdeen Angus Cattle Society, so grass-fed beef can be guaranteed. Sausages are home-made on the premises without preservatives or additives, pies are hand-made by a local-ish piemaker whose products are much in evidence in surrounding shops and judging by the steak and kidney I ate on the hoof, as it were, they are well above average quality. He has game in season, will order Norfolk Bronze turkeys, organic meats and free-range pork as requested, stocks free-range eggs and Home Farm preserves, has recently added fruit and vegetables, and supplies the Royal Opera House and some tennis players, 'although only the Germans seem to eat meat nowadays'!

W Gardner & Sons

157 Arthur Road Wimbledon Park SW19. Tel: 0181 946 2215
Mon-Fri 8am-5.30pm (closed Mon & Wed 1-2pm), Sat 8am-3.30pm

Wimbledon's 'oldest established Traditional Butcher's Shop' has been in the hands of Ian Michael Rooke for a third of its 90-year history. Times have changed and Ian has adjusted with them. His beef is Perth Fresh Meat Quality Assured (grass-fed), his pork, chicken, turkeys (Norfolk Bronze) and eggs (Martin Pitt) are free-range, his sausages homemade and gluten-free. Pies are those good ones also to be seen in Robert Edwards. And he has a good sideline in pickles, chutneys and jams, Paul Newman's spaghetti sauces and salad dressing. Here's to another 30 years.

Delicatessens

The Coffee Shop

38a High Street Wimbledon Village SW19. Tel: 0181 947 5341
Mon-Sun 8am-7pm

This small family concern had become the place to pass the time of day in 'the Village', even before owner Paul Lippner got the proverbial itch after seven successful years as a café. Last autumn he expanded into deli-wares, and now offers cheeses, oils and vinegars, pastas, salamis and pâtés, in addition to the teas and coffees, patisserie, cakes, croissants and bread (baked by girlfriend Marta Brennan) which made it such a popular place originally. Watch out for an ever expanding deli range, as Paul is always ready to try new things out. In the summer months, some 20 pavement tables give excellent views up and down the Village High Street which often seems more of a thoroughfare for horses than for cars (there are two riding schools close by). The whole caboodle is ably run by sister Miranda.

Giuliano

45 The Broadway Wimbledon SW19. Tel: 0181 543 7366
Mon-Fri 9am-7pm, Sat 9am-6.30pm

The ancient but functioning pasta-making machine and flour-dustbin just inside the door attest to the Italian-ness of this pleasant deli, which is well-stocked with what you'd expect. A small Sicilian-run London bakery makes all the bread, which Giuliano claims is 'the best for miles around'. The pasta goes into the home-made lunchtime dishes, such as tagliatelle, gnocchi and ravioli; the bread, especially the ciabatta, is the wrapping for enormous sandwiches. Neapolitan Giuliano is keen on cheeses and particularly anxious that Brits should realise that Dolcelatte is just a mild Gorgonzola – to this end he keeps a cheese book behind the counter. Of interest among the many cheeses are Fontina, soft and mild from Val d'Aosta and the basic ingredient of a Piedmontese Fonduta; a smoked cows' Mozzarella; and Taleggio from Lombardy, exceptionally creamy and mild but developing piquancy if left to mature. There's a fridgeful of home-made puddings and ice-creams – tiramisu, tartufo, cassatta, bomba strega and pasteria di grano, a traditional Easter cake of Ricotta, lemon zest and orange water.

Morse & Hardy

8 Leopold Road Wimbledon SW19. Tel: 0181 944 7007 Fax: 0181 944 7006
Mon-Fri 10am-7pm, Sun 9am-6pm

This smart young deli - five and a half is nothing in deli years - is tucked away roughly equidistant between Wimbledon and Wimbledon Park tube stations. From February to September it saves local food-lovers wearisome trips to the centre of London, as it stocks Neal's Yard cheeses, Carluccio's own-brand goods and Maison Blanc cakes, as well as the tubbed Orkney herrings, Slack's oak-smoked Cumberland sausage, Robson's kippers from Craston, Dickinson & Morris award-winning pork pies, luxury jams (carrot, rhubarb and prune, and walnut) from Alsace, hand-made Belgian chocs, Chocolate Society drinking chocolate and biscuits (it seems Wimbledonians cannot get enough of these), Calissons d'Aix (the French almond delicacy), etc. From October to January (well, that's if anything's left after Christmas), it really comes into its own. Previously hidden shelves are opened up and piled high with French and Italian luxuries, hampers galore, wonderful gift items. Perhaps all this quality is not surprising since co-owner Kathryn Morse is an ex-Fortnum & Mason buyer.

Greengrocer

Roots

76 High Street Wimbledon Village SW19. Tel: 0181 944 5105
Mon-Sat 7am-7pm, Sun 9am-6pm

Although this is self-service, the staff, headed by owner John Mendez, are very helpful, pointing out what's at its best to picky customers, most of whom they seem to know personally. Apart from the fruit 'n' veg (some organic in winter months only), all of which looks fresh and healthy and, when I went, included rarely seen fresh horseradish, kohlrabi, red onions, cob nuts and lovely big artichokes, there's also a small but interesting bread selection, delivered daily – scofa, ciabatta, farmhouse, and a half-brown-half-white cottage loaf for warring couples who will not compromise!

South East

With the exception of treasures such as Criterion
Ices and Kennedy's Sausages, the main gastronomic
advantage of south-east London was, until recently,
its proximity to the 'garden' of Kent. Today, those
venerable retailers have been joined by up-market
traiteurs, fancy sausage shops and brave new delis.

The first French charcuterie/rotisserie in the
south-east suburbs opened too late for inclusion in
the body of this book: Le Parc Franglais (94 Wickham Road, Beckenham, tel: 0181 650 0355). This
exciting new venture is run by ex-Savoy,
ex-Mosimann's Club Christian McClintock — may
he survive until the next edition.

Beckenham

Baker

Sponge Kitchens
106 Wickham Road Beckenham Kent. Tel: 0181 650 0062
Mon-Sat 6.30am-5.30pm

Located opposite the wonderfully exotic Chinese Garage, this outlet often boasts a queue extending into the street. The business was started by Alan Stewart's father just after the war and used to sell only sponges. Now they have 'only 200 different items', ranging across the taste spectrum from an authentic-tasting tarte aux pommes with a deep filling of freshly ground almonds to pineapple tart, a confection of Scottish origin consisting of pineapple pieces in butter cream with an icing top ('very sweet and sickly for people who like that sort of thing'). Battenburg Cake, a cheery mainstay of 1950s teatime, is made with a real almond paste surround and sold by the slice. The shop's breads, however, are very much of the 1990s with ciabatta, sun-dried tomato and multi-grain varieties on sale. They are used for a variety of well-stuffed sandwiches. A half-ciabatta overflowing with Cambazola and salami made a very satisfactory lunch. Other fillings include the chicken and Rondele cheese, Brie and bacon, and the ubiquitous chicken tikka. Branches at Station Approach, Hayes, Kent, and Bromley Road, Downham, Kent.

Butcher

Parhams
96 Wickham Road Beckenham Kent. Tel: 0181 650 0521
Mon-Wed 7.30am-5pm, Thur-Fri 7.30am-5.30pm, Sat 7.30am-1pm

Trading on this suburban site for over 70 years, Parhams sells only Scotch beef in cuts ranging from porterhouse steaks to oxtail. 'High-class beef for a high-class area,' declares manager Leslie Colley. The burghers of Beckenham can also treat themselves to magret of duck, Dutch veal escalopes and guinea fowl. The shop's modestly priced turkey and tarragon sausages are first-rate. A beguiling range of meat and fruit pies for baking at home are made at the back of the shop by Sue Newall. A meaty treat comes at Christmas when the owner Alan Emus buys a champion beast from the Smithfield Show. Last year it was a Supreme Champion pig.

Cheesemonger

James's Cheese Shop
188 High Street Beckenham Kent. Tel: 0181 650 1411
Mon-Sat 9am-5.30pm

Run by John Sanders since 1988, south-east London's oldest cheesemonger stocks mouth-watering names from the pantheon of British cheesemakers – Keen's Farm Cheddar, Lance Appleby's Cheshire, Mrs Kirkham's Lancashire – plus many specialities from James Aldridge, who founded the shop in 1982 (hence the name). Now based in Surrey, Aldridge is the UK's leading affineur (cheese finisher/maturer). Don't miss his River Eden, a tiny smoked cows' milk cheese with fresh garlic, or the rind-washed Tornegus, a Duckett's Caerphilly 'massaged' in white wine for seven weeks. An outstanding Continental selection includes many chèvres, such as Camembert and delectable Crottin de Chavignol, which serves suburban dinner parties as both gastronomic highlight and conversation piece (the name translates as horse droppings). The shop also bakes its own bread (generously filled rolls available at lunchtimes) and stocks a good range of biscuits, pickles and wine.

Coffee/Tea

Importers
180 High Street Beckenham Kent. Tel: 0181 658 9049
Mon-Sat 9am-5pm. Mail order

Early on weekday mornings, the Importers shop imparts a delicious aroma to this otherwise unfragrant suburban thoroughfare. Some 19 varieties of raw coffee beans are roasted on a daily basis, using a rather antiquated gas appliance in the window. They range from a sharp Brazilian espresso, which delivers a rousing caffeine buzz, and Colombian Condor (a useful secondary source of income for the notorious city of Medellin) to the legendary Blue Mountain coffee from Jamaica — its stratospheric cost, around four times as much as other coffee beans, is due largely to its popularity in Japan. The shop, which is part of a chain established in the 1930s, also sells a couple of dozen different sorts of leaf tea. These are mainly the traditional black liquor which fuelled the Empire, such as the malty Lattakari from Assam and Tukvana Darjeeling, described as being 'rather like muscatel grapes'. There are a handful of green teas, including a refreshing infusion from Taiwan called Oolong, said to have a 'peach-like character'. They also stock all manner of fruit-flavoured teas, including passion fruit (particularly successful) and mango.

Delicatessen

Giuseppe's Delicatessen

53 Beckenham Road Beckenham Kent. Tel: 0181 289 8565
Mon-Fri 8am-6.30pm, Sat 8.30am-5.30pm

A native of Naples, Guiseppe De Vai set himself an uphill task in November 1994 when he opened a deli/coffee bar to bring a taste of the warm south to windswept wastelands between Beckenham and Penge. But, after a very slow start, commuters have taken to popping in for fresh tortellini (choice of parma ham, mushroom, quattro formaggi and spinach/Ricotta fillings), a selection of cured meats and cheese (including both Roman and Siennese Pecorino) and excellent fresh Italian bread. Home-made treats include tiramisu (with free earthenware pot) and the sustaining Neapolitan speciality arancini, which resembles a Scotch egg but, being made of rice, tomato and Mozzarella, acutally tastes of something. Guiseppe's pride and joy is a 1950s Gaggia espresso machine, which he says is 'like an old Ferrari'. A machine of similar vintage made the fortune of Soho's Bar Italia. If only Guiseppe's was on Frith Street, it would be packed.

Sausages

Villagers Fine Sausages

91 The High Street Beckenham Kent. Tel: 0181 325 5475
Mon-Sat 8.30am-6.30pm

Opened in October 1995 by Brian Stevens and Ron Etheridge, who jointly have 40 years' experience in the butchery trade, this outfit produces sausages to over 100 recipes. Around 40 different kinds are available at any one time and freshly cooked samples are usually on offer. They will also make special sausages if requested. While I was in the shop, Ron agreed to make a special batch of Bratwurst for a customer. All the sausages are made on the premises, are high in meat and low in fat, and only use natural ingredients, fresh herbs and spices. One testimony to the healthiness of Villagers' bangers is that the third partner in the business is Dr Wilson Mills, who is a GP. His wife received the accolade of having a cocktail sausage named after her. Villagers' imaginatively titled output includes a purplish pork banger called the Goodhew ('red cabbage swimming with apples and cayenne'), a pork and spinach job called Bruto's Fear (surely it should be Blutto?) and a pork and prunes sausage called Cavalier. Why? 'Because it contains brandy,' I was mystifyingly informed. Perhaps they meant Musketeer. Other tempting specialities include wild boar, venison, duck a l'orange and vegetarian cheese sausages.

Bermondsey

Delicatessen/Oils & Spices/Seafood

Le Pont de la Tour

Shad Thames Butler's Wharf SE1

Food Store

Tel: 0171 403 4030
Mon-Fri 9am-8.30pm, Sat-Sun 10am-6pm

Oil and Spice Shop

Tel: 0171 403 3434
Mon-Fri 12pm-6pm, Sat-Sun 10am-6pm

Smoked Fish and Crustacea Shop

Tel: 0171 403 7573
Mon-Fri 12pm-8pm, Sat-Sun 10am-6pm

Squeezed into elegant nooks in Sir Terence Conran's Pont de la Tour restaurant complex are these three out-of-the-way boutiques. The most appropriately located is the Oil and Spice Shop, for this area was formerly occupied by warehouses of the London spice trade. Enter and you're hit by a potent whiff of the souk, an amalgam of celery, curry, anise and pepper from the brightly coloured piles on display. The shop stocks 90-odd spices and around 60 different oils, including, you'll be pleased to learn, 'an oil pressed from olives grown on Terence's estate in Provence'. (It may be irksome to some that the oil in question, made by Henri Bellon in Fontvieille, is excellent.) There are also about 40 different vinegars, ranging from a tiny phial of Aceto Balsamico Tradizionale, rare as angel's tears and costing £80 for 100cc, to tangy fruit vinegars from Wendy Brandon of Dyfed. Her jams and preserves are also prominent in Sir Tel's Food Store, a superior sort of deli with a smallish section of cooked meats and cheeses from Neal's Yard. But the real reason for coming here are the 50 varieties of rustic-style bread (20 available at any one time), baked somewhere in this rambling conglomeration of posh nosheries by Stuart Powell. Worth a trek across town to buy, they are fairly priced for the quality. The parmesan (a tricky loaf to make) captures the rich, slightly nutty flavour of the cheese perfectly, the rosemary is aromatic and generously flecked with the herb. Though it sells three kinds of smoked salmon plus gravadlax and a few interesting pickles, the Smoked Fish and Crustacea Shop is a bit of a disappointment. The stock is meagre and, aside from a few special offers, the prices could only be afforded by Terence himself. A plateau de fruits de mer will set you back £15 per person (orders must be for a minimum of two and there's a deposit for the plate).

Blackheath

Baker

Village Bakery
44 Tranquil Vale SE3. Tel: 0181 318 1916
Mon-Sat 8.30am-5.30pm

Preparing to open Blackheath's only baker's shop in 1978, Peter Squire was astonished to find a pair of large old bread ovens at the rear of his new premises. It turned out the site had been a bakery until 1935. This proved to be a good omen because the shop has been packed ever since. Maybe Peter's impressive baking skills have something to do with it as well. 'He's the top man, a real professional,' says Fergus Clague from Handmade Food (see page 222) next door. 'Their little Sacher Tortes are wonderful.' Other Continental specialities include baguettes made from 100 per cent French flour and light and dark rye bread. Flour for the shop's English loaves comes from Bartley Mills, a small traditional mill at Bell Yew Green in Sussex. 'We do make good bread,' Peter modestly acknowledged, 'but you should get here fairly early. It tends to sell out.' Amid a host of pâtisserie, a large, deep-pan Kent Bramley apple pie struck a tempting local note.

Butcher

G G Sparkes
24 Old Dover Road SE3. Tel: 0181 858 7672
Mon-Sat 8.30am-5.30pm

A 40-year-old family-run business, 90 per cent of whose meat is organic. Lamb and free-range eggs come from David Wooley in Lincolnshire, bacon and ham from Maynard's Farm in Shropshire, justly very famous for its excellent cures (telephone first about the bacon, as Maynard's is a small producer which does not deliver – someone from Sparkes has to go to him). Home-made sausages include such exotica as Martini and Mozzarella (a Sicilian Christmas speciality) and an unexpectedly scrummy chicken curry with tomato, as well as more traditional British recipes. The number of locals of Italian ancestry has ensured that this very British butcher has become expert in such things as fegattini (chopped liver burger wrapped in caul fat) and crepinetti (seasoned free-range pork flattened into astonishingly thin steaks). Additional stock features gulls' eggs in praline, dark-chocolate-covered roasted walnuts, home-made pesto sauce (that Italian influence again) and a few organic cheeses – the Welsh Llangloffan is a good bet.

Delicatessen/Caterer

Hand Made Food
40 Tranquil Vale SE3. Tel: 0181 297 9966 Fax: 0181 265 1235
Mon-Fri 9am-6pm, Sat 9am-5.30pm

Since May 1994, Fergus Clague's small shop has considerably cheered up an area that for all its 'villagey-ness' and evident affluence is peculiarly lacking in distinctive food shops. As its name implies, Hand Made Food specialises in prepared foods, all cooked on the premises in the small back kitchen. There are chicken/apricot and duck/orange pies, coq au vin, fabada (a Portuguese bean and pork dish like cassoulet), fish and cottage pies, duck/pistachio and sweet potato/aubergine terrines, pecan pie, banoffee pie, tarte au citron, and bread and butter pudding. All kinds of parties, from dinner to wedding to christening to garden, are happily catered for. Fergus only buys his UK cheeses from independent traditional farmhouse producers, such as Appleby's and Mrs Kirkham's, as well as a fair selection of Continental and Irish varieties. Bread comes daily from a baker in Catford, and on Saturdays from Clarke's and Neal's Yard. There's a good range of D J Jardine's American sauces and salsas, and, among the more esoteric items, mouth-stripping home-pickled cherries, well worth trying with cold meats and cheese even at £16/jar (that's a very large jar), and the organic sea-salt from L'Ile de Noirmoutier on France's Atlantic coast. The thyme-flavoured variety, according to Fergus, is excellent for roasting salt-wrapped sea bass, but its price (£1.75 for 150g) suggests that the wrapping would cost nearly as much as the fish. However, the salt is absolutely delicious sprinkled sparingly over roast baby new potatoes or a tomato salad.

Fishmonger

L & W Marshall

13 Tranquil Vale SE3. Tel: 0181 852 1060
Tue, Wed, Sat 8am-4.30pm, Thur-Fri 8am-6.30pm, Sun 10am-3.30pm

Neil Perram and his nephew Paul Arnold took over this long-established outlet last year. Dick Bellamy has continued working in the shop which his brother Reg ran for 37 years. The new regime have expanded the range somewhat, now selling fresh tuna and marlin. Traditional tastes are catered for in the form of jellied eels and whelks. Brixham sprats, oysters and two types of clams were on sale the day I called. Free-range poultry from local farms is also available.

Bromley

Fishmonger

Cope's

6 Widmore Road Bromley. Tel: 0181 460 3343
Mon-Sat 8am-5.30pm, Sunday 9am-5.00pm

Much of the impressive array on Cope's old-fashioned marble slab has circumvented the customary route via Billingsgate: the tuna comes direct from the Seychelles ('via a contact') twice a week, the rainbow trout from 'a man who goes fly-fishing for us down in Hampshire'. Alongside the rainbow was a fish similar in shape but lacking its irridescent band: the rare blue rainbow trout, introduced from the US about two years ago. (Whatever happened to the sublime brown trout, native to our waters?) Geoffrey Cope reckons his is the oldest unchanged shop in Bromley. He has been here for 33 years and it was a fishmonger before that. He still retains the old smoking kilns, in which are smoked haddock, salmon, buckling and kippers. He also prepares fish however the customers request it: whiting skinned and curled; Dover sole filleted. The shop has a game licence and sells wild boar, venison and rabbit in season.

Sausages

Kennedy's Sausages

161 High Street Bromley (16 other outlets). Tel: 0181 460 3330
Mon-Fri 8am-5pm, Sat 8am-4pm

No, it's not another trendy sausage outlet. The only 'flavours' sold here are pork, beef and, er, pork and beef combined. The 17 Kennedy's shops scattered across the high streets of south-east London are one of the unsung joys of the area. Each week they sell 17-20,000 lbs of sausages. Though Alex Kennedy opened his first outlet in 1877, the style of the chain appears to be set in the 1930s. Their fittings include marble counters, mirrors, mahogany fittings and rococo gilt lettering. The reason for their enduring success is a wonderfully creamy banger, well-spiced, with not too much in the way of padding. They are the epitome of the English sausage, the kind that Graham Greene pined for during his years of exile in Antibes. Freshly made stocks arrive twice a day at each shop from Kennedy's plant in Peckham. 'It would be an absolute disaster to change,' says managing director Andrew Kennedy, the fourth generation of the family to be involved in the business. 'In a changing world, something that stays stable has its attractions. We have an extremely loyal customer base.' The shops also do a line in steak pies, sausage rolls and suchlike, but the real jewel in their crown is the sizzler. They're not available by mail-order or from any other outlets.

Camberwell

Novelty Cakes

Margaret's

224 Camberwell Road SE5. Tel: 0171 701 1940
Mon-Sat 9am-5pm

Though it might be thought a little ungallant to remark upon the fact, Margaret has been a top cake decorator long enough to have been responsible for the extravagant five-decker job dished out at King

Hussein of Jordan's first wedding. In 1994, a more modest confection for the nuptials of Sheridan Morley featured in the pages of *Hello!* magazine. Formerly head decorator at Selfridges, Margaret's toothsome artworks are by no means restricted to the celeb market. At the time of my visit, she had just completed children's cakes in the form of Mickey Mouse and a Ninja Turtle. She was putting the finishing touches to a dart-board and a stunning wickerwork basket filled with perhaps 50 red roses, both entirely made of royal icing. This demanding technique is gradually making a comeback in the face of fondant icing. 'It melts in the mouth and you get a perfect finish,' Margaret explains. 'Customers can either search through a pattern book for a cake they like or have one custom-made following discussions with Margaret's partner Bill. She can supply the cake base (fruit or Madeira) or use a customer's cake.

Market

East Street SE5
Tue & Fri 7am-5pm, Sat 7am-6.30pm, Sun 8am-2pm

An almost medieval squeeze off the Walworth Road, with some 245 pitches mostly selling traditional English fruit and veg. The market has a reputation (not always merited) for economy. Plenty of local colour in true South London vein – a gangland slaying occurred in an East Street boozer only a couple of years ago.

Deptford

Butcher

Halal Butchers
109 Deptford High Street SE8. Tel: 0181 694 2350
Sun-Fri 7am-8pm, Sat 5am-8pm

The largest and best-stocked among half a dozen Halal butchers on Deptford High Street has been thriving for 15 years. It is the place to come if you want to tackle one of those take-no-prisoners hearty meat dishes advocated by Digby Anderson in his Imperative Cooking column in *The Spectator*. The manager Rana invited me to 'a seat in my office': two inverted plastic buckets in a corner of the shop overlooking a couple of huge tubs filled with smoked cows' feet. The shop sells goat, cocks, breeder chickens and mutton (from sheep that are around 13 months old; lamb is around 13 weeks old). These are all rich in flavour but demand long, slow cooking. 'Eighty per cent of all the meat we sell is for stews,' explains Rana. 'Pot roast is a traditional food in Africa and the Caribbean.' There is also a comprehensive range of multi-coloured viscera, including ox and goats' tripe, and a peculiar portion of innards called The Bible comes in sheets and is, according to Rana, 'very strong stuff'. If you fancy preparing a pot of Mannish Water (Caribbean soup made from bulls' genitalia, and said to be an aphrodisiac) for your next dinner party, it's worth noting the early opening on Saturdays.

Emporia

Eunice Tropical Food Shop

133 Deptford High Street SE8. Tel: 0181 469 3095
Mon-Sat 7am-7pm

This is a tiny, pungent patch of West Africa which has pitched down in south London for the past decade. It is a great place for a gastronomic safari. Eunice was out when I called, so her affable husband Kwame Donkor showed me round, carefully spelling out the names of the produce much to the amusement of regular customers. 'These are pona yams from Ghana and Nigeria – the top of the range,' he said, pointing to a cupboard packed full of roots. Another similar-looking root is cassava, which has to be grated and the starch squeezed out before cooking (one variety actually contains a toxin, so if in doubt stick to the sweet, yellow-fleshed kind). It is also available in dried form, known as farina, which is mixed with mashed potato to make fufu, a staple carbohydrate dish of West Africa. Dried green vegetables, included a bitter leaf called ukazi and an okra-like pod called ogbono (the kernel of the African bush mango), both used in soups and stews. But the shop's main speciality is dried fish – mainly black, curly, rather whiffy lumps which include catfish, mudfish, talapia and stockfish. There are also dried snails, de-shelled and curled round a short stick, which look like one of the least likely foodstuffs imaginable. I was tempted by a Nigerian patent medicine called Alafia Bitters, which the label claims 'eradicates piles. Very powerful against sexual weakness, barrenness and constipation'. Presumably its extraordinary range of application causes the manufacturer some problems, for it is known as 'NOT A JOKE brand'.

Laurie's

86 Deptford High Street SE8. Tel: 0181 691 0514
Tue-Thu 9am-6pm, Fri 8am-7pm, Sat 8am-6pm

Something of a Deptford institution, Laurie's has been selling an extensive range of West Indian produce for the best part of the last quarter of a century. There are yams a-plenty, the soft varieties from Martinique, Jamaica and Brazil (cook for about 10 minutes and use as accompanying vegetable) and hard ones from Ghana which are used in stews; green plantains (for making porridge, or cooked with mackerel in a dish known as 'rundown') and the somewhat sweeter yellow kind; green, pear-shaped christophene or chow-chow, a rather watery-fleshed member of the squash family; and the gnarled-looking fibrous tuber dasheen. Paul, who works in the shop, thinks people are daunted by the look of such vegetables but points out that, when cooked correctly, they are just as tasty and as healthy as more familiar European ones. He is knowledgeable about the staples of the Caribbean diet and will bend a willing ear about the advantages of Mother Edward sweet potatoes from Jamaica ('much drier and better eating than Israeli ones, lovely baked in their skins'). He is knowledgeable too, the difference between soursop, which is used in punches, and sweetsop, which 'looks like the backside of a dinosaur but is sugary-sweet inside'; the neasberry, a brownish fruit which tastes like a mixture of figs and dates; the 30 different kinds of mango – robin, hairy, beef, Julie ('one of the most sought-after'), Tommy Atkin, black (which is really green-skinned). It's all very instructive and should convince the die-hardest at least to try.

Fishmonger

Deptford Codfather
47 High Street SE8. Tel: 0181 692 3292
Mon-Sat 8am-5pm

One of three fishmongers on Deptford High Street, the Codfather is part of a chain which owns its own fleet on the south coast. That's why, according to manager Simon Baldwin, we're the cheapest in London'. The familiar harvest from our own shores is augmented by a host of exotica – the shop sells up to 40 different varieties. They include huge red snappers from the Seychelles, trevally from New Zealand, golden and black tilapia (aka St Peter's fish and similar to koi carp) and yellow croaker. A few unusual offerings come from nearer home: baby shark (known as hush puppies or smooth hounds) with its beautifully mottled, rather abrasive skin and a big fresh-water bream , caught in salmon nets on the Blackwater River near Galway.

Market

Deptford High Street SE8
8.30am-4pm

A sprawling mixed market with 141 stalls, and 40 more on Saturdays, about half of them selling foodstuffs with a good choice of European and Afro-Caribbean fruit and veg. Lots of pulses, too.

East Dulwich

Cheesemonger/Delicatessen

The Cheese Block
69 Lordship Lane East Dulwich SE22. Tel: 0181 299 3636
Mon-Fri 9am-7pm, Sat 9am-6pm, Sun 10am-1pm

Now in its fifth year, The Cheese Block keeps over 250 cheeses in stock. Most bear a little explanatory tag, rather in the manner of the bottles in Oddbins. So we learn that the ivory-coloured Beaufort 'develops a very fruity and scenty flavour typical of the Tarantaise high mountain pasture', Langres is 'regularly washed with marc de Champagne', while the colourfully named Stinking Bishop is more prosaically 'washed in pear wine'. The proprietor B. Roa ('my first name is too long to pronounce, everyone just calls me Roa') passed me a crumb of Roquefort Troupeau, the best of its kind around, according to him. It was indeed a morsel of cheese heaven, but at around £12/lb you might think it ought to be. Stock includes most of the popular English farmhouse cheeses and several Pecorini. But on the Friday afternoon when I called, most customers were popping in for organic wholemeal bread, made by a specialist baker. 'Maybe only 500 people in London are eating it,' claims Roa. There's also a huge range of condiments, olives and cooked meats.

West Dulwich

Delicatessen/Traiteur

La Gastronomia
86 Park Hall Road SE21. Tel: 0181 766 0494
Mon-Sat 8.30am-6.30pm

This is the largest of the three delicatessens run by the Policane family. What makes them so outstanding are Danny Policane's homemade Italian specialities produced in the kitchen at the back of this shop. Perhaps his flagship dish is the stuffed vegetable: aubergines, courgettes, peppers and tomatoes all come in for the treatment. Not cheap but they look and taste delicious. There are also pancakes filled with spinach and Ricotta, cauliflower and potato, Ricotta and ham. Home-made antipasti include artichoke hearts, aubergine and mushroom and grilled, marinaded aubergine. There are half a dozen different types of olives, including Greek split olives with garlic, lemon and herbs. I plumped for the delicious herby Kalamata olives which had dinner guests swooning. Other pickles include sweet baby onions in balsamic vinegar and the sliced aubergines with wild mushrooms and sun-dried tomatoes. The shops are well stocked for pasta, salami and condiments. They all produce freshly baked bread from small ovens on the premises. Other branches are at 135 Half Moon Lane, Dulwich, SE24 (0171 274 1034) and 18 Westow Hill, Crystal Palace, SE19 (0181 670 0717).

Greenwich

Butcher

Dring's
22 Royal Hill SE10. Tel: 0181 858 4032
Mon-Fri 8am-5pm, Sat 7.30am-4pm

How many butchers can claim to have had their sausages praised in the House of Lords? The late Lord Ted Willis apparently bought Dring's Cumberland every Friday and recommended it to fellow peers. Brothers Dave and Bob have run this small, delightfully old-fashioned butchery for the past 30 years. All their beef comes from Scotland and is hung for a minimum of two weeks, and lamb comes from the West Country. Lambs' kidneys arrive in their fat and are prepared by the brothers. As Dave says, 'there's nothing worse than dodgy kidneys', and this is a particular treat for those, like me, who love kidneys baked in their fatty jackets, or like to render the fat for subsequent potato-roasting. They are adept at all manner of Continental and specialist butchery. All the meat in the shop is British, with the exception of magret of duck from France and Dutch veal liver. Around Christmas, customers must prepare themselves for a 20-minute wait. The shop sells around 550 turkeys, including Bronze birds and geese from Judy Goodman's farm near Worcester.

Cheesemonger

The Cheeseboard
26 Royal Hill SE10. Tel: 0181 305 0401
Mon-Wed, Fri 9.30am-5pm, Thur 9.30am-1pm, Sat 9am-5pm. Mail order

Michael Jones celebrated his 10th anniversary here in 1994 by winning the accolade 'Best Cheese Shop in London and the South East'. He specialises in unpasteurised cheeses from England, France, Italy and Spain, telephoning his man in Paris on a Monday or Tuesday for delivery in Greenwich on a Wednesday. All the top-name UK producers are here – Keen's, Appleby, Kirkham, Duckett's – as well as excellent examples of lower-volume cheeses, such as smoked Wedmore (chive-flavoured Caerphilly), the recently saved Lanark Blue, and Orkney. His range of French chèvre is impressive, and the fresh brebis (ewes' milk cheese) as good as you'll get this side of the Channel. He gets no-fat fromage frais direct from France which certain customers buy in bulk the day it arrives. He also stocks a selection of pickles, biscuits and bread.

Delicatessen/Caterer

Food Parcels

20 Royal Hill SE10. Tel: 0181 858 2268
Mon-Thur 9am-5pm, Fri 9am-5.30pm, Sat 9am-4pm Local delivery

Mike Speller, who claims to have taught Fergus Clague of Hand Made Food (see page 222) everything he knows, has spent eight of his 12 years as a traiteur/caterer in Greenwich, where he has established a loyal and satisfied clientele. His main business is the provision of gourmet 'fayre' (the irritating spelling perhaps an unavoidable by-product of his name) either fresh or frozen, dishes that are happily free of gimmickry with recognisable names such as cassoulet, fish crumble and beef Wellington. Hearty pâtés come in minimum 1kg (2lb) quantities (10 servings). Vegetarians are not forgotten, although their choice is not as wide. All food is made on site. Otherwise, the shop has a selection of English tracklements, home-made jellies, relishes and pickles, and Duskin's apple juices. Food Parcels can also supply specialised hampers for such events as Glyndebourne or Twickenham – available from Greenwich Direct Marketing, 93 Trafalgar Road, SE20 9TS (tel: 0181 293 0225, Fax: 0181 858 6105).

Health Food

Greenlands
Unit 3A Greenwich Market SE10. Tel: 0181 293 9176
Open every day 10am-6.30pm

L ocated in the heart of Greenwich's 1737 market near a sign which quite reasonably admonishes 'A false balance is abomination to the Lord but a just weight is his delight', this small but richly stocked shop was established two years ago by the charming Steve Chong and his formidably well-informed assistant Ian. The bread selection includes a 100 per cent rye sour dough and Irish soda bread made by Loaves and Fishes of Dalston. There are prize-winning vegetarian sausages (basil and tomato; tarragon and mushroom; spinach, leek and cheese) made by Wicken Fen of Ely and the serious-looking Goats' Milk Acidophilus yoghurt from Rozbert Dairy. Ian says that Clipper Green China Tea is 'hugely popular' but if you're desperate for organic, a Japanese version is also available at twice the price. This is where I first discovered the products of Tropical Wholefoods. These are tropical dried fruits and fungi produced by indigenous people in Africa using low-tech equipment supplied by the company. The results, particularly the sun-dried pineapple and mango are heavenly. Available at Wild Oats, Notting Hill; Bushwacker Hammersmith and other health stores.

Sausages

O'Hagan's Natural Sausages
192 Trafalgar Road SE10. Tel: 0181 858 2833/3433
Mon-Fri 9am-5.30pm, Sat 8.30am-5.30pm

B ritain's banger boom started in this small, easily overlooked shop on the Woolwich side of Greenwich. In 1988, Bill O'Hagan opened the 'world's first specialist sausage shop' and the idea has spread like mustard on a hot dog. But there is a strong case that the first is still the best. This shop sells around 1,000 kilos of sausages a year and rather more than that amount is supplied to pubs and other trade customers. You can see them being made at the back of the shop and the ingredients meat, fresh herbs and vegetables are high quality. Over 50 different types are made – ranging from pork with apricot and cognac to highly spiced Moroccan lamb – of which 30-odd are customarily available in the shop. The shop's best-selling sausages are O'Hagan's Specials and the garlic-laden Toulouse.

Lewisham

Delicatessen

Gennaro's Delicatessen
23 Lewis Grove SE13. Tel: 0181 852 1370
Mon-Thu, Sat 9am-6pm, Fri 9am-6.30pm, Sun (Dec only) 10am-4pm

This Aladdin's cave of a deli, shelves crowded with everything from coconut milk to white truffles in oil, has been a Mecca for Lewisham gastronomes since Gennaro Masiello opened his doors in 1982. Imagine Richard Dreyfuss with a radiant smile and genial disposition and you've got Gennaro, beaming even on a Saturday when the shop is bursting at the seams and ad agency types from Blackheath are bellowing an unending litany of dinner-party demands. As one of the best-stocked Italian shops outside Soho, Gennaro's cheese counter offers Parmigiano Reggiano and a choice of half a dozen different Pecorini. Over a dozen salamis nestle in the cooked-meat section, including piquant fennel-seed salame, oval schiacciata (it means squashed) from Rome and Coppa di Parma, a sausage made from the neck of the pig.

Emporium

Turkish Food Centre
227 Lewisham High Street. SE13 Tel: 0181 318 0436
Mon-Sat 8am-9pm

Aficionados rate Turkish cooking as one of the world's great cuisines, and this newly opened storehouse of the raw ingredients is a paragon among ethnic food stores (there are twin branches in Dalston and Haringey). Combining bakery, butcher, greengrocer and supermarket, it is stocked to the rafters, is well-ordered and spotless. The vegetables sparkle with crunchy freshness and include three types of hot green pepper, Turkish lettuce and spinach, flat-leaf parsley and kolakas root (used like a potato). Baked exotica ranging from lahmacon (a kind of proto-pizza of mince on crisp pastry) to pide bread, a great flat mattress of a loaf costing just 50p. Sweet-toothed customers can choose from a dozen different types of baklava. The deli counter offers four sorts of fresh feta cheese cut from block and ten varieties of olives. The butchery tends towards the hearty, with lambs' spleen, tripe and testicles making a tempting display for devotees of viscera.

Market

Lewisham High Street SE13
Wed, Fri & Sat 8.30am-5pm

Sixty-four stalls, mainly staple fruit and veg, though there are some seasonal bargains with stalls given over solely to raspberries, strawberries or mushrooms. Two stalls at the Catford end are devoted to fish and shellfish. The nearly permanent mini-market is good for halal meat and Afro-Caribbean items

Nunhead

Baker

J F Ayre
131/133 Evelina Road SE15. Tel: 0181 639 0648
Mon-Sat 6am-5.30pm

33/34 Market Square, Bromley. Tel: 0181 466 8883
Mon-Sat 8am-5.30pm

One of south London's busiest bakeries for over 40 years, Ayre's expanded to a second large outlet in Bromley in 1994. According to director Vincent Ayre – still in his 20s, he is the major dynamic force in the company – the shops sell 396 different lines. As well as making the classic English breads, the company's Danish head baker has introduced a wide range of specialist loaves, including four types of dark Bavarian rye (plain, caraway, fruited and walnut), a yoghurt loaf and sunflower-seed. The company's *pièce de résistance* is a Swiss Muesli loaf, 'Beautiful but horrendously expensive, because of the whole roast hazelnuts,' as Vincent admits. Similiar demanding standards for ingredients apply to all Ayre's output. The Mozzarella in the filled rolls is made from buffalo milk and the salame is Milano. On the pâtisserie counter, mammoth German torten (raspberry or chocolate mousse on a sponge base) strikes a Wagnerian note among more homely stodge. One item enjoying a sudden surge in popularity is the celebration cake. A maestro of the icing nozzle called Ron is responsible for decorating 250 custom-made cakes each week. Anything goes, as long as it's in good taste – they often get asked for parts of the body but, with good humoured laughter, nobody would say which.

Fishmonger

F C Sopers
141 Evelina Road SE15. Tel: 0181 639 9729
Tue-Thur 8.30am-5.30pm, Fri-Sat 8am-5.30pm, Sun 9am-2pm

South-east London's best (but not cheapest) fishmonger has been run by the aptly named Bill Whiting for the past 35 years. A delightful and genial man, he is exceptional in his trade for both the quality of his produce and the fact that he doesn't seem to bear any grudge towards the supermarkets. He says that his shop is doing very well, pointing out that supermarkets can't compete on freshness. Bill insists that his shop has always specialised in quality, ensuring that fish comes from areas noted for those varieties: crabs from Cromer, cod from Peterhead ('without doubt, it's the best cod you can buy – people are always saying that they've never had fish like it'). He disapproves of shops which go for the cheap ticket, following the sound advice of his 'old guvnor': never sell anything to anybody that you wouldn't eat yourself. From his diversely populated slab, I plumped for a large English squid. 'Look at that, pure white,' Bill pointed having cut off the head and tentacles, and peeling off the creature's purple epidermis. 'You only get squid like that in England. It'll taste lovely.' And, with a little help from Rick Stein's *Taste of the Sea*, it more than fulfilled his prediction.

Southwark

Baker/Pâtisserie

Konditor & Cook

22 Cornwall Road SE1. Tel: 0171 261 0456 Fax: 0171 261 9021
Mon-Fri 7.30am-6pm, Sat 8.30am-1pm

Master-pâtissier and baker Gerhard Jenne's pretty purple-painted shop is so tucked away between The Cut and the river that he is hard to find indeed. But when you do, there are some treats in store: lemon crunch, orange and lavender, chocolate, hazlenut and raspberry cakes; raspberry and banana slice; croissants and steamed prune buns; chocolate brownies with walnuts; crisp and dry orange or Parmesan or Gruyere sablés; chocolate, orange and almond bombe – these are all made on the premises and are of an extremely high standard. This list must surely mark him out as an imaginative 'English-style' baker, which is what he would like to be known as, although apparently some customers expect a more robust German style of baking ('konditor' is German for pâtissier). Gerhard started two years ago, uses nothing but free-range eggs and natural butter in his baking, and has been kept alive by the useful proximity of London Weekend Television, IPC Magazines, the Young Vic, the Royal Festival Hall and other large local employers. There is a ready-to-go counter in the back room: moussaka, pizza, etc, plus a few provisions such as Duskin's apple juice. Breads come via Gailforce (see Baker and Spice) and are mostly Sally Clarke's. Birthday cakes, amusing and scrummy, are made to order (clients have included Charlie Watts, Les Jaggers and various Royals). Theatre-goers will come across Gerhard's foods at the Young Vic, whose catering he took over last August. Gerhard may well be Southwark's best-kept secret (I only discovered him thanks to word-of-mouth recommendations), and one that undoubtedly deserves to be better known.

Fishmonger

Aberdeen Sea Products
Unit 2, Toulmin Street SE1. Tel: 0171 407 0247
Mon-Thur 8am-1pm, Fri 8am-5pm, Sat 8am-1.30pm

Max Angle Seafoods
1 Kennington Lane SE11. Tel: 0171 735 1931
Tue-Fri 8am-4pm

Operating for the past eight years as a wholesale supplier to many top London outlets and restaurants (Fortnum & Mason, Harrods and The Savoy, for example), Aberdeen Sea Products also has a thriving retail operation at its Toulmin Street outlet (fish is kept under refrigeration so you might have to ask for what you want) and recently expanded by taking over the long-established Max Angle fishmongers. Most of the stock is turned over on a daily basis – they are among the relatively few London outlets where absolute freshness is guaranteed. 'Customers can obtain exactly the same fish we supply to our trade customers at a very reasonable price,' says Matthew Angle, the company's youthful, appropriately named owner. At the time of my visit, the stock at Toulmin Street ranged from halibut and turbot to herring and sardines from the South Coast. There were also some tempting fish kebabs. Smoked salmon comes from Aberdeen, is a medium smoke, sugar-free cure, 'between a light London cure and a heavy Highland smoke', and according to Matthew the best you can get. But the shop's *pièce de résistance* was a shoal of tuna. Five huge blue-fins, freshly caught in Oman, were beached in the cold room. The company supplies many Japanese restaurants and the blue-fin is the best for raw consumption as sushi or sashimi. Particularly prized is its light-coloured belly meat, which constitutes just three to five per cent of total weight. You can try this gastronomic treasure at the normal price of around £5-£6 per 500g/1lb, something that is well worth visiting SE11 for.

Sydenham

Delicatessen/Caterer

Foodissimo
60 Sydenham Road SE26. Tel: 0181 244 2443
Mon-Fri 9.30am-6pm, Sat 9am-5.30pm

Giancarlo Nassimbeni was manhandling a vat of rat when I called: seven pounds of ratatouille for a party up the street. As well as catering for Sydenham soirées (anything from pasta and sauce at 30 pence a portion to a large plate of assorted salami for £5) since 1993, the shop stocks a good range of breads, fresh pasta and rice. There are fresh Italian sausages and some unusual cooked meats, such as smoked, roasted prosciutto with herbs. Cheeses include Ricotta in both sheeps' and cows' milk versions, matured Provolone and Spanish Manchego. A mixture of items from around the world results in some interesting gastronomic cross-overs. For example, there are pasta-like noodles from Sri Lanka known as string hoppers and a kind of Sardinian poppadom called pane carasau. Made from hard corn, they have a 38-cm/15-inch diameter. You brush them with olive oil before popping them in the oven for a few moments.

Ice-Cream

Criterion Ices
118 Sydenham Road SE26. Tel: 0181 778 7945
Mon-Sun 10.30am-5.30pm

With marvellous, sophisticated flavours which would grace and amaze any dinner party – and at about half the price of most premium brands – Criterion Ices not only merits a detour to Sydenham, it makes it an absolute necessity. Run by the Valenti family, the company celebrated its 75th birthday last year. They make around 30 varieties of ice-cream on the premises, using Jersey and Guernsey cream. What makes them outstanding, apart from depth and the accuracy of flavour, is that the adult ices are not over-sweetened. Criterion's Continental

Roast Coffee has a café-au-lait dryness, its Stem Ginger is spicy and abundantly spiked with chunks of the preserved fruit, while its Clotted Cream flavour captures the slightly baked, concentrated creaminess of the original dairy product. Criterion's latest is a Cinnamon ice-cream, but not all its output is aimed at the carriage trade. Honeycomb is lapped up by the gallon and Turkish Delight with Chocolate Chips (a combination which could hardly be found wanting in the sweetness department) is another favourite lick. They also produce half a dozen sorbets, of which the mango and passion fruit varieties have a surprisingly luxurious richness considering they are fat-free. There are even two chocolate varieties for the insatiably sweet-toothed.

West Norwood

Delicatessen

Helen's Salt Beef Bar
43 Norwood Road SE27. Tel: 0181 670 8790
Mon-Sat 9am-5.30pm

Unpretentious deli run by Helen Hashai who left Czechoslovakia in 1968. Her home-cooked salt beef was described by one devotee as 'the best in south London' not that there is a huge amount of competition, to be honest. Taken in a rye sandwich with a dab of mustard, a sample tasting proved to be pleasantly lean with fine texture and flavour. She also cooks her own ham, roast beef and turkey. Selection of Continental bread.

Fishmonger

Gunn's
326 Norwood Road SE27. Tel: 0181 670 0880
Tue, Wed 9am-1pm, Thur, Fri 9am-5pm, Sat 9am-3pm

Run by aimiable brothers Brian and Eddie Gunn, this traditional fishmongers has been in the family for over 25 years. Specialists in home-smoked fish, they have pale and enticing sides of smoked haddock and cod on display, together with fresh-boiled crabs. Bought on a daily basis from Billingsgate, stock includes conger eel (its head, ferocious at decapitation, glaring through the window when I visited), sea bass and Dover sole. They also have live eels, very much a luxury item these days at £6 per 500g/1lb. Prices, in general, are moderate.

Baker

Thompson's Bakery

368 Norwood Road, SE27. Tel: 0181 766 7288
Mon-Sat 9am-6pm

Connected to the West Indian bakery of the same name in Brixton, but actually owned by the effervescent Liz Mallender, this happy, bustling joint had just celebrated its first birthday when I visited. And may there be many happy returns. In addition to Thompson's hard-dough breads and buns, and English bloomers, wholemeal and granary loaves, Liz meets the needs of the local community with salt-fish fritters, chicken tikka pasties, Jamaican patties, samosas, bhajis, filled rolls, curried goat and cow-foot stew. Everything is made, if not by Thompson's, by local producers.

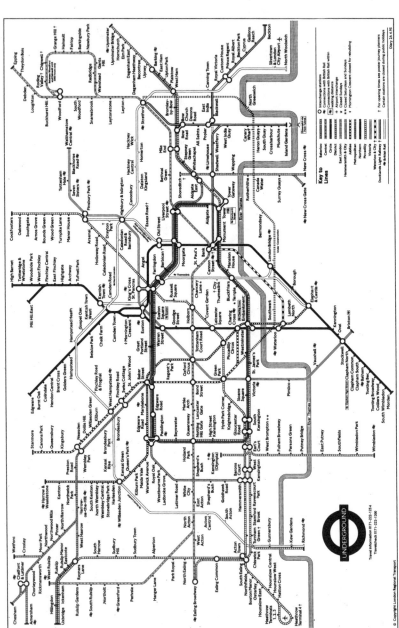

LRT Registered User No. 96/2353